D0436120

BROTHERS EMANUEL

BROTHERS
EMANUEL

....

A Memoir of an American Family

EZEKIEL J. EMANUEL

Random House New York

Copyright © 2013 by Ezekiel J. Emanuel

Published in the United States by Random House, an imprint of
The Random House Publishing Group, a division of
Random House, Inc., New York.

RANDOM HOUSE and colophon are registered trademarks of Random House, Inc.

Emanuel, Ezekiel J.
Brothers Emanuel : a memoir of an American family / Ezekiel Emanuel.
p. cm.
ISBN 978-1-4000-6903-3
eBook ISBN 978-1-58836-993-2
1. Emanuel, Ezekiel J., 1957–   2. Emanuel, Rahm, 1959–   3. Emanuel, Ari, 1961–
4. Emanuel family.   5. Brothers—Illinois—Chicago—Biography.   6. Jews—
Illinois—Chicago—Biography.   7. Chicago (Ill.)—Biography.   I. Title.
F548.54.E63A3 2013
977.3'110430922—dc23
[B]
2012033580

Printed in the United States of America on acid-free paper

www.atrandom.com

2   4   6   8   9   7   5   3   1

First Edition

Book design by Liz Cosgrove

To my loyal and wonderful brothers
Rahm and Ariel
I love you schmucks!

An autobiography is the truest of all books; for while it inevitably consists mainly of extinctions of the truth, shirkings of the truth, partial revealments of the truth, with hardly an instance of plain straight truth, the remorseless truth is there, between the lines, where the author-cat is raking dust upon it which hides from the disinterested spectator neither it nor its smell (though I didn't use that figure)—the result being that the reader knows the author in spite of his wily diligences.

—Mark Twain, in a letter to William D. Howells, March 14, 1904

Contents

BROTHERS EMANUEL

BORN TO PROTEST

Rahm.

That is my first memory in life.

He looked harmless enough, bundled in a blanket and struggling to focus his eyes. My cousin Gary and I were fairly impressed with his grasp reflex—all babies will grab on to a finger as it touches their palm. Since this was his only real trick, he seemed pretty useless. My mother, however, acted like he was extremely precious and treated him with so much care that it was clear that she loved him every bit as much as she loved me. Although I could not form the words, or express the feelings they evoked, part of me knew that here was a competitor.

In December 1959, Gary was five years old and I was just two. Two skinny kids with the same dark brown hair, brown eyes, and strong chins, we looked like brothers and spent so much time together that we felt like brothers, too. For months my parents had been trying to prepare me for the arrival of a real sibling. They had given me a doll to play with and encouraged me to take care of her. And when the baby, a little boy they named Rahm, finally arrived, they encouraged me to help take care of him, too.

On this particular morning, Gary and I were jumping up and down on our convertible sofa. It was a monstrous, ugly piece of furniture covered in indestructible black Naugahyde. When opened, it practically filled the living room in our first Chicago apartment and the metal that held the mattress was so thin and springy that when we used the sofa as a trampoline we could make the whole frame shake.

My mother had made breakfast, dispatched my father to care for patients at Michael Reese Hospital, and fed and diapered the baby. Dodging the toys on the floor—including that doll, which I had beheaded—she brought the baby into the living room and called to us to stop our gymnastics and come look at him. We did as we were told, inspecting the snuffling, wizened little creature with very dark skin, a snubby nose, and a wild spray of black hair.

"I'm going to put Rahmy down here and you boys can watch him for a little while. Take care of him," said my mother. Clearly, she hoped we might like being the big boys in charge for a few minutes. My guess is that she also needed a little break.

We seemed agreeable enough, so she laid Rahm down on the sofa bed's mattress and surrounded him with pillows to make him secure before leaving the room. It took us only a few seconds before we decided to climb back up on the bed and invent a new game that might have been called "Bounce the Baby."

We positioned ourselves on either side of the little bundle and timed our jumps so that we landed simultaneously. The mattress bowed and the metal bands that held it were loaded with enough energy to bounce Rahm on the surface of the bed.

Instantly, we grasped the situation's potential. With enough effort, and perfect timing, we might bounce Rahm off the mattress and onto the floor. We couldn't restrain ourselves, and we were too excited to remember to be quiet. The noise we made as we jumped like a couple of jackhammers brought my mother running into the room.

"Stop! Stop right now!"

It's not so easy to stop bouncing once you get going. As Gary and I crashed together, my mother scooped Rahm off the bed with a sweep of her arm.

Tall, with long brown hair and a beautiful warm and open face, my twenty-six-year-old mother was young and strong but the sight of her second-born son being launched into the air had sent her heart racing. As Gary and I tumbled to a stop, she took a moment to catch her breath and choose her next move. Though we had behaved like idiots, my mother knew we were too young to have formed any malice aforethought. As a devotee of the pediatrician and author Benjamin Spock, who appealed to her with his radically sympathetic approach to childrearing, she had vowed to control the impulse to scream, hit, or punish us.

"Boys," she finally said, "babies aren't grown-up enough to play that way. You could have hurt Rahmy if he fell off the bed, or you fell onto him."

She was right, of course. And she tried to correct us, without berating us. Few mothers would have exercised the restraint my mother showed that morning, and fewer still would have had such confidence in Spock's advice that they would have followed it so closely, and with such conviction, in the heat of battle.

Later, she bundled us three boys up and bounced a stroller down the stairs so we could walk a few blocks in the stinging cold December air to a local market. Along the way we passed some of our neighbors, older Jewish women who clucked in Yiddish, assuming she did not know that they were saying something disparaging about the "hillbillies" with all their kids.

Low rents and easy access to public transportation had made our neighborhood popular with poor whites from Appalachia who flocked to Chicago seeking jobs. Distinctive in the way they talked, and dressed, these newcomers had met their share of bigotry and the term *hillbilly* was a put-down. My mother, who refused to use the word, startled the women with a little Yiddish admonition—"Ich bin a yid," which means "I am a Jew"—to remind them of the ugliness of prejudice and their own ignorance.

In this one morning, the very first memory of my life, Marsha Emanuel had confronted, as a matter of routine, most of the responsibilities and issues that would define her adult life. She had risen early

to cook breakfast, care for three kids, and see her husband depart for
a day's work that might not end until late in the evening. Before noon
she had saved Rahm's life, taught Gary and me some life lessons, confronted bigotry on the sidewalk, and done a little shopping. All this
would be repeated, in a rough way, for at least four thousand more
days until the Emanuel boys—me, Rahm, and soon-to-come brother
Ariel—started to be more self-sufficient. In that time, we would begin
to define ourselves and begin to imagine our places in the world. The
process began, of course, in the tiny community that was our family
and in the even smaller circle that we made as brothers.

.....

As in most families, especially in generations past, our mother was the
parent of record and spent much more time with us than our father,
Benjamin, did. Certainly he was very involved in our upbringing, and
his parenting style—lots of hugs, kisses, jokes, and play—was unusual
for the sixties. But he was the sole wage earner in the family, and as a
young, poorly compensated medical fellow at Michael Reese Hospital, he worked more than seventy hours per week to support us.

My earliest memory of my father finds me standing at the window
of the same apartment where Rahm was nearly bounced to the floor.
Heat pours out of a steam radiator that squats below the window and
my cousin Gary fidgets beside me. My nose is pressed against the glass
as I stare down on a city street that is white with salt and banked by
snow pushed off the traffic lanes by city plows. My father, on crutches
after breaking his leg while dancing at a bar mitzvah, crosses North
Broadway and hobbles to a spot where a sign lettered in faded yellow
and green paint marks the stop for the 151 and 153 buses.

Gary and I watch as big cars with swooping tailfins slowly creep
past. Within minutes a flat-faced city bus glides to a halt at the stop
across the street. When it departs in a puff of diesel exhaust, my father
and the others who had been standing there have disappeared.

More than a half hour would pass before my father arrived at the
hospital, which was on the South Side of the city. His research group,
led by a famous Harvard-trained autocrat named Dr. Jack Metcoff,

had begun by testing Chicago's first kidney dialysis machine on dogs. At the start of 1960 they moved to clinical trials using human beings. The demand for treatment, including emergency cases of attempted suicides by poisoning, was so great that the fellows worked around the clock. On any given day, my father wasn't likely to return from work before I was asleep for the night. I saw that a man's work was important, that he must pursue it tirelessly, and that it might require certain sacrifices, like being away from the warmth and comfort of home.

Of course I had mixed feelings about Rahm's arrival. But as Rahm grew stronger, crawled, and then toddled after me, I enjoyed him more and more. He wasn't as much fun as a puppy (we'd get one of those later) but he was just as physically expressive. When he was upset, his brow would become furrowed and his whole face seemed to darken. When he smiled, the corners of his mouth turned up sharply, his eyes sparkled, and a dimple would form on his cheek. It was a charming but also mischievous look, the kind that lets you in on a secret joke. The Hebrew word for a kid with this look is *shovav,* which means "little devil," and Rahm *was* a shovav. His tendency to show his feelings would stay with him for life and evolve to the point where he could communicate a whole range of emotions—puzzled, content, annoyed, you name it—without saying a word. In many staff meetings at the White House, when he was chief of staff and I was working on health-care reform at the Office of Management and Budget, I would see him turn down the corners of his mouth just a bit to show his displeasure with an idea. Or his brow would tighten when he was about to chastise someone. And he remains one of the great subtle eye rollers, especially when someone else is making an observation about political machinations he finds obtuse. What might come as a shock to most people is that as a baby and through his early childhood, Rahm barely spoke at all. When we were young children, I frequently spoke for us both.

"Rahm, do you want something to eat?" my mother would ask.

"He's not hungry right now," I'd reply. He'd just as easily go along if I said, "Yes, he wants two pieces of toast with margarine and lots of jam."

Rahm was similarly passive when it came to play, choosing to sit back and observe and only participate when invited or encouraged. In part his attitude may have been connected to the fact that I was far more aggressive. I was perfectly happy to talk for him and to think up things for both of us to do, like sitting on the window seat drumming on pots with wooden spoons.

For my parents, however, Rahm's slowness to talk and relative passivity became a concern. During her pregnancy with him my mother had undergone general anesthesia to have a benign tumor removed from her breast and she worried about how the drugs might have affected him. When he was born he was, at six pounds, eleven ounces, her smallest baby. When he reached age two he seemed unusually quiet to my parents. They took him to a specialist to see if his verbal skills were developing normally. It turned out that there was no developmental delay. He could talk perfectly well. He just seemed perfectly content not to—and leave the talking to me.

It seems to me now that during those quiet early years Rahm learned from and about the world not by physically engaging it the way I did, but instead by carefully observing it from a safe distance. Rahm studied his environment and dissected how people interacted; he asserted himself only when it was necessary. But back then I thought of him as kind of a blob, too slow to keep up with a hyperactive, hyperverbal kid like me. When he finally started using full sentences at the age of three and a half, my mother's anxiety disappeared. But she made the mistake of once telling him how she had worried over the prenatal effects of the anesthesia. Ever the politician, he latched on to this confession and, when it suited his purpose, would say, "You owe me, Mom." She'd feel guilty, and he'd get what he wanted.

Rahm stayed small as he grew into adulthood and when we were young his size did make me feel protective, especially when we left the apartment. On any given day, we would take an outing—a walk to the park, maybe a stop at a store—but every once in a while we'd bump the baby carriage down the stairs and take a bus downtown, or perhaps to the South Side. From all appearances my mother was just another homemaker schlepping her kids to a museum or a department store. Many times we actually went to those kinds of places. But on other occasions we went to the Board of Education building on Clark Street to join picket lines or to South Side schools where black parents lay down in the street to block the delivery of temporary classrooms. Called Willis Wagons, after the superintendent of the city schools, Benjamin Willis, these trailers made it possible for the school system to expand classrooms at black schools, maintaining segregation as Chicago's black population grew and hundreds of thousands of whites moved to the suburbs. They were both the symbols and the instruments of the city's racism.

My mother wasn't, as she says, a "lie-down-in-the-street kind of person." As a mother, she recalls, "I had to make sure I wasn't arrested, because I had children to worry about. And, believe it or not, I also had in my mind the idea that I had to get home to make your father dinner."

My mother saw nothing inconsistent in her traditional desire to look after her husband and children and her radical politics. She began her civil rights work before most people had ever heard the word *feminism* and in those early years she was focused on racial justice. She later confessed that she felt some twinges of resentment over the sacrifices—setting aside her education, career, and other ambitions—that she made for her family, but her protests were on behalf of others. At neighborhood schools, she stood with black parents who gathered by the hundreds in the street to demand equal access even as white neighbors gathered to jeer. I did not understand the issues, but I knew that something important was happening and that it involved people of many different ages and races who were united in a way that felt good.

After she had put in an hour or so at one of these protests, my mother made sure we caught the Chicago Transit Authority bus home in time for her to make dinner and get us kids into bed. More than once we would return home with the same bus driver who had dropped us off. He'd greet my mother with some benign remark—"Had a nice time shopping?"—and she would smile as if that were exactly what she had been doing.

In the time when my mother began standing up against prejudice and racism the vast majority of white Americans rarely thought about civil rights. When polled they denied that the country even had a serious racial problem. They believed, instead, that America really did offer equal opportunity, and that discrimination was an unimportant exception and not the rule. At the same time the majority simply knew that a woman's place was in the home and certainly not on the sidewalk carrying signs and singing freedom songs, and absolutely not with her toddlers in tow. This was, after all, a nation that had waited until 1920 to give women the vote and as of the early 1960s still did not guarantee women equal access to employment and education. Many prestigious universities and colleges, such as Yale and Princeton and my own Amherst College, did not yet admit female students. Women who stood up for themselves and others were routinely criticized as selfish, man-hating battle-axes who certainly must be inadequate wives and neglectful mothers. However, in my family there was nothing strange and everything right about standing up in public for what you believe, especially if justice was at stake. Indeed, standing up was a tradition for us.

Six months before my mother was born, our maternal grandfather had joined the first big American protest against Hitler, a march of fifty thousand that helped unify Chicago's Jews against the Nazis. Herman Smulevitz understood the way that bigotry can become violent. He was born in Russia in 1902, at a time when mobs of anti-Semites were attacking Jewish communities in murderous pogroms. We were told that he stowed away alone on a ship that brought him to America at the age of ten. After landing in New York he began searching for his father, who had abandoned his mother, remarried, and settled in Indiana. When he finally arrived at his father's home, exhausted and bewildered by all he had experienced, Herman's stepmother refused to take him in. He would forever call her the *machashaifeh,* which is Yiddish for "witch."

Big and strong for his age, and toughened by all he went through, young Herman eventually found refuge with an uncle in the Jewish community around Maxwell Street in Chicago. He worked odd jobs until he enlisted in the army near the end of World War I, where he saw combat only as a champion boxer. Nearly six feet tall and weighing 250 pounds, he had a long reach and huge hands with fingers the size of Polish sausages. This physique, joined with his life experience on the streets of Chicago, made him plenty tough.

After the war, Herman labored as a lumberjack and did track work for a railroad. In 1927 he married a Romanian immigrant named Sophie Lampert. In just six years they had three daughters—Shirley, Esther, and Marsha. A son named Shelden came in 1940, followed by Leslie in 1948. In this time Herman worked as a grocer and a union man who used his muscle, when necessary, to organize steel mills and meatpacking houses. Herman, who taught himself to read English, devoured newspapers and books and held strong opinions about what he read. He was a loud and sometimes profane man who would say almost anything to win an argument.

As a child, Marsha Smulevitz stayed out of the fray, watching her older sisters argue in vain with their father and noticing that her younger brothers were often scolded in a way that seemed to diminish them. She feared her father, resented his bullying, and was devastated when he demanded that she give up the money she had saved for college to pay for her brother Shelden's college tuition. She complied, but never got over losing her chance to continue her education after high school.

But as much as my mother hated his authoritarian streak, she also listened to what her father said about standing up against injustice. The contradiction inherent in a bully who urges the oppressed to challenge their tormentors was obvious, but it did not make the message any less important. She sought out moments when she might experience the struggle for justice herself. The first chance came on a Thursday afternoon in December 1946. She heard that some whites were organizing to take action against black veterans who planned to move their families into a new public housing project that had been planned as an integrated community. She hopped on her brother's bike and went to see what might happen.

When my mother arrived at the apartment complex, hundreds of whites, mostly women who were homemakers, stood in the street to block two black vets who had arrived with moving trucks filled with their belongings. Dozens of police officers were at the site and they helped the drivers inch their trucks through the crowd of angry onlookers. When the trucks stopped, the police officers moved in to protect the men as they tried to unload their stuff. The crowd surged forward. Some of the women screamed threats and racist insults. Others threw rocks and dirt.

Just a thirteen-year-old girl, my mother was shocked to see adult women shrieking with anger, and the police swinging batons to move them. When one of the trucks got stuck in the mud and its wheels began to spin helplessly, the driver switched off the motor and the men inside ran to a nearby office. Rocks rained on them and the vehicle. The truck's windows were broken and eight people were injured in the melee as more stones flew and the officers pushed the crowd back.

In that moment, my mother promised herself that she would always support anyone who sought equal rights. Back at home she kept what she saw that day to herself because she knew that her father would never approve of a girl taking such a risk. As she became an adult and went out into the world she developed some courage to go with her convictions. By the time I came along she was comfortable arguing with my grandfather even when he banged on the table and shouted. The noise he made when he slapped his big sausage hand down inspired me to call him "Big Banger." Actually I pronounced it "Big Bang-ah," but he did not frighten or intimidate me.

Big Bangah got most excited when the subject was elections or party politics. He was a rabidly loyal Democrat, because the Democratic Party represented the workingman. He believed Franklin Roosevelt had literally saved America from the Great Depression and had, in World War II, defeated the most evil entity in history. A true Chicagoan of his generation, Herman believed that whatever policy the Democratic Party pursued, he was for it. If he could have, he would have controlled every vote in his family and delivered them to the Democrats each election day.

My mother was more discerning. She was a liberal and a Democrat, but she had no patience for politicians of any party who blocked civil rights legislation. She also gave credit to those Republicans— Nelson Rockefeller, Everett Dirksen, and others—who took the right position on civil rights.

Any time my mother praised Dirksen, Rockefeller, or other open-minded, moderate Republicans she got a fierce response from Big Bangah. More than once these arguments developed such intensity that the sound and the fury could make one or both of them come a little unhinged.

One of the most memorable of these battles would arise in the fall of 1966, as Republican Charles "Chuck" Percy challenged the incumbent Democratic senator Paul Douglas. Douglas was my grandfather's kind of Democrat. He was an intellectual and a political activist who also was a friend of the workingman. He had taught economics at the University of Chicago before entering politics as an anti-machine candidate, in a losing campaign for mayor. A long shot, he had won election to the U.S. Senate in 1948 with a campaign that stressed Truman-style anticommunism as well as civil rights, social programs, and public housing. Since then, he had been a Democratic stalwart, which included supporting John F. Kennedy's decision to send "advisors" to Vietnam and Lyndon Johnson's escalation of the confrontation with the Chinese-backed North Vietnamese.

As the 1966 election drew near, American deaths in Vietnam surpassed five thousand and troop levels approached four hundred thousand. Public opposition to the war was still small, but growing, with protests occurring in many cities. My mother, who was deeply affected by all this, told her father that she was thinking of voting for Percy, who opposed the war. Percy was the blond-haired, blue-eyed chief executive officer of a huge company called Bell & Howell. A product of the best local schools and the University of Chicago, he lived in the ultrarich lakeside suburb of Kenilworth, where Jews, Catholics, and blacks were even less welcomed than Democrats. Add all of his advantages to his GOP credentials and stir in the exclusionary taint of Kenilworth and Percy was a man of the ruling class whom Herman could not abide and he let my mother know it. We boys stood back and watched as our grandfather's voice grew louder during a Friday night Shabbat dinner.

"If you are going to vote for that man," he finally said while swinging his arm to point at the door, "then get out of my fucking house!"

My mother, insulted and furious, turned on her heel and slammed the door as she left. She was on the sidewalk, fuming and talking to herself, when she realized that she had just been ordered to leave her own home.

On election day, my mother walked us all to the polling station, which was in a basement-level community center of some sort. We always joined my mother on the trip to the polling station, so she could show us democracy in action. She checked in with the registrar, who knew her by name, as is the tradition in Chicago politics to this day, and then brought us three brothers with her down the narrow hall that led to the voting machines. While we waited for a booth to open up, I remember Rahm and me pulling the various switches on the instructional voting machine model. We then followed her to one of the machines, where we three boys crowded in around her. She pulled a big lever to close the curtain behind us.

Inside that booth, Rahm, Ari, and I watched as our mother flipped all the switches along the Democratic Party column except for the one marked "United States Senator," where she paused, and then flicked the little lever for Percy. I howled, "Mommy! You can't! That's Percy!"

As my cries echoed through the polling station, I reached up to pull the Douglas lever and change my mother's vote. She slapped my hand as if I had touched a hot burner on the stove and then quickly yanked on the red handle that recorded her votes. The curtain opened. The privacy of the booth evaporated, and around us people paused and just stared. My mother herded us like chickens, pushing with her hands until we went out the door and up the few steps to the street.

Percy won, upsetting Douglas by 56 percent to 44 percent.

.....

For us, the result of the 1966 election provided more to argue about and debate, but no matter what was said, including "get out of this fucking house!" the hard feelings that arose in the heat of verbal battle always dissipated quickly. This was just the way things worked in my family, where you could speak with intense passion, and even insult your opponent, and no one took it too seriously or personally. Indeed, I soon learned that when you took the time to argue with someone it was a sign of respect for their ideas. Where I came from, just nodding and smiling when someone expressed views was the ultimate insult. If people weren't yelling about politics in our house then they were arguing about music, or movies, or food. None of the excitement— not the yelling, the pounding on the table, or the slamming of doors— bothered me at all when I was little. It was sort of like growing up next to an airport runway, where everyone in the neighborhood becomes accustomed to the noise. In our home, everyone shouted and argued about everything.

The exception to this rule was my father's mother, whom we called Savta, which is Hebrew for "grandmother." A small woman with silvery hair and big glasses, Penina Emanuel wore her hair in a stiff bob cut and her wrinkled face showed the signs of a life spent under the Mediterranean sun. She had been widowed in 1955 when doctors misdiagnosed my paternal grandfather and namesake Ezekiel's heart failure as influenza. I remember her as a serious and intelligent woman who wore neither makeup nor jewelry, except for a plain watch with a black leather strap on her left wrist. I don't think I ever saw her wearing anything but a dark dress with long sleeves. Her shoes were always the same—black or brown with a single strap across the top that was fixed with a plain button.

Old-fashioned in every way, Savta drank her tea Russian-style, in a glass that was placed in a silver-handled holder called a *podstakannik*. She was a neat freak who made her bed so carefully that it was hard to tell that anyone ever slept in it. Everything had to be in its place.

The one great exception to these rules came when she got out the flour and other ingredients and let us help her make stuffed pierogies. On these occasions she would roll out the dough, we would press a cup down on it to cut a circle, and then we'd fold the dough over a dollop of meat, or mushroom, or some other stuffing she had prepared.

During these escapades she didn't mind that we were loud, sprayed flour all over the counters, floor, and our faces, and tussled over who got to handle the various ingredients. She may have even smiled amid the mayhem.

These memories of cooking stand out because otherwise Savta rarely smiled and I'm not sure I ever heard her laugh out loud. From an adult perspective I can guess that she never got over the deaths of her husband and her eldest son, Emanuel—whose name she and Ezekiel adopted as the family's last name in his memory—and the loss of her life in Israel. As a child I only knew that she was a quiet, almost ghostlike figure in our house who spent much of her time alone in her room—reading the Israeli newspapers or Hebrew books—and almost never talked. When she did appear she hovered in the background of things, flashing looks of disapproval at my mother, who would ignore them until she couldn't and then demand that my father find someplace else for Savta to live.

For his part my father cajoled and deflected. What was he going to do? He was stuck between two strong-willed women. One talked and the other didn't, but they both communicated very clearly, issuing contradictory demands. In his usual kick-the-can way he refused to make a choice. He listened to our mother yell and did nothing. In the meantime Savta waged a quiet war of wills with our mother. She demanded that my mother refer to her as "Mrs. Emanuel" whenever she spoke of her in public and she stubbornly refused to learn to speak English, even though she was fluent in many languages and obviously understood English quite well.

In a family where everyone seemed to be loudly protesting something at all times, Savta's silent boycott of the English language was her form of resistance. She might come to America to live with her son and his wife, whom she never quite accepted, but she sure as hell wasn't going to learn the language. She would speak Hebrew with her son and get along with my mother and us boys by speaking a little Yiddish, which we were expected to understand. To my mother's dismay, at every meal she commanded us in Hebrew to stop talking and eat, which trained us to gobble down our food. This habit became even more ingrained as we boys grew older and our urgent need for calories and competitive drives led us to consume our meals with grabby abandon. He who reached first got the biggest piece of chicken or the last green pepper slice in the salad.

But I'm getting ahead of myself. Before Savta had her chance to carry out her silent protest in Chicago, she had to decide to leave Tel Aviv. She made this choice only after concluding that her only surviving child—my father—wasn't likely to come back to live in Israel any time soon. In the spring of 1960, she wrote that she would be coming before the end of summer. This news was one of several factors that motivated my parents to move out of the cramped little apartment on Broadway. One of the others was a rat.

.....

After failing to make a go of it in Israel my parents returned to Chicago to find housing in scarce supply. With little money and no credit, they grabbed the first affordable place they could find—a crummy flat on Broadway.

The entrance, stairs, and hallway of the building were filthy. Peeling paint left flakes on the floor and cracked plaster awaited repairs that were never made. Inside their apartment they dealt with more of the same. The walls hadn't been cleaned—forget fresh paint—in many years. The wiring was balky, the faucets all dripped, the sinks were rust-stained, and when the winter wind blew it rattled the windows and sent a chill through the whole building. These conditions were commonplace in certain parts of 1950s Chicago, where the building codes were strict but the officials charged with enforcement used them to collect bribes or punish those who refused to pay. Month after month, my parents pestered the landlord about the cold, the broken fixtures, the many repairs left undone. My father was especially concerned about the possibility that children would eat the paint chips falling from the walls and get lead poisoning. Still the landlord, who was also a rabbi, did nothing.

The last straw came on a night when my mother heard Rahm crying in his crib. Assuming he was hungry or needed to be changed, she got herself out of bed and turned on the light. Rahm was not alone. There in the crib was a sizable rat. In shock, and then anger, my mother shooed the thing away from her baby. As it crawled out of the crib and then ran across the floor she thought she saw another. She shouted for my father, who came running. He checked my brother to make sure he had not been bitten—he hadn't—and then listened as my mother told him what she saw. He banged around to make sure no rats were still lurking in the apartment, but they had obviously escaped through the same hole that had let them in.

Although my mother and father had already started planning a move, the rats made the matter urgent. Thanks to several raises in his salary, my father had a bit more money to spend. He signed a lease on a larger apartment just around the corner on West Buena Avenue. The four-story brick building was divided into eight big units with high ceilings and tall windows. Our apartment, which was on the second floor, came with two bedrooms, a living room, a dining room, and, off the kitchen, a third bedroom with its own bath. Designed as a maid's quarters, it would be perfect for my grandmother. She booked passage to America at the end of the summer of 1960.

That summer, my mother helped form a neighborhood chapter of the Congress of Racial Equality (CORE), which months earlier had gained national attention with its support for sit-ins at segregated lunch counters across the South. These protests, which went on for days, inspired support around the country. With me by her side and Rahm in a carriage, my mother joined a picket line at a Woolworth's store in Chicago. She was one of just a few whites who joined a crowd of black patrons inside who occupied the lunch counter for hours on end, to show their support for what was happening in the South.

For my mother, a bus ride and an hour or two on a picket line was a rather routine activity and since I started attending protests with her at a very tender age, it seemed normal to me, too. I thought nothing of the fact that we were among very few white people in these crowds. I did notice there were not a lot of other kids at these demonstrations.

When we got home from these protests we fell into a fairly typical domestic routine. My mother got dinner ready for when my father returned from the hospital. She cooked the usual things—chicken, pasta, lots of vegetables—but her best dishes were kugel and cheesecake. One of the things she never served was fresh milk, because she believed it was contaminated by the radioactive strontium 90 in fallout from atomic bomb tests. If we ever drank milk it was the powdered stuff that came out a sort of bluish white when you added water and stirred it with a spoon. This is probably why to this day none of us brothers really likes milk nor drinks it regularly.

While my mother cooked, Rahm and I busied ourselves with books, crayons, or games. Our play was intense; we both had boundless energy that made us push, shove, run, hide, and wrestle constantly. It was this energy, which my parents tried to accept as much as possible, that posed the biggest challenge to anyone who tried to take care of us. Although she was young and energetic, there were days when Rahm and I ran my mother into the ground. Things would only get worse when the third brother eventually came.

.....

There were just two Emanuel brothers to contend with when my grandmother arrived in New York by ship in September 1960. My father met her there and on the train to Chicago he told her that a third grandchild was on the way. Savta was actually upset about the imminent arrival of a third child, who would only tie her beautiful boy closer to the American woman who had stolen him from her. This is not to say that she did not love her grandchildren, at least in theory. She did. However, she loved her only remaining son above all others. And no woman, and especially no American woman, would ever be good enough for him.

In America, Savta tried to impose some order on the household she joined, but she would not have much impact.

.....

In the days before my mother was to have her third child I became more excited by the hour. When she and my father finally went to Mount Sinai Hospital for the delivery, Rahm and I could barely contain ourselves. We talked nonstop about the brother or sister we were expecting.

Our frenzy this day was heightened by the uneasiness Rahm and I felt because of our father and mother's prolonged absence. We had never been separated from them for so long and had been told that we would see, or at least hear from, them "soon." Hours and then an entire day passed with nothing but occasional calls from my father, reporting that the baby had not yet arrived. What we did not know was that things were going very badly at Mount Sinai. The umbilical cord was wrapped around the baby's neck, which threatened both the oxygen and blood supply to the baby's brain. The delivery was not progressing, and the situation was touch-and-go. In 1961, cesarean deliveries required general anesthesia and a lot of cutting, which were two things my parents and the hospital staff wanted to avoid. They kept this option in reserve as my mother went through a labor that lasted for thirty-two painful, frightening hours. Emanuel brother number three, whom they named Ariel—Hebrew for "lion of God"— finally arrived on the morning of March 29, squalling and healthy.

When the phone rang in the kitchen Savta grabbed the receiver and put it to her ear. Rahm and I were playing a game that involved running in circles through the kitchen, dining room, and walk-in pantry. Savta listened carefully and then called, "Jonny! Jonny!" (My full name is Ezekiel Jonathan Emanuel and Jonny was what everyone called me back then.)

With Rahm following hard on my heels, I stopped to take the phone from my grandmother and heard my father's voice on the other end. He said everything was all right and there were now three Emanuel brothers.

"Just what I ordered!" I told my father.

Two

CONTROLLED MAYHEM

"Dai shovavim! Dai!"

"Stop, you devils! Stop!" Savta shouted at us in Hebrew, but Rahm and I ignored her. We pushed and pulled on my father, who sat firmly on the family room floor with his legs crossed and fought back by tickling and kissing us on our necks.

The big challenge of these wrestling matches was to try to shove our father over onto the floor. One by one we would attack him from behind. Being left-handed, he would reach across his right shoulder, grab us under our arms, and flip us over in one smooth motion. We got the thrill of being suddenly upside down and the delight of landing in his lap, where we would be cuddled and tickled until the next "attacker" made his move and my father would have to defend himself again.

These attacks welcomed my father as soon as he arrived home from work. To my grandmother's eyes this was a gross display of indulgence and disrespect. We were dangerous little beasts ganging up on her beautiful son. The wildness did occasionally result in a gouged eye, a bloody scratch, or a twisted ear, but my father was equal to the challenge.

For my father, laughter and a little workout provided a much better antidote for the stress of work than a martini or a highball, which were the popular agents of relaxation for his generation. (As far as I can recall, my parents never drank hard liquor and only had wine or beer in the house for occasional parties or holidays.) My dad also knew that we needed ways to discharge enormous amounts of emotional and physical energy. Controlled mayhem did the trick and also wore us out so we would fall asleep quickly after we got into our beds.

Our dad also believed in giving us generous amounts of affection. In this he was very different from the typical American father of the era. In the 1950s and 1960s, many parents were generally standoffish with their male children, and acted as if they were raising a generation of would-be soldiers. I remember some of my friends' parents who would shake their children's hands at bedtime. Our dad hugged us and kissed us so much that some friends and relatives complained that he was going to turn us into sissies or homosexuals. But my dad didn't care. Let them raise their kids in a reserved and reticent way. He grew up in Israel and his boys were going to be hugged and kissed by their father, and know they were loved.

In time, medical science would discover that both affection and exercise raise the levels of certain hormones—the ones that make us feel relaxed, content, and secure—and aid the development of a healthy mind and body. The positive effects have been seen in studies following babies well into adulthood. For my pediatrician father, this proof was not necessary. He understood, innately, that children—most especially boys—need to express themselves through movement, touch, and even aggression. Like my mother, he valued the individuality of even the smallest child.

In his practice and outside it, my father approached children with the same interest and respect he might bring to meeting any adult, and he was truly delighted by the experience. With a little boy he might ask, "How do you know you are a boy?" and listen very seriously as, in one case, a four-year-old explained, "I know I'm a boy because I wear a kippah at temple." My father would answer, "Good thinking," because he wanted to establish a bond of respect and trust. He knew that a child who trusted him might one day say a few words that would be the key to a diagnosis. Better to be the doctor a kid would confide in, than the one that she fears.

Sincere conversations also gave my father the chance to observe a child's movements and thought processes and learn about his personality. Anyone who has spent time with newborns knows that while they all go through the same developmental stages, they come into this world as individuals with widely varied temperaments. Brave babies seek out novelty and show a remarkable ability to adapt to new sights, sounds, and people. Others are wary, and easily overstimulated. Most occupy a spot between the poles, meeting the world with their own peculiar need for both security and new experiences. Similar variations can be seen in a host of traits including levels of anxiety, attachment, fear, and even boredom. Parents can sense the differences in children and know that these differences require them to be flexible caregivers. There's nothing to be gained, and much to be lost, in trying to bend every child to match a one-size-fits-all notion of what it means to be a boy or girl of a specific age. Better to set a few parameters and then go with the flow. Call it jazz parenting.

Analytical, logical, and objective, I asked a great many questions about how things worked and found comfort in the answers. For example, when I learned that one of my father's young patients—a kid like me—was diagnosed with leukemia I asked endless questions about how the disease developed and how it might be treated. I was very worried about this boy, but also needed to know that it wasn't infectious and I could not just "catch it" and suddenly fall deathly ill myself. I was reassured as my father and mother answered every one of my questions in a way that helped me accept that leukemia was a rare condition and could not be transmitted from person to person like strep throat.

My way of considering things was accompanied by a powerful tendency to experiment—poking, prodding, testing—and to talk, and talk, and talk about everything I saw and felt. Talking about something from all the possible angles was the way I would come to understand the world and elucidate my own views. To their credit, my parents only occasionally reached the point of exasperation where they begged me to be quiet.

In contrast, Rahm was quiet and observant, while Ari was forceful, rambunctious, highly social, and hyperactive, and did more moving than talking. He was, in everyone's eyes, the best-looking of the brothers, a child so cute he could break a window or a lamp and get away with it, flashing his mischievous smile that said, "You can't possibly stay angry at me, can you?"

Loud and physically fearless, Ari walked and talked early in order to keep up with his big brothers, and plunged into life with boundless energy and courage. His one concession to dependency was a pink pacifier that he used to soothe himself right up until he was about to go to kindergarten. As a toddler with the pacifier in his mouth he greeted one of my mother's fellow civil rights activist friends, Roz, a grown woman, with the question "Onna fight?"

We grew up in a home where the adults enjoyed being parents. In fact, our mother considered raising us to be the most important job she would ever have—her calling. Although she endured lots of ribbing for it, she made an intense study of what the experts said and applied it with her own variations. She was very deliberate in her parenting, always keeping in mind that our development, especially our emotional and intellectual development, depended on our early life experiences. She wanted us to feel that the world was a safe place, where we were loved and free to express our thoughts and ideas. And she endeavored to give us many diverse experiences.

When it came to feelings, matters were a bit more complicated. We could show love and flashes of other emotions like envy, jealousy, pride, dejection, or remorse. But as I realized later in life, when problems arose we did not have many ways to discuss them deeply. The emotional vocabulary in our family was limited. We were never encouraged to articulate our deeper feelings. Indeed, discussion of how we felt tended to be brief, if not monosyllabic. After a fight or an argument our mother often required us to hug each other and kiss and say we were sorry. In this realm, physicality trumped words. So early on we internalized the notion that it was easier to give someone a kiss or a hug or a punch than to struggle to elucidate and articulate the nuances of our private feelings and emotions. We were not unique in this way, but for people with a proclivity for talking a lot, this gap in our verbal repertoire is a paradox.

Considering the demands of a household that churned with activity from dawn to dusk it is possible that my parents just did not have the time or energy to resolve our resentments or jealousies. To keep order, our mother issued as few rules as possible, but enforced them consistently. She encouraged us to say what we thought in whatever language adults might use. If they cussed, we could cuss, too. And if a decision was under consideration—where to go on vacation, what movie to see—our input was often solicited.

She also did her best to encourage our interests, which we tended to choose ourselves. The experience of having choices and the ability to influence decisions in the family makes a child feel empowered and secure rather than dependent and impotent. It is no wonder, looking back, that we grew into assertive adults who were willing to take risks. We were raised to develop our own opinions and believe in our ability to make good judgments.

This confidence was reinforced by the remarkable amount of freedom our parents gave us from a very young age. In the early 1960s, before milk cartons were decorated with photos of abducted children and supervised "playdates" became the norm, I led my brothers, Rahm and Ari, on expeditions around the neighborhood. Although I was barely six and my brothers were two and four, I was allowed to lead them to the end of the block, across a street—we were always taught to look both ways—and through an underpass beneath Lake Shore Drive, to a public rock garden where we pretended to assault a fort. More often we played on the sidewalk in front of the building or went to the little fenced-in playground in the middle of our block on Buena. The playground offered sandboxes, swings, and slides and enough grass and shrubbery to make the perfect setting to play war or cowboys and Indians.

Every kid who happened along could join in. The neighborhood was pretty diverse with whites of various ethnicities. There were a few Jews, some Italians, Irish Catholics, and the kids who had come to the North with their parents from Appalachia. On sunny days, we would play until we were summoned inside. When the weather did not allow us to go outside we managed to conduct raids and combat missions indoors.

Sometimes our pretend fights became real. When Ari was still sleeping in a crib, Rahm and I would climb onto the top level of our bunk bed and jump into it with such force that it rattled the hardware that held it together and bounced Ari off the mattress and into the air. The bunk beds were a definite center of aggression. The difference this time was that, unlike Rahm when he was an infant, Ari loved it when we landed in his crib like airborne troops.

We also waged an endless series of skirmishes and sneak attacks. We built forts using pillows and blankets arranged on the lower bunk, which then became strategic ground that had to be defended. Usually Ari and Rahm attacked me, throwing pillows and trying to wrestle me onto the floor. If they prevailed, they would take possession of the little bunk bed Masada, reconstruct its fortifications, and defend it from my attacks as a giant, a monster, or a roaring dinosaur.

Little boys have always been fascinated by fighting and they seem almost biologically driven to act out elaborate mock battles complete with imaginary wounds and melodramatic deaths. Our mother, who was a self-described pacifist, refused to let us have any toy guns, even squirt guns. But there was nothing she could do to prevent us from shaping our fingers into pretend pistols, which we could use to "kill" each other. We did. Many times each day. And at night, when the room was illuminated by one of those little night-lights that plug directly into the wall socket, we prowled in the shadows to make sneak attacks. As a grown man, Rahm would tell me he was never afraid of the dark, or monsters, "but I was scared of the people in the room." Considering his size, he may well have been wary, if not afraid of, Ari and me, but I remember he held his own during all sorts of combat.

Our father, who was working hard to establish his practice and make us solidly middle-class, often came home after dinner had been served because he had to make house calls, visit patients in the hospital, or handle appointments on Monday and Thursday nights, when the office was open until 9 P.M. Depending on the time, we would mob him in the dining room or he might help with baths and getting us into pajamas so that my mother could give us each our nightly time alone with her. This habit of making sure she spent fifteen or twenty minutes with each of us, either talking or reading to us, was something she started when Rahm was a toddler and it probably went a long way toward making sure we each felt we received the individual attention we needed. As she explained it to me once, "Every child should feel like he's as special as an only child, for at least a little time every day."

Maintaining this routine was not always easy. Our wild play sometimes produced real bruises and bloody wounds that required serious intervention. When I was five, I once missed the seat of a children's chair and hit the back of my head on a cast-iron radiator with a Tootsie Pop in my mouth. The impact knocked three teeth out of my mouth and left a fourth dangling by a little strand of tissue. A few years later, Rahm suffered a terrible hand injury. My friend Georgie announced that he had learned some dirty jokes and was eager to share them. We were in the vestibule of his building next door, and he and I decided to dash outside to exclude Rahm from hearing the jokes. Rahm rushed to follow us, and the huge oaken door slammed on his hand.

He was screaming in pain, two fingers crushed and spurting blood. I took him home as fast as I could and there my mother wrapped his injured left hand. In the cab en route to nearby Edgewater Hospital, she struggled and sometimes failed to stay composed. The hand surgeon who unwrapped Rahm's hand found the two fingertips dangling from shreds of skin. He stitched them back together as well as he could, although to this day they look a little lumpy, as if the tips were hastily pasted on.

I still have a sense of guilt about this episode. Even after all this time some part of me feels I failed in my duties as a big brother. But this would not be the last time Rahm suffered a serious hand injury.

Hands seem to be our family's Achilles' heel. Years later Rahm would cut his finger on his right hand at Arby's and require amputation. And one Sunday on the way to friends' house for brunch I was caught between my brothers in the backseat of my father's Pontiac Grand Prix as Ari and Rahm wrestled over an opened can of mixed nuts. Suddenly the tips of two fingers on Ari's hand were sliced almost completely off by the sharp rim. Blood spurted on all three of us. Possessed, my father drove straight to Mount Sinai Hospital emergency room, where he made a perfect repair himself.

Fortunately, despite constant and intense physical play, deep wounds and broken bones requiring hospital trips were the exception, not the rule, for our day-to-day lives. Our more common mishaps were minor ones, which nevertheless led to howls of complaint. When my mother ran out of patience with our whining, her frustration turned to anger. We would be so lost in whatever frantic game we had concocted that we failed to notice the growing tension and her outburst would surprise us.

Every kid who has ever pushed his mother past the breaking point knows the shocked feeling that comes when you hear her voice reach that certain decibel level and feel the slap of her open hand on your behind or cheek. Tall and strong, my mother could make herself into a physically imposing presence, especially in the eyes of someone who is four feet tall. The leverage supplied by her rather long arms meant that her swats were delivered with a surprising amount of power.

Worse than the physical punishment were the long silences that followed. Time passes slowly for children. My mother could seethe for hours, sometimes even for days, after breaking. The mix of feelings we experienced when this was going on—guilt, confusion, anxiety, loss—was excruciating. Our mother's dark mood cast a pall over the entire household. Worst of all, we felt powerless to affect it. No apology, dandelion bouquet, or handmade card would make her smile if she wasn't ready and willing.

Years later my mother would tell us that for every time she lost her temper or retreated in silence, there were a hundred moments when she was afraid we would push her over the edge and she managed to keep her cool. Of those times when she whacked us or gave us the silent treatment, she would say she was protecting us from something worse. "You boys would drive anyone crazy," she would say. "Believe me."

As adults we were able to imagine some of the pressure she felt, especially in the period when she had three hyperactive preschool kids and one judgmental mother-in-law, all jammed into a three-bedroom apartment. Savta could not have been much help. She wasn't particularly interested in taking care of us, and she often voiced her disapproval of her son's marriage and criticized my mother's efforts to be a good wife and parent. She once offered my mother ten thousand dollars to leave our father. My mother never figured out if this was a joke or not.

A lonely widow deprived of her lifelong friends and familiar surroundings in Tel Aviv, Savta would not have been happy in Chicago under any circumstances. As the overprotective mother of one living child, she wouldn't be satisfied with anyone who married her son. Benjamin Emanuel could have proposed to Golda Meir and Savta would have found something lacking. In Marsha Emanuel, she believed she saw an ambitious American who would weigh her precious son down with too many children and grandiose expectations for the privileged kind of life she saw on American television. Big cars and suburban houses represented to Savta a trap that would prevent her son from returning to Tel Aviv to live. And she was certain that his wicked wife would force him to choose this American life over Israel, which meant that she would have to accept either exile in the United States or life without her son in Tel Aviv.

What Savta did not understand was that my father was the one most devoted to the American dream of a home in the suburbs, two cars in the garage, and a climb up the social ladder. He liked both the challenges and the opportunities of working in the country with the most technologically advanced medicine. He also enjoyed the culture, comforts, and opportunities that surrounded him in the richest country in the world. Sure, he loved his homeland, and he imagined that he might one day return. But it was my mother who longed for Israel the most. After all, in the short time she had lived there she had had more close friends than she had ever known in America and gold had literally rained down on her from above.

Three

THE EMANUELS

The story of the gold begins in Odessa, on the Black Sea, long before my mother and father were born and, indeed, before the family was even called by the name Emanuel. As pogroms and civil wars blazed across the Russian Empire, hundreds of thousands of Jews fled to Western Europe, America, and to what was then called Palestine. Today, millions of families in America and around the world can trace their stories back to these displaced Jews of Russia and Eastern Europe. To others, these events can seem like distant history. To us they are both shrouded in faded memories and deeply personal dramas filled with danger and heroism and lessons that echo in our own attitudes and perspectives.

I was told that my father's relatives left their home in Odessa in 1905 after selling substantial landholdings. With their fortune converted to gold coins and diamonds, they immigrated to Jerusalem. At that time my ancestors went by the name of Auerbach. My father's father, who was also named Ezekiel, opened a pharmacy financed by an old friend from Odessa who was passing through Palestine on his way to settle in Rome. The pharmacy supported his wife; his eldest son, Emanuel; and the younger Benjamin, who was born in Israel in

1927. Ever suspicious and fearful, Ezekiel hid away the gold coins and jewels against an uncertain future. He told no one, not even his wife, Penina, where he put them.

While not political activists, the Auerbachs were Zionists who supported the ultimate creation of a Jewish state that would be a bulwark against the anti-Semitism and terror they had seen in Europe. Before this dream could be realized, they and other Jewish pioneers who had come to Palestine would have to wait out the British occupation, which had begun at the end of World War I. The Jews and Arabs of Palestine both resented British rule, but during a period that ran from 1930 into the 1940s the Arabs were the most violent in their opposition to both the occupation and to the Jewish immigrants who came fleeing anti-Semitism, oppression, and then Adolf Hitler. Thousands of Arabs and hundreds of Jews died in clashes with each other and with the British authorities. One of them was my father's older brother Emanuel.

In November 1933, the same month when Marsha Smulevitz was born in Chicago, Emanuel Auerbach was standing on the edge of a conflict between protesters and police in Jerusalem when a bullet ricocheted off the pavement and struck his leg. The wound itself was not life-threatening, but it soon became infected. With effective antibiotics, yet to be developed, Emanuel would have lived. Instead he died of the infection. He was buried in the Mount of Olives Cemetery, which is in East Jerusalem and overlooks the Old City. Soon after their son's death, Ezekiel and Penina changed the family name to honor their son. On a visit to Israel in 2010, my eldest daughter and I, with the help of an ancient Arab caretaker of the cemetery and a right-wing Jewish settler cabdriver, eventually located the grave, which no one in the family had seen since at least 1948.

Ezekiel and Penina never really recovered from Emanuel's death. My brothers and I learned this not from my father but from people who knew him as a child. They described my father's parents as serious, almost grim people who devoted themselves to their business and lived very quietly. As my father's grade school classmate and lifelong friend Batya Carmi recalled, "He grew up as an only child but under the dark cloud of his dead brother."

To slip from under that cloud, Ben spent as much time as possible away from his parents' store and the apartment. Little interested in academics, but sociable and friendly, he was more like Ari and Rahm than me. Even he would admit that in school he "tried to get the most for the least effort," which was something he would later say many times about Rahm, another second child.

We boys loved to hear about our parents' childhood, and storytelling was frequently part of our bedtime ritual. We visited my parents' bed, en masse, just about every night. Usually our mom read a chapter from a book, but whenever we could get our father and mother to tell us stories from their own lives we were especially attentive.

In later years I was struck with how world events affected the course of my father's life. As a boy he lived at one of the great flashpoints of history and, while he escaped the Holocaust, he nevertheless knew what it was like to be the subject of violent hatred. He also participated in the founding of Israel and its development as a frontier nation. But as important as these aspects of his life were, my brothers and I were far more intrigued by the tales that revealed our father as a shovav like us.

The Ben Emanuel we learned to know from those stories was a class clown, a middling student, a fantastic dancer, and an avid movie fan. (In one of his stories his best Shabbat white shirt was ripped to shreds in the frenzy outside the theater prior to the local premiere of *Flash Gordon*.) He told us about long days spent at the beach, lots of dances, and a class costume party where he dressed up as Charlie Chaplin. From then on his nickname was Charlie, which stuck, so much so that Batya still calls him that.

Together, the stories they painted revealed a footloose, Huck Finn kind of kid in a sunny Tel Aviv that was more small town than big city. It was Hannibal, Missouri, on the Mediterranean, a place where a boy could roam from the shore to the markets to the cinema and get into mischief without encountering any serious trouble.

Hovering over it all, of course, was the tension between the Jews and the Arabs and their shared anger at their British overseers. The bigotry that simmered in Tel Aviv was both conceptual and personal. For example, when my father's aunt, a nurse, married an Arab doctor she had met in a hospital, the couple went to great lengths to obscure their relationship. The doctor, who eventually became a high official in the health-care system, actually hid behind closed doors when people visited his home because both sides—Jews and Arabs—suspected he was some sort of spy. The man, whom my father knew only as "Dr. Ayoub," eventually played a key role in his life, but for years he lived in the shadows.

Dr. Ayoub's fears were well-founded. Both the Jews and the Arabs operated secret security organizations that acted with deadly force, and he correctly feared assassination from both sides. More commonly, Arabs and Jews clashed spontaneously in the streets, with small incidents escalating into brawls that sometimes brought gunfire and fatalities. A smart kid who kept his wits about him could flee before getting caught up in these melees. My father succeeded at this, escaping the fate that befell his brother in order to serve the Zionist cause in a much more prosaic way—clearing land at a distant kibbutz.

Like many other young Israeli men, my father waited out World War II, nursing dreams of a better future that included a sovereign Jewish state. And like most of his peers, he joined a paramilitary group that was preparing for a war of independence. His most dangerous activities involved handing out literature, and plastering political posters on the walls of city buildings at night. The only violence he experienced was when a British officer on horseback caught him trying to paste a propaganda poster on a building. The man beat him with a stick, giving him the only wounds—a series of bruises—he ever suffered in the Zionist cause.

When World War II ended and negotiations over Palestine's future began, my father looked for a chance to escape the shadow of his brother and see something more of the world. Restrictions imposed by the British authorities made it almost impossible for young men to travel abroad except to study in disciplines unavailable locally. Medicine was one of those disciplines. My father applied to study at several medical schools in the United States and Europe. Given his lackluster grades, his acceptance at the rather exclusive University of Lausanne in Switzerland was a bit of a surprise.

Whenever my father's stories focused on his life after adolescence, Ari, Rahm, and I would pay extra-close attention because this was when the juicy stuff, full of obstacles, adventure, and sex, entered the picture. A good example was his passage to Lausanne. In 1946 the British navy policed shipping in the Mediterranean and often sent migrating Jews back to their ports of embarkation. A few captains used daring tactics to evade or outrun the blockade. More than once these races ended with a ship aground on the shore and people leaping into the water and swimming in the Mediterranean to beaches. Against this backdrop, our father very nervously boarded a Romanian ship docked in Haifa for a voyage to Marseilles. His suitcase contained just two suits and a wool coat. In his wallet were a few British pounds. Just before the lines were cast off, police officers stormed onto the ship demanding to see Benjamin Emanuel. When they found him, they took him ashore to a little military post. Terrified, my father was sure he would be denied permission to leave. Instead the officers explained that a friend, Dr. Ayoub, had asked them to make sure he was treated well. Relieved, my father assured them that he was quite happy and returned to the ship. The voyage to Marseilles took more than four days, and traveling to Lausanne by train across the war-ravaged countryside took the better part of another week.

Benjamin Emanuel arrived at the medical school in March. He had no place to live, and was months behind the other students. Somehow he managed to persuade school officials to let him try to catch up with his classmates. He found shelter with a local family but this arrangement was only temporary. "They wouldn't let you bring women home," he explained, slyly. In a matter of weeks he found a new place to live with an eclectic group of ten fellow students—French, Caribbean, South American—who occupied most of a small apartment building. It was an easygoing group that shared chores like cooking and cleaning. As my father would recall, the toughest job involved keeping the coal-fired stoves that heated the place supplied with fuel that was stored in the basement.

Adopting a regimen that would see him through his entire education, my father rose every morning at six and studied in his room until noon. In the beginning, he focused on learning French, since all of his classes would be conducted in this language and he knew none of it at all. With the help of the French *Reader's Digest* and a translation dictionary he would pass his first oral exam—which was given six weeks after his arrival—with little difficulty.

The six-hour workday plan left my father with plenty of time to go to movies, hang out in cafés, date young women, and generally have fun—or, as he would tell us, "live the life of Riley." The apartment in Lausanne became the scene of many parties, late-night political debates, competitive chess matches, and romantic escapades. Whenever he brought up the subject of Claire, the beautiful Swiss girlfriend who almost became his wife, my mother gave him a look that instantly changed the story line. But she did let him tell us—many times over the years—the famous "breast cream" story.

The tale begins with a young woman who wanted to win a local beauty contest but was worried that her breasts were too small. With their very best "Trust us, we're doctors" demeanor my father and his suite mates told her about a new cream they were developing at the medical school that could augment her chance for victory. It was such special stuff that it had to be applied "just so," which meant that she would have to drop by the apartment every day for weeks so these would-be doctors could carefully and methodically rub it in. She agreed to the plan. The cream was only ordinary moisturizer, but after weeks of the treatment, when she actually won the contest, their "patient" credited the special cream.

In the breast cream story, and most of his other memories, my father is usually the instigator for adventures that involve a host of characters from different backgrounds and cultures. He liked and admired most of his fellow students, except for the Americans. Part of his feeling stemmed from the fact that they were rich. Living off the GI Bill and a very favorable postwar exchange rate, the American students could afford cars and meals in restaurants. The other source of my father's resentment was the feeling that they studied "like parrots," memorizing facts without mastering concepts. Most performed poorly on their exams and many were still in Lausanne, acting like perpetual students, long after my father graduated.

My father's graduation was delayed by Israel's 1948 War of Independence, and an escapade that made him seem to us like a character from a James Bond movie. The tale began as Zionists prepared for the war by expanding the paramilitary organizations of Haganah and Irgun. Both secretly bought arms on the world market and recruited Jews, especially those who had fought in World War II, to help acquire them. In February 1948 my father and three friends were approached in Lausanne by an operative who went by the name Ben David. He wanted them to accompany him on an arms-purchasing mission. My father instantly volunteered and joined the others for a train trip to Vienna and then on to Prague, where Czech officials were prepared to sell thousands of World War II surplus rifles to the Jewish paramilitary.

Secret negotiations had led to an agreement on the shipment, which would be made in defiance of a United Nations ban against the sale of military hardware to either Arabs or Jews in the former Mandate of Palestine. Officials all over Europe were on the alert to stop this kind of trade. My father and his mates could be arrested and imprisoned at any moment.

Their first stop was the Rothschild Hospital, which was on a street called Währinger Gürtel in the sector of Vienna controlled by U.S. forces. Once home to a neurological institute headed by Viktor Frankl, the hospital occupied a massive five-story building that had been built in the 1870s and subsequently expanded to serve a growing Jewish population. Shut down as Jews were rounded up during the Holocaust, it became after the war a center for displaced persons. Tens of thousands of Jews from around Europe had transited through the building on their way to Israel.

On the day my father and his nervous friends arrived at the hospital they were told to go to the top floor and knock on a closed door. It opened into a room where a couple of men sat at a table. Surrounding them were piles of banknotes from various countries, stacked from floor to ceiling. The quantities were enormous and must have amounted to tens of millions of dollars.

Ben David was handed a big valise full of this cash, which would travel with the group to Prague. There they would meet their Czech contacts, confirm that an additional sum of money had been transferred by wire to pay for the arms, and inspect the weapons. They were also given a map showing various banks in the city and told to look in the potted plants in front of each one for a cache of diamonds that had supposedly been hidden by some wealthy Jewish man before he was captured by the Nazis.

The train route north to Prague covered about two hundred and fifty miles. Inspectors at the border checked the passports, travel documents, and belongings of some passengers who were seemingly selected at random. My father and his mates were passed over. Once they arrived in Prague, they found a room for the night, and rested anxiously with their valuable luggage. In the morning, on February 25, 1948, they located the banks and searched all the potted plants, but found no gems in the dirt. When Ben David then tried to make contact with the Czechs, he discovered that during the day, the communists had completed a bloodless coup. All the officials who had agreed to the arms sale were forced out of power. Anyone who had come to Prague to do business with them would be wise to escape. Ben David and his confederates did just that, catching the first available train and crossing the border before it was closed.

The story of the secret mission to Prague, the room full of money at the Rothschild Hospital, and the coup that put our father in danger made him appear bold, dashing, and brave to us. He always emphasized the fact that the whole adventure was a bust, and he never figured out why Ben David needed four clueless Jewish medical students from Switzerland to accompany him. We overlooked these details in favor of fantasies about secret drops in planters, storerooms filled with cash, clandestine rendezvous, and wartime intrigue. The truth probably lay somewhere between the two.

One message of this story for us boys was the idea that when duty and adventure call, you say "Yes!" even if your role is unclear and you don't understand all the details of the plan. And it came back in full force when President Obama asked Rahm to become his chief of staff. Rahm hated the idea. He had rapidly risen in Congress and thought he had a chance to become the first Jewish Speaker of the House in due course. Giving up his House seat would end that dream. Every day after the offer Rahm would call me and shout into the phone, "I don't want to do it! I don't have to do it!" All the while he knew he had no choice, he had to do it. It was his duty. Indeed, he was shouting at me precisely because he knew he was going to serve the president regardless of his personal preferences, and secure in the knowledge that I would never be insulted.

Soon after my father's safe return to Lausanne, he decided to go home to Tel Aviv and join the forces fighting to create the new state of Israel. He reported to a camp on the French Riviera where volunteers from all over the world, including some non-Jews who believed in Zionism, were being mustered. After a brief orientation, he boarded a small ship bound for the Israeli coast, which ship ran into a storm that caused so much seasickness my father recalled "I needed hours to wash all the vomit off of me." When he finally arrived, he was first assigned to work as an orderly in a mental institution but soon transferred to active military service on the southern front, near the border with Egypt.

Perhaps because my mother was such a pacifist, the war stories he told us downplayed the fighting, but we heard enough to understand that he had received very little training before he was assigned to what passed for Israeli artillery: a unit that patrolled in jeeps mounted with machine guns. His most daring mission involved an assault on Gaza, where the Egyptian army, which invaded when the Israelis declared their independence, had established a base. The Israeli Defense Forces (IDF) battle plan called for various units to attack from the south and east. My father's group won a series of skirmishes as the Israeli forces encircled the Egyptians and cut their supply routes. With little opposition, my father's unit advanced westward past the border and reached the Egyptian coastal town of El Arish. There British airplanes dropped leaflets warning them to pull back or face an aerial attack. They beat a rapid retreat. So much for my father's heroism.

When he spoke of the war my father usually omitted any reference to being shot at by the enemy and firing back. In the first tellings of the war stories, especially the one about the Gaza attack, he said he drove the jeep and when the shooting started he merely fed the ammunition to the machine gunner. Eventually, when we were older, he confirmed that he had taken his turn at the trigger.

Our father harbored no doubts about the Zionist cause or the need for a strong Israeli military posture and he was proud to have done his duty. But he did not talk about the damages his unit inflicted on the other side, and never said anything to suggest that fighting was anything but serious, even dreadful business. In short, he spoke about war in the way of a father who hoped his sons would never see one. If anything, our father's war stories offered lessons on the unpredictable nature of life and the unexpected consequences that can arise from the choices we make.

.....

The Israeli victory at Gaza left the Egyptian army trapped in the city and forced its government to negotiate an end to the war. My father left the IDF and returned to Lausanne to complete his medical studies. During his final year in medical school, my father was elected president of the student body. Charming and compassionate, he negotiated with the dean—a famous physician called Blackie—on behalf of classmates who had trouble in their studies. He never forgot the student who outpointed him on the final exam to graduate first in the class. "A big round Syrian guy who never went to the movies, never even took a walk," my father would say. "But he was all right. So I came in second. Big deal."

Always forward-looking, my father set his sights on internships in the United States, which was the best place for a young doctor to learn the practical skills he needed. A weeklong voyage brought him to New York City, where my father arrived with a treasured Parker ballpoint pen and twenty-five dollars in his pocket. The immigration officer who checked his papers said, "A Jewish doctor in America? You'll be married in a month or two." My father took just enough time to gape at the skyscrapers before getting on a bus bound for Cincinnati and its world-famous children's hospital.

Welcomed into a training program populated by a mix of Americans and foreigners, my father found that the ones trained in the United States were far ahead of him in practical skills. This was most apparent in the emergency room, where the others knew how to take histories, examine patients, and perform dozens of procedures. In Europe, medical students were trained in the theory of medicine, not to perform practical duties. Lost and insecure, he bumbled along for a few months making lots of mistakes. Some of these errors were as minor as a misplaced intravenous line. Others, like an extremely crude circumcision, would have a lasting effect.

Fortunately, senior doctors helped my father catch up. His extensive medical knowledge and reasoning skills from Switzerland combined with the trial by fire in Cincinnati eventually made him an excellent practitioner. He was an especially good diagnostician, distinguishing common conditions from the unusual cases that needed special attention. During a six-week rotation in a polio ward, where patients were confined to iron lungs, he learned the finer skills of relating to families in crisis. The experience taught him that his own psychological survival required that he maintain some professional distance to avoid having his heart broken every day.

In his off time, my father took in the wonders of America. Like most immigrants he was amazed by the abundance of food, the music, the beautiful women, and other diversions that were difficult to find in postwar Europe. After a couple of Cuban doctors taught him a costly lesson about poker he decided he preferred jazz clubs to gambling and he spent many a night in Cincinnati's black neighborhoods, where the live music, performed by some of the greats, such as Louis Armstrong, could be heard all night long.

Despite being in Ohio, Cincinnati was, at the time, very much a southern city, where whites and blacks rarely socialized together.

Raised in Israel and having spent six years in Europe, where there were few blacks but they were well integrated into society, my father was completely oblivious to this racial taboo and could never understand why anyone cared. But he raised a few eyebrows when he began to date a black woman. Indeed, he was called in by the head of the hospital and informed about the color line. If he wanted to stay on staff, he was told, he would have to end the relationship. He continued to see the woman surreptitiously until the relationship ended in its own way. He raised many more eyebrows when a local mobster learned that my father had been flirting with his girlfriend.

The woman in question had been hospitalized for a nose job. The plastic surgeon assigned my father to change her dressing daily. She was so beautiful that my father did the job three times a day. He and his patient hit it off so well that eventually her boyfriend became concerned.

Based across the Ohio River in Covington, Kentucky, the local Mafia wasn't exactly Murder Inc., but it was a force to be feared. And though he did not realize it, my father's flirtations were so dangerous that they quickly became the talk of the hospital.

Matters turned serious when two suspicious men pulled up to the hospital in a fancy new Buick Roadmaster and entered the lobby. They asked an alert hospital receptionist where they could find Dr. Emanuel. She saw bulges that she took to be guns in shoulder holsters inside their coats, and while they walked toward the elevator she quickly called the chief resident, a very proper British physician.

The chief resident immediately recognized the danger, quickly located my father, and, with no time to spare, took him down a back stairway and out to the staff parking lot, where he stuffed him into his car. They raced to the train station, where the chief bought my father a ticket to Toronto, jabbed a few dollars into his shirt pocket, and watched him board a northbound train. Here was my father on a speeding train with only the clothes on his back and a few dollars in his pocket. As the train chugged northward my father, an Israeli, realized that he had no passport to show at the border to enter Canada.

My father was not particularly handsome. As my mother described him to her parents, he looked liked he ran into a brick wall nose first and had slightly buck teeth. However, my father always has been attractive because of his energy, warmth, charm, and talent for finding some connection with people from all cultures and walks of life. He rarely observed social formalities and niceties—something he has passed on to his boys. He was prone to getting involved in various shenanigans, some of them quite dangerous. Characteristically he depended on his considerable charm and humor to get him out of jams. This adventure was no different. He struck up a conversation with a couple who were traveling back to their home in Rochester, New York. Once they heard about my father's tale and current predicament, they invited the young doctor with the funny accent to stay with them. During that stay he tried twice to cross into Canada but was turned away both times.

After two weeks spent hiding out in the couple's Rochester home, my father returned to Cincinnati to discover that he was still a hunted man. The chief resident recommended a permanent move. My father went to the interns' quarters, collected his belongings, and fled to Chicago. The move would be the most important one he ever made.

.....

In Chicago my father learned they needed pediatricians at Mount Sinai Hospital. Occupying more than a full city block and overlooking Douglas Park, Mount Sinai had been founded in 1919 to serve the Chicago Jewish community of North Lawndale at a time when that area was home to thousands of recent immigrants from Eastern Europe, including my mother's parents. It was also created to aid the training of Jewish doctors, who were excluded by the major university hospitals in the city. Interns and fellows at Mount Sinai followed the kind of demanding program you would have found at any American teaching hospital in that era, which is why Benjamin Emanuel was dead on his feet on a late night in October as he delivered a young patient to the X-ray department, which was near the emergency room.

An attending physician believed the boy had a condition called intussusception, in which a portion of the intestine telescopes into another, interrupts blood flow, and can cause a life-threatening perforation. Benjamin was sure his boss was wrong, but what he thought did not matter. He handed the boy over to a tall, dark-haired radiology technician who listened to his request for films and then told him she wasn't very busy and could develop the pictures for him. He went into the hallway, climbed onto one of the spare emergency room gurneys, and closed his eyes to get some rest.

An hour passed as the X-rays were taken and developed. When she was finished, technician Marsha Smulevitz brought them out to show to the doctor, whom she found asleep on the gurney in the hallway. She playfully released the lock on the wheels of the gurney and let it roll down a ramp through the emergency room doors and into the cold night air. The young doctor awakened amused, not annoyed, and grinned as he pushed the gurney back to where it belonged.

A quick scan of the images confirmed that the doctor who had sent him on this radiological errand was wrong. The boy did not have an intussusception. My father then considered the funny young woman who had brought the pictures and decided it would be a good idea to invite her for breakfast. That first breakfast lasted for hours and led to a game of pool in the residents' lounge. At the time nurses and technicians were forbidden from entering this little haven for male physicians, but Ben Emanuel wasn't much for observing such rules.

Soon after, the couple had their first formal date, at an Italian restaurant called Papa Milano's. In the days that followed, they spent every spare hour together. She told him about her family, growing up in Chicago, and her strong views on civil rights and equality. He told her about his brother Emanuel and his adventures around the world.

Marsha was amused by Ben's stories but more taken by his attitude. He loved medicine and had worked hard at becoming a good doctor, but he did not want to be treated like a god, which was a status too many people were happy to grant any physician in a white coat. Marsha was so impressed with this mensch that after just a few days she called her mother and said, "I think I met the man I'm going to spend the rest of my life with." Then, less than two weeks after the gurney ride, he asked her to marry him, and one day settle in Israel.

She said yes even though, as she recalled, "I knew everyone would think we were crazy."

My mother's parents, noting that Marsha's older sister Esther was unmarried, said that tradition required a low-key event. Hoping to give the groom's parents time to travel from Israel, they set a date ten months into the future. However, Ezekiel and Penina did not make the trip. Heeding her parents' advice about avoiding a big show, Ben and Marsha paid for the rabbi and caterer themselves and were married on August 21, 1955, in my aunt Shirley's apartment. By this time, my father was finished with his residency and ready to go into the world and make some money.

A job offering $450 per month plus free room and board brought my parents to Elgin State Hospital, a sprawling old redbrick campus thirty miles west of Chicago, where more than a thousand psychiatric patients received little more than custodial care. Appalled by the conditions he found, my father began reviewing cases. He discovered that many of the patients had been improperly diagnosed and some had been committed on no basis other than that their families did not want them. He discharged as many of these patients as he could. He also helped a researcher who was conducting a study on the use of the stimulant Ritalin, with comatose patients. They found it could rouse some patients out of their torpor.

When his one-year contract ended my father considered the hopelessness of the state mental health system and left Elgin for a chief residency in pediatrics at St. Louis Children's Hospital. With this training my father could have picked from a number of job offers, including one from a prominent St. Louis pediatrician that would have made him a partner in a prestigious private practice. But he thought about his mother living alone in Israel and decided it was time to return.

Although my mother's parents begged her to stay in America, she agreed to go to Israel. She and my father traveled by train to New York and then sailed to Naples, Italy. There they used some of the money they had saved while living at the mental institution in Elgin to buy a little Fiat 500 that traveled by ship with them to Israel and a new life.

.....

In 1957 Israel was an eight-year-old democracy with murderously hostile neighbors on three sides and a population that included roughly
two million Jews and about eight hundred thousand Arabs.

When they arrived in Tel Aviv, my parents found few comforts.
Food, especially meat and eggs, was being rationed and apartments
were so scarce that they had to crowd in with Penina. However, the
country buzzed with an abundant sense of idealism and purpose.
Hundreds of thousands of immigrants, many of whom were displaced
by the Holocaust and came with absolutely nothing, were busy creating a brand-new government, army, public institutions, and an entire
economy. Entrepreneurs competed to serve an ever-growing demand
for their goods and services while rural settlers established farms, or-
chards, and dairies. In this environment, people felt they were part of
something momentous. They were.

My mother loved everything about Israel, from the warmth of the
Mediterranean climate to the variety of the people she encountered.
She became very friendly with a family in her building, named Connor, who had fled Germany for Russia and eventually settled in Harbin, China. With the rise of Mao they had been forced to flee again,
and wound up in Israel. One of the Connor daughters married a
man who had also come to Israel from Harbin. He had made a fortune
on pearls he had managed to smuggle out of China. Stories of pearl
smuggling and narrow escapes were commonplace among the Jewish
settlers. Indeed, everyone had endured so much hardship that it seemed
silly to waste time on picayune differences. Friendships were formed
quickly as everyone sought a sense of connection and community in
this new place. Mrs. Connor welcomed both of my parents to visit her
apartment whenever they needed anything. One day when my father
popped in to say hello he found her cooking in nothing but her apron
and her underwear. Her false teeth sat in a glass. Terribly self-conscious
about her dentures, she immediately lifted the apron to cover her
toothless mouth.

The building was also home to a family named Yacoby, who were

Kurdish Jews from Iraq and became my parents' lifelong friends. Mr. Yacoby owned a jewelry store in nearby Jaffa, which became a trading center about five thousand years ago. In a place so ancient, one senses the mortal realities of our existence. Mr. Yacoby certainly seemed filled with a certain existential perspective. He often said that he would live only as long as his antique watch continued to tick. He did not know that at night his son slipped it off his wrist so he could keep it in good repair.

Like Mr. Yacoby, many of our neighbors in Tel Aviv delighted my mother with their stories, insights, and warmth. When she wasn't with them, she took long walks through quiet neighborhoods and along the Mediterranean shore, which was only a block away from our apartment on Mendele Street. Sometimes she went with friends to explore the countryside. On many afternoons she worked in the family drugstore. Pretty, friendly, and never prudish, she became the favorite of shy men who needed condoms.

While my mother enjoyed everything about her life in Israel, my father struggled to find satisfying work in a country that was overrun with doctors. When a job in a hospital turned out to be little more than a record-keeping assignment, he accepted a national health service post serving five frontier kibbutzes. The post came with a jeep, a driver, a pistol that did not work, and a schedule that required him to be in a different little clinic every day. Most of his patients had nothing wrong with them but came looking for a letter authorizing them to travel to the city for tests, or a specialist's care. This allowed them to get transport for a day of shopping or sightseeing in Tel Aviv. When he turned them down, they complained to his boss. Others had grown accustomed to getting prescriptions for antibiotics even when they did not need them. When my father prescribed rest but no medicine for viral illnesses, they complained as well. His supervisor told him to just write the prescriptions so that the complaints would stop.

The one person who did not complain to my father about her medical condition, although she could have, was my mother. She arrived in Israel pregnant and was thrilled by the prospect of becoming a mother. She experienced very little morning sickness or other discomforts, and

often said she never felt better than when she was expecting. But like
every woman in the last trimester, she needed the bathroom during the
night.

Nighttime bathroom trips became trickier when a bulb in the ceiling light fixture burned out. My father, who is utterly incompetent
(even negligent) when it came to the simplest household repairs, never
got around to replacing it. After stubbing her toe for the umpteenth
time, she got tired of asking. She got a chair, dragged it into the hallway, placed it under the light, and climbed up. As she loosened the
bulb a shower of coins fell out of the fixture.

She had discovered a cache of nineteenth-century forty-franc
French gold coins—people called them Napoleons—that my grandfather had hidden many years before. The discovery surprised my
grandmother, who remembered hearing something about her husband
hiding the coins. He had died without telling her where they were, and
after a brief search she had given up looking for them. Now that a
small fortune in coins had been found, my parents and grandmother
put more than a little effort into looking for more. They found a few
more in the ceiling lights of the pharmacy, but with all their tapping
on walls, peering inside electrical outlets, and drilling of holes, they
failed to turn up the mother lode, which they suspected lurked somewhere in the building.

With gold falling on her head and her baby arriving right on schedule on September 6, my mother was content. She and my father named
me Ezekiel Jonathan Emanuel—Ezekiel to honor my grandfather and
Jonathan because my mom liked it. Unhappy with the idea of calling
a baby by a prophetic Old Testament name, my mother took to calling
me Jonny. In the back of her mind she also thought that this name
would serve me better if we ever moved back to America. It was 1957,
after all, a conformist time when names like John and William were
the norm and something as exotic as Ezekiel would provoke a lot of
teasing.

Israel would always be our second home. As boys we returned frequently for the summers. Rahm and Ari both spent time in Israel as
young adults—Rahm after college and Ari during high school. I would

take my eldest daughter there when she was six months old for her first trip, and then when her sisters arrived, we would often spend a month during the summers in an apartment overlooking the Mediterranean so they could learn Hebrew in an *ulpan*, jump the waves, shop in the markets, and soak up Israeli life and culture. After graduating from college, my eldest would spend a year in Israel learning Hebrew, studying how to care for the terminally ill, and making friends with peace activists from both Palestinian and Israeli sides. All three brothers and our families would finally reunite in Israel for the bar mitzvahs of Rahm's and Ari's eldest sons in 2010.

For a while I was raised by the little village that was our apartment building. Everyone fussed over me and a young woman named Zeeva became my regular sitter for the times when my mother and father both worked. As Zeeva would remember, I was a very vocal and curious baby. I took my first steps at nine months and was running a few weeks later. At around this time they would put me outside on the balcony of the apartment with little bowls filled with steamed vegetables for me to gnaw on. I would stand with one hand on the ironwork of the balcony and wave a piece of broccoli while delivering a lecture like a Roman emperor to anyone who would listen.

Esther, my mother's unmarried older sister, came to help my mother with her new baby and she too fell in love with the life in Israel's city by the sea. We might have all stayed, permanently, if Israel had more to offer a young doctor with my father's interests and ambition. He wanted to be a pediatrician, but Israel needed general practitioners, so that was what he was asked to do. The longer he served as a GP for frontier kibbutzes the less likely he was to get into pediatrics. His prospects grew even worse when the government sent him to a military outpost near Jerusalem to care for a contingent of police and soldiers.

The base was on an isolated hilltop near Jerusalem called Mount Scopus. All the surrounding territory was controlled by Jordan, which meant the outpost was accessible only with the aid of United Nations peacekeepers. Israeli convoys were permitted to supply the base but the Jordanian troops periodically barred them and gunfire was common between them and the Israeli Defense Forces. Every once in a while the Jordanians wounded one of the Israeli sentries and it would be up to my father to scamper out to get him and then fix him up. The Jordanians suspected that the Israelis were secretly fortifying their positions, which was against the agreement governing the situation. In fact, the IDF troops *were* working every night on fortifications, but given the gunfire coming from the other side, you could hardly blame them.

While my father was there, he came under regular gunfire and risked his own life scurrying into the line of fire to help the wounded. Sometimes this happened in the middle of the break periods when the troops would make up teams and kick a soccer ball around a patch of dirt. My father, who was usually in the game, would run to the wounded player and help carry him to safety. Since he was acting as a medic, the snipers left him alone even when he returned to rescue the ball.

Because he spoke fluent English my father also sometimes served as liaison with George Flint, a Canadian officer who oversaw the UN peacekeepers. Flint came every day with mail during a two-month period when the Jordanians blockaded Mount Scopus and my father and all the other Israelis were trapped there. At one point, he told my father he had been cleared to return to Canada but was staying on to arrange to ship a car home, duty-free.

Thanks to Flint and the intervention of higher-level UN officials, the blockade was ended and my father was able to return home to discover that the two-month-old baby he had left behind was now six months old. Sporadic Jordanian attacks on Mount Scopus continued, however. In May 1958, Lieutenant Colonel Flint was killed by a Jordanian sniper as he waved a white flag and tried to escort some wounded Israelis to safety.

The worry my father's deployment caused my mother, the stress he experienced being separated from us, and the difficulty he faced in his effort to find work as a pediatrician began to weigh heavily on them. My father tried to start a private practice, adding this work to his job for the health ministry, but Tel Aviv already had too many physicians and he saw few patients. When my mother became pregnant with Rahm in early 1959 they began to think hard about their options. Israel did not really need another pediatrician, especially one practicing outside of his field in order to just get by. At the same time, opportunity remained in America, where medicine, science, and technology were reaching new heights. He might even be able to train in a subspecialty like pediatric kidney disease.

A return to America offered my mother a chance to be close to her family, old friends, and familiar comforts, but ironically enough, she was the one who was resistant and reluctant about returning to Chicago. In her fantasies, she refused to leave Tel Aviv and ran away with friends to make her point to her husband. But in the end, she understood why he wanted to go back to the States and agreed to it. It helped her to know that my father was hoping to come back someday. In fact, it seemed almost inevitable that he would become an experienced pediatric specialist in America and then, when conditions were right, return to Israel with a notable academic reputation, forcing the Israeli medical establishment to give him a spot where he could conduct research as well as see patients.

Four

AMERICA

In 1959, Chicago's Michael Reese Hospital welcomed my father. He was soon a leader in the dialysis program, and an attending physician in the pediatric wards. Ambitious and eager to make money, my father searched the blocks south and west of the hospital for a convenient spot where he could see private patients but also get back to the hospital quickly when he was needed. A tiny storefront that could have suited a candy shop became the home of his one-man general practice. The neighborhood, which was about twenty-five blocks south of downtown, had changed dramatically in the previous decade as upwardly mobile Jewish families moved out and poorer black families moved in. Since several doctors had left along with their patients, the area needed physicians.

In the beginning, the patients may have been taken aback by this young Jewish doctor with a thick foreign accent. They also had to get accustomed to the idea that he was not available on a predictable schedule. If, for example, the staff at the hospital called to ask for his help, he would have to close his office and rush over there. But those patients who did get to see him at that storefront clinic found my father was the kind of doctor who offered good care and as much respect as he received. Chicago was a melting pot of immigrants, and my father spoke four languages well and several others sufficiently so that he could communicate with people of many nationalities. Consequently, he quickly became a popular doctor in a city of many immigrant families. He proved himself by being right with almost every diagnosis, and by being fair about payment, which meant that his patients paid only what they could, and some paid nothing at all. Either way, they got the same level of care and, when necessary, house calls, hospital visits, and after-hours research by my father in the medical library if a difficult case required it. My father welcomed these tough cases because they broke up the monotony that can come with seeing one patient with an ear infection or strep throat after another. They required a little detective work and sharp action when a definitive diagnosis was finally made.

A good example arose when one mother brought her two-and-a-half-year-old son to the office with a fever, cough, headache, and blurred vision. The boy, whose name was George, had both tuberculosis and meningitis. The meningitis, which could cause brain damage and death, was the most urgent problem. My father suspected it was caused by a fungus called cryptococcus. Lab results proved he was right and a search of the literature turned up just a few cases when patients were cured with a new drug—amphotericin B—developed from bacteria found in the soil along the Orinoco River in Venezuela. The drug was not commercially available but my father somehow managed to get it and George was saved.

George, whom my father followed for years, became the subject of one of dozens of case studies and papers he published in professional journals. This academic output was quite remarkable for a doctor who worked seventy hours a week seeing patients in the office, at the hospital, and in their homes. The variety and pace of work suited my father, but the pay was low and as our family grew he longed to spend more time at home. He solved both these problems by leaving the hospital and practice on the South Side and partnering with another physician in an office that was much closer to our home and had a wealthier clientele. He got privileges at most of Chicago's North Side community hospitals and began seeing newborns in the maternity ward who became patients in his practice. He still worked hard, often seeing two dozen patients in an afternoon when his partner saw no more than ten. This happened in part because my father was filled with kinetic energy. Entering the exam room, he would minimize salutations with the parents and focus immediately on the children and the presenting problem. His typical visits were so short the nurses at the hospitals called him "Speedy Gonzales." Despite his speed, and because of his openness and charm, his reputation grew as many mothers requested him personally.

When he was working, my father's style was very relaxed and matter-of-fact but warm. A little blood, a little vomit, or a little crying was nothing to him. But if he could avoid tears, he made an effort to do so. For example, he often used a little misdirection, like an old-fashioned magician, to remove stitches without a child realizing it. "Are you tough enough to do this without crying?" he would ask. While he talked, and the child was screwing up his courage, my father had already begun to work. Before they could answer the threads would be out and he would delight his patient by declaring, "You did it!"

He taught parents to trust their instincts, be attentive, and enjoy their children because they grow up fast. One mother told me that my father showed up on the maternity ward, gave her son the once-over, and said, "Hug, love, squeeze your baby." Desperately nervous about how to handle her first child, she said, "That's it?" My father answered, "You're going to be fine, and he will be, too."

The mother and father who told that story about Ben Emanuel's five-word introduction to parenting discovered that his advice, and the Spock-style confidence he showed in all parents, made perfect sense. They made him the pediatrician for their first son, and two more children, who all stayed in his practice until they became adults. Over time I would hear many similar stories.

Dr. Benjamin Emanuel's no-nonsense style helped him build one of the biggest practices in the city. Most of his patients were middle-class, but many were so poor that he gave away a great many free checkups, doses of penicillin, and free samples of other medications he received from drug company representatives. The only rich or famous people he saw in his office tended to be big-league ballplayers who played games at nearby Wrigley Field and lived in the neighborhood. He knew so little about American sports that he had no idea that Billy Williams and Ron Santo played for the Cubs and he called the football star Dick Butkus "Dick Bupkis." (He wasn't even aware enough to use his connections to finagle tickets for a game or two.) The "Bupkis" kids and all the others got my father up and going in the morning. He loved talking to children of every age. To him, they were never boring.

Although he still planned to go back to Israel one day, he liked everything about his life in Chicago and allowed himself to think about climbing the economic ladder. The American dream, as he saw it, included the chance to work hard at something you loved, and to provide for your family. He wanted financial security, proper schooling for his kids, and a few of the things, like travel, theater, and music, that he always considered essential to a full life. He may have been happy to serve the poor, but he did not think it was necessary to be one of them.

My father's first big-ticket purchase was a fancy hi-fi—one of those big stand-alone console models—which he bought so he could listen to classical music records. He put the stereo and the vinyl albums in his little study alcove off the living room. After declaring that this was the one pleasure he allowed himself, he barred us from touching the stereo system or going into his office.

At the time it seemed a bit strange that our father never taught us much about music or skiing, which he had enjoyed in Switzerland. Later he would explain that the money and time required for ski trips just weren't available when we were young. And when it came to music, he just could not imagine how his three hyperactive boys would manage to sit still long enough to listen to a prelude, let alone a whole symphony.

To his credit, our father did eventually introduce us to chess, which he played extremely well. These after-dinner and Sunday afternoon games were played either at the dining room table or in the living room, where the board was set up on the round, white marble coffee table. Our father sat on the edge of the sofa and we plopped ourselves on the floor.

These chess games were not idle fun. My father did not believe in falsely building his sons' self-esteem by purposely letting us win or larding on the excessive praise. He played to win and teach us by real competition. Sometimes he would simply stop the game and then show us, with quickly moving hands, how the next dozen moves would inevitably lead us to defeat.

"You will move here. I will move there," he would say as his thick fingers quickly and nimbly shuffled the knight, bishop, pawns, and other pieces, showing us how the game would "inevitably" evolve. "And then this, and then I would checkmate."

During these demonstrations he would repeatedly admonish us with two messages. "Think three moves ahead!" he would say every game. "Imagine all your opponent's possible responses before you make a move. Think about how I am going to respond if you move your knight that way." He would then show us a few possible counter-measures he might take to thwart our strategy. "Play the moves out in your mind before you move your piece," he said.

The second imperative was easier for us to learn: "Remember what Napoleon said: Offense is the best defense."

My brothers and I never checked whether Napoleon ever uttered such a sound bite, but we surely absorbed it. And it certainly fit with our personalities and natural tendency to take the "fight" side of the fight-or-flight response to danger. Hyperactive and distractible, none of us ever got good enough at chess to even come close to beating him. For my father, chess was about seeing problems in a sophisticated way and learning to plan multiple moves ahead. These games—and my father's urgings—reinforced our natural tendency to be aggressive in whatever we set out to do. Winning became so important that we each deliberately sought out the particular hobbies, sports, and career interests that fit our abilities and in which we could excel. Life was about competition, and if you couldn't finish at the top in one pursuit, you found the game where your talents allowed you to win.

.....

While my father gradually became one of the more popular pediatricians on the North Side of Chicago, my mother was the center of our days. Happily, she found on West Buena Avenue a kindred spirit in another young Jewish mother named Carol Glass. Like my parents, Carol and Bill Glass had three sons. They were roughly the same age as Rahm, Ari, and me, so they were ideal playmates.

I'm told I introduced myself to her at a small playground near our apartment. She was sitting on a bench watching her two older kids on the swings and slides while my mother sat on another, watching me and Rahm. I walked over and handed Mrs. Glass an orange and asked her to peel it for me because "my mommy cannot do it." In fact, she had told me to do it for myself. Mrs. Glass thought this was hilarious. She and my mother became friends on the spot and formed an alliance that made mothering just a little easier.

What little spare time my mother had she devoted to civil rights activism. My father solved the problems of individuals. When a black or immigrant family was facing discrimination and couldn't get a white pediatrician to see them, my father would gladly care for the children—and reduce his charges or simply waive the fees if they were poor and couldn't afford it. By contrast, when my mother saw discrimination she began organizing. Her tendency was to start a political movement, protest, and make systemic change. I think as we grew up, we boys became frustrated by our father's approach of repeatedly addressing the same problem posed by many individuals, and learned from our mother to devote ourselves to addressing larger social issues.

Early on, my mother opened our apartment for meetings of the local CORE chapter, which attracted dozens of blacks and whites, many of whom were Jewish. CORE pushed for integration at public facilities like city beaches and for access to housing. But with Willis Wagons dotting the landscape and schools in white areas emptying out, education remained the movement's primary focus.

Looking back at it decades later, the stubborn attitudes of local officials seem truly astounding. Superintendent Benjamin Willis, for example, refused to acknowledge that the schools were segregated even though the district had kept the races separate for years. He would not say whether he thought racial separation in public education was a good idea or a bad one. However, every day seemed to bring new revelations of the district's inequities and more protests at administrative offices and school buildings. On certain occasions, when civil rights leaders called for boycotts, schools in many neighborhoods closed for lack of students.

Officials responded defensively to protests and criticisms, digging in for what promised to be a long fight on behalf of the status quo. All the signs suggested the Chicago Public Schools system would be in turmoil for many years. My parents, who wanted us to learn Hebrew in case we moved back to Israel, expected to send us to a private Jewish day school. Still, they recognized the value of the city schools and committed themselves to the cause of change for the benefit of everyone in the city.

All this activity was a direct reflection of my mother's deeply held moral code, a set of beliefs that was born in her father's labor union activism, reinforced by her bike trip to that first housing protest, and hardened by the discrimination she felt, saw, and read about in the newspapers. Most Jews who joined the civil rights movement were motivated at least in part by their own ongoing, personal experience with prejudice and bigotry. In Chicago, 1961 began with a midnight bombing at the doorway of the Anshe Emet synagogue, which was just a few blocks from our home. Although we weren't members, we attended Anshe Emet on the weeks when we did not go to the small shul my grandfather had helped to found in nearby Albany Park. The blast at Anshe Emet damaged the synagogue building and broke more than a hundred windows in the neighborhood. No one was hurt, but the crime, which was never solved, reminded everyone that hatred and anti-Semitism were alive in the world and good people were called to stand against it. This imperative lent a sense of purpose and urgency to the organizing meetings that took place at our apartment.

In the same way that other kids spied on adult dinner parties, Rahm and I would hang on the edges of these political planning sessions, watching, listening, and learning. When these gatherings took place in our living room, which most did, we would crawl behind the crescent-shaped part of the sectional sofa that occupied a corner of the room and hide under the triangle-shaped table that filled the empty space between the arc of the upholstery and the plaster walls. There was enough room for two of us, although a few legs and elbows might stick out, and if the adults were engaged in the issues and talking loudly they could not hear when we whispered or made the tabletop bump against a wall. Eventually we would forget to be quiet. Once discovered we would be subjected to lots of oohs and aahs and "they're so cutes" before we were shuffled off to bed.

At that time, the specifics about policies and tactical discussion went over our heads, but we felt, deep down, the emotions behind what was being said. The main thing was that people were suffering and anyone who cared about right and wrong had an obligation to speak up and demand better. In this crowd, indignation was infectious, and the sight and sound of so many different people speaking so passionately stirred the heart. Here were grown-ups who believed that it was possible to make the world a better place and to achieve it by pointing out the unfairness and the suffering and seeking a solution through dialogue. Undoubtedly this experience of eavesdropping on activists helped instill in us both a moral sensibility and the desire to do something about a problem whenever we could. It is not hard to see Rahm's devotion to improving Chicago Public Schools and my work on universal health-care coverage as outgrowths of witnessing these meetings in our house.

.....

Because they often worked on school issues, the CORE people talked a lot about children, but very few kids ever came to these sessions with their parents. The exceptions were the Deans. Roz Dean had been high school friends with my mother's sister Esther. She had joined CORE along with her husband, Alan, who was black. When meetings were held at our house during the daytime they often brought their sons Michael and Clifton. The two families became close. We spent many

Saturdays and Sundays at their home and they often came to see us. Michael and Clifton played with us in the alley behind the house and on the sidewalk out front. I think this must have been where I first heard the phrase "nigger lover" muttered by someone passing by on the sidewalk.

In this time, from 1961 to 1967, Chicago was one of the hot spots in a national civil rights movement that was gathering strength. The tactics used at protests were expanded to include passive resistance and participants expected to be arrested. Many people received special training—they were taught to make themselves limp and heavy—right in our living room. Afterward we would play at this activity, imitating the adults we saw lying like rag dolls on the floor of our apartment.

Although we were too young to understand exactly what my mother was doing as she left for a few hours of marching, we noticed that she returned with a lot to discuss. On three or four occasions she stayed away overnight because she had been arrested. These arrests, as I later learned, were usually part of a plan. CORE trained volunteers in the methods of civil disobedience and passive resistance. When the protesters respectfully refused police orders to stop their picketing and move along, the officers had no choice but to charge them with disorderly conduct and take them into custody. As they tried to do this, the protesters would go limp and fall to the ground. By relaxing as much as possible they made their bodies difficult to handle, which turned any effort at mass arrests into a laborious spectacle of teams of police officers hauling people one by one onto paddy wagons and buses.

Arrests increased the chance that a protest or demonstration would get media attention. They also signaled that the issue at hand, whether it was education, housing, employment, or anything else, was so serious that otherwise law-abiding citizens were willing to go to jail in order to be heard. Although there were few of them, the presence of women, especially white women who could be mothers, added an important touch of diversity to these scenes.

My mother's first arrest was in Chicago, and probably occurred around 1963, when people all over the country attended demonstrations to show their support for Martin Luther King Jr. and the campaign for racial equality that blazed across the South. My mother spent one night in a Cook County jail after she was arrested with many other civil rights protesters. A friend helped my dad take care of us while she was gone. Having seen pictures and TV film reports of police using nightsticks and turning dogs and fire hoses on protesters, we were a little anxious, but with enough reassurance we were able to go to sleep and by morning she was back at home.

On two other occasions, my mother was arrested in Evanston, a wealthy northern suburb that is home to both Northwestern University and the Woman's Christian Temperance Union. The first time she was dragged in by police who had responded to complaints about pickets disrupting traffic at a real estate company. She was released by a judge who said she would be dealt with more harshly if it happened again. The second time someone reported that she was back at the real estate agency and was the "ringleader" of a protest. Finding herself in serious trouble, my mother called on a family friend who was a lawyer. She expected that Jerry Jaffe, an older man with a quiet legal practice, would help her find a younger attorney who knew his way around the criminal courts. Instead he took up the cause himself. He got my mother released and then told her, "Thanks for reminding me why I became a lawyer in the first place."

Although a middle-aged lawyer might have gotten a certain charge out of my mother's case, she did not take any of these incidents lightly. Jail is jail, even if you know you won't be there for very long, and she worried about us at home. Indeed, we were so accustomed to her attention and our nighttime routine that we were always upset by her absence. And though my father supported her unequivocally, there were times when our grandfather Herman thought she was risking too much. He knew the tough-minded people who were standing against integration in places like the Back of the Yards neighborhood on the South Side. They had shown him their willingness to fight during union battles in the 1930s and '40s. Herman had no doubt that they could turn violent if they felt provoked. He was afraid that my mother would find herself in the wrong place at a moment when shouts were answered by rocks, fists, and baseball bats.

Years before, when she had been more or less forced to give up her own shot at an education, my mother had been a girl unable to speak on her own behalf. Now she was a woman who saw that the political system was bullying powerless children in a similar way and she had discovered she could do something about it. Having found her voice, both in the civil rights movement and as an adult with her own family, my mother stood up to Herman. She told him she knew how to take care of herself and would continue her activism. The lessons she taught us through her courage and assertiveness were as important as any other form of mothering. They also showed us that people can evolve and grow and that women can be full and multifaceted human beings, not just nonstop caregivers. In these ways marching and shouting and getting arrested were a way for our mother to express who she was.

The subtext of my mother's civil rights work, especially the bit about women as fully engaged human beings, was not something Herman would have grasped in a conscious way. I don't think that even my mother understood, at that time, all the factors that drove her to fight for kids and families who were being oppressed. But she made it very clear that she was not going to stop attending the protests or welcoming the neighborhood chapter of CORE to our home.

Herman's worst fear—that my mother would be harmed during a protest—was never realized, but his daughter *was* occasionally manhandled by white police officers who resented having to move limp and heavy protesters who lay on the sidewalks practicing passive resistance. They could not understand why this woman, who looked like their wives, was mixed up in racial politics. "Lady, what are you doing here?" they would ask. "What does it look like I'm doing?" she would reply before challenging them with the charge that they were disrupting a perfectly legal protest.

Under my mother's influence, I became the kind of kid who evaluated everything he saw and heard and did not assume that anyone's word was final just because he or she wore a uniform, a badge, or a doctor's white coat. It was my right, perhaps even my obligation, to determine if people were being fair and not just accept their authority. Of course, a small child's world, especially one in which adults are loving and patient, is just and fair in a way that the real world can never match. Growing up is often a matter of confronting this reality, and adjusting to it. As a young child I was truly disturbed, for example, when I realized that many people in America and around the world lived with hunger and without basic shelter or medical care. However, I was relieved to know my parents were doing what they could to help solve these problems. Then came the Passover afternoon when we got in the Rambler to drive to my grandparents' house for a Seder.

We had driven just a few blocks when I said, "Daddy, how do you make money?"

"When babies get sick, I take care of them."

"You mean you take money for making babies well?"

"Well, I don't take much, Jonny. And I have to take care of our family, you know."

He was right, of course, but I was outraged by the thought that my father required payment for his services as a doctor. For the rest of the ride I sputtered questions about parents who were poor and could not pay and demanded to know why everyone could not just get medical care for free. All he could do was explain that he did help many people for free, but that doctors had to care for their families, too, and that meant that someone had to pay.

When we got to my grandparents' home I ran upstairs to tell the Big Bangah how terrible it was that my father was taking money from the sick. He declared, "My daughter is raising a socialist."

No doubt our neighbors would have taken Herman's statement as a fact, not a joke. In their eyes we were radical. And while the landlord insisted the reason was all the noise we made on the ceiling of the first-floor apartment with our running around, there probably was something more to his refusal to renew the lease on our apartment on Buena Avenue. He did not like the big, mixed-race meetings my mother was having in our apartment. Those sessions were no bigger or more troublesome than a typical dinner party or cocktail hour, but the neighbors who hissed "nigger lovers" at us on the sidewalks found them intolerable. And I'm sure they let their discomfort be known to the landlord.

.....

In mid-1963 a moving van pulled up to our building on West Buena Avenue and our furniture and other belongings were loaded up for a two-mile journey north to a quiet block on Winona Street, on the northern edge of the neighborhood called Uptown. The four-bedroom apartment my father found for us took up the entire first floor of a building, so there were no downstairs neighbors to be bothered by our pounding footsteps.

With nine rooms, the place on Winona was as big as many suburban houses and came with high ceilings and heavy moldings. Even better, for us boys, was the location. It was half a block from the park along the lakeshore and two blocks from the beautiful sandy beach at Foster Avenue.

My parents made some definitive statements with the way they divided up the space. First, they made sure that a small room that faced the street was reserved for my father as a study where he could read, listen to music, and do paperwork. After taking the biggest bedroom for themselves they moved my grandmother into a small bedroom/bathroom suite off the kitchen, which had presumably been designed for a maid. We three boys were crowded into a single bedroom, with an attached half bath. Rahm and Ari slept on bunks. I had a single bed. The fourth bedroom was set aside as "the children's study."

Equipped with three desks, each with a lamp and chair, and a shared bookcase, the study room was where we were expected to do our homework and any other extra projects we might choose to do. No one talked about this being an unusual arrangement, but my guess is that in 1963 very few families would have devoted an entire room to the academic pursuits of three boys under the age of six. My parents did it, and their choice signaled the value of study, work, and achievement.

In time they would reinforce the importance of academic excellence by carefully reviewing our schoolwork and consistently emphasizing the value of getting good grades, which would eventually help us enter top colleges.

It was around this time that my parents also began talking about how I ought to become a doctor when I grew up. I was the firstborn child of an immigrant who himself was a doctor. Plus I was a goody-goody and got good grades in all my school subjects, and I especially liked science, where I could literally poke and probe nature. Thus, because of my brains and curiosity and our immigrant status, it seemed almost predetermined that I should be a doctor. That I was going in the medical direction relieved Rahm and Ari of any career pressure. In this Jewish family, one doctor son would be both necessary and sufficient. I always thought those two owed me big-time for giving them this freedom of choice.

Outside our apartment, the neighborhood was full of families from different ethnic and religious backgrounds. In this way, Uptown was like countless neighborhoods in postwar America where families of varying backgrounds found shelter for a time as they climbed the economic ladder. Shared aspirations for middle-class comfort, safety, and status meant that we all had much in common. However, there was no denying that our differences bred prejudice and often led to conflicts, especially with kids who recently arrived from Appalachia. These boys and girls had definite feelings about "kikes" and "nigger lovers" and were aggressive about expressing them.

We did find friends in the building next door, however. Georgie, the Italian-American kid who was involved in Rahm's finger-smashing incident, introduced me to the rituals of the Catholic Church as he practiced during the week for being an altar boy on Sundays. I let Georgie put me down on my knees, hands folded in prayer, while he uttered some Latin prayer or other. I had no idea what was going on. In our building, the other tenants included a Greek-American family and a couple named Downs, with sons named Sean and Tommy and a daughter named Ana Maria. Mr. Downs, whose first name was John, was an "artist/reporter" for *The Chicago Daily News*. Seven years younger than my father, he was reflexively conservative and rarely questioned authority. His mind began to change as he got to know my parents and heard about the issues discussed at the organizing meetings at our apartment. But he never joined them. He preferred, instead, to observe and report for the newspaper and, when off duty, to enjoy our family's friendship.

John Downs was a real, all-American dad in a way my father never was. He grew up on a Wisconsin farm. He drove a sporty white Thunderbird with red leather seats, played baseball with us, and put up a basketball hoop on the garage in the alley. On any given Saturday he might announce that he was headed for "the country" and invite anyone so inclined to come along for the adventure. Rahm, Ari, and I were always game. Often we would wind up at some farm outside the city where John simply pulled his car up to a barn, honked the horn, and asked if we could have a look around. Invariably the proud farmer would take us on a tour and we'd get to see lots of cows, pigs, and perhaps a few horses. Exotic sights to us city slickers.

One summer, John enlisted us in the design and construction of a wooden go-cart from scrap lumber and a set of wheels stripped from an old grocery cart. He then had the brilliant idea to challenge the kids in the building next door to build a similar contraption so we could race in the cobblestone back alley. We made up pairs of pushers and drivers and clattered up and down the brick alley for hours. On other occasions, the alley was the site for kickball or Wiffle Ball games. When John returned from trips to see his wife's family in Texas, he demonstrated the fine art of setting off M-80 firecrackers. Our father, who was more cerebral and not handy with tools, and, quite frankly, too busy for hanging out in the alley, would never have done any of these things. But to their credit, my parents never discouraged us from hanging out with other adults, learning from everyone we met.

Thanks to neighbors like John Downs and the large number of kids being raised in nearby apartments, our little stretch of Winona was a busy and happy place. We would think nothing of running down the block and pounding on a door to find out if a friend was up for a visit or a game. When Downs's daughter was born, Rahm, who loved babies, would show up unexpectedly and report, "I'm here to feed Ana Maria." Apparently Mrs. Downs had once told him, "Of course you can feed her sometime," and Rahm held her to the promise, many times over.

.....

Although people tend to idealize the past—everyone was friendly, every neighborhood was perfectly safe—I know that the few blocks around our apartment were an oasis of safety and kindness. Eddie wasn't just the manager of the drugstore. He was someone who looked out for us when we passed by his shop and let us stop inside to dry off when we got caught in the rain. However, even in a safe neighborhood the city posed a few dangers. In the early 1960s robberies and muggings occurred regularly in Lincoln Park. More danger waited three or four blocks to the west, in areas where gangs were starting to take control of certain street corners. Then there were the anti-Semites, who seem to exist in almost every place and time. Ari, Rahm, and I experienced our first brush with this problem when I was in third grade. Eight or nine of us were playing in the alley behind our apartment when one of the boys called Rahm a kike.

My "Take it back!" was answered by the oldest kid in the group, who happened to be a girl. "Don't you dare take it back," she ordered. When the offender stood firm, with his chin thrust out, I took a swing at him. He swung back and in an instant we were punching, scratching, and wrestling with each other.

Rahm and Ari were six and four at the time so they just stood on the sidelines yelling as the other boy and I threw punches and wrestled on the ground. Neither of us did much damage, but doing damage was not the point. The point was that we had been insulted and bullied and we would not stand for it. There would be more fights in the future, and Rahm and Ari eventually battled at my side. After each fight, we would walk home talking heatedly about who won and who lost and how *they* were wrong for starting the fight in the first place. My mother and father were not alarmed when we got into these scrapes. I think they understood how they happened and knew that as long as we were small and the injuries were minor, it was good that we stood up for ourselves.

It would be hard to say that the kids we fought with in the alley had a real understanding of the bigotry they showed. These fights were mostly based on the idea that we were somehow *supposed* to hate each other because we were different. We *were* different in some obvious ways. We came from different religious backgrounds. The other kids also noticed that we seemed to get a lot of breaks from school that they did not get. This was especially true early in the school year when our Jewish day school closed for Rosh Hashanah, Yom Kippur, and Sukkot. Considering their own struggles to get back into the discipline of academics after summer vacation, our Jews-only holidays made us seem unfairly privileged.

Also, I have no doubt that some of the resentment that was focused on us rose out of insecurity and fear. Many of the newcomers to the neighborhood came from Appalachia seeking jobs and fleeing rural poverty. In Chicago life for them was strange, uncomfortable, and filled with rejection. Scorned by people who called them hillbillies, the kids who cursed at us were scared and lonely and angry and we were convenient targets for their built-up rage. As the sons of a foreign-born doctor who lived in a big apartment, we probably represented everything that seemed unfair and out of reach.

What the kids from Appalachia failed to understand was that we were outsiders, too. In the 1960s Jews in America were a distinct minority subject to plenty of discrimination. Sometimes the effects were direct. For example, my father was not given privileges at certain hospitals, like Northwestern. In other cases you just knew that parts of society were unfriendly. Many of Chicago's private clubs were closed to Jews in the 1960s and Jews were still excluded from certain suburbs.

To my parents' credit, we did not spend any time worrying about where we might be excluded. Instead, we considered ourselves full citizens and believed we had the responsibility to fight for all the cherished rights this status confers. We also assumed that the country we loved belonged to us just as surely as it belonged to the descendants of the *Mayflower* families. Perhaps the only difference was that my father possessed a "recent immigrant's" sense of wonder and excitement about discovering opportunities for earning one's way to unheard-of wealth and security. It was in this spirit that we began a series of long-distance driving vacations that allowed us to see the breadth of both the American landscape and its culture.

For our first big road trip, my father rented a small camper, the hard-shell kind that you pull behind your car, and loaded up our blue Rambler station wagon with blankets and food and drinks. The whole family, including Savta, piled in and he pointed us toward U.S. Route 66. In the city that we left behind, civil rights leaders were planning for a mass rally at Grant Park, where, in a few days, Mayor Richard Daley would be booed off the stage by ten thousand angry citizens. Another speaker would be drowned out by voices in the crowd, including some that cried, "Kill him!"

.....

As Chicago simmered, we Emanuels spent two weeks traveling to Colorado for a vacation. We traveled in classic American family road trip fashion, with a few variations based on my father's priorities. He always preferred adventure over creature comforts, which meant, for example, that we tried to avoid restaurants. Since my brothers and I could eat, literally, a dozen or more sandwiches per day, this meant that our mother got no vacation from her duty as quartermaster and cook.

The seating arrangements inside the sky-blue Rambler typically found my father behind the wheel while my mother sat in the backseat, where she could tend to Ari and Rahm, who were both in car seats. These were rare at the time, but because my mother was a stickler for car safety we used them religiously. Savta sat in the front passenger seat by the window and I squeezed between her and my father with an American Automobile Association planner called a "TripTik" in my hands. These little booklets contained maps with yellow highlighted routes that could guide you through an entire road trip. I loved being the navigator who kept track of the passing landmarks and was authorized to raise my voice above the din of conversation to bark an

order to "turn right!" or declare, "We're going the wrong way!" My
role as navigator was a source of envy for Rahm and if he pestered my
parents enough they would tell me to let him handle the TripTik for
a while. During one of these moments he screamed, "Stop!" When
my father testily asked why he should stop, Rahm noted that the road
we were traveling was gray-black and the route on the map was colored yellow. "Dad needs to find the yellow road!" My father was not
pleased, to say the least.

As anyone who has taken a long family car trip knows, our adventures were also mixed with other kinds of stress and occasional mishaps. Besides being responsible for our care and feeding, our mother,
who also had to keep her eye on a not-so-cheerful mother-in-law, inevitably suffered a meltdown or two per trip. And the first one frequently occurred at the start, just so everyone knew who would be
dictating the emotional tenor of the trip. My father never saw the reason to spend a lot on hotels or motels. "You just lay your head down
and leave the next morning. Why do we need a fancy room?" he would
always say. Typically, very few of the motel rooms he selected were
ever up to our mother's higher but not very stringent standards. The
same was frequently true for restaurants. Whenever she was unhappy
she would start complaining about something and end up delivering
an endless monologue of criticism. Observations on the mildew in a
motel shower, the chilly air in the camper, or the ugliness of the campground would be followed by more generalized complaints about how
we were inconsiderate and unkind and ungrateful.

In the early days, my father would catch much of the heat because
he botched the plans for the trip, ignored her advice, or failed to be
helpful in some way. When Ari, Rahm, and I were the focus of these
rants it was because we were too loud or fighting too much. I know
now that these outbursts came from a woman being pushed beyond
her capacity. She never liked camping, and considering that she had to
take care of us, these adventures hardly amounted to a vacation for her.

At the time, however, we boys were usually shocked by our mother's emotional storms, which arose suddenly and were followed by a
stunned silence that could last a hundred miles or more. Sometimes

we would pray for a little mishap to break the tension. Not infrequently, we got one.

On the 1963 expedition we hit just about every tourist attraction you can name between Chicago and the foot of the Rockies without major incident. As we approached the mountains, my father directed our attention out the window and reminded us to appreciate the view, which included massive stands of Douglas fir and blue spruce climbing up the mountainsides and, in the distance, snowcapped peaks. Simultaneously, my safety-conscious mother told him to forget about the view and keep his eyes on the road.

The gawking was easy on the gentler slope of the foothills. When we reached steeper inclines and the two-lane highway became a series of switchbacks, my father had to focus more intently on the challenge of keeping the car and trailer moving forward. Signs that warned KEEP IN LOW GEAR were new to him. He did not understand that he was supposed to slip the handle of the automatic transmission out of drive and into the slot marked "L" to prevent a stall. As the incline got steeper and the sheer drop beside the road grew more terrifying, the car shuddered and stalled. He slammed on the brakes to keep us from sliding backward.

"Get out and put some rocks behind the wheels!" he screamed with panic in his voice.

My mother and I scrambled out of the car and searched for the biggest rocks we could find. These chocks stopped the slip-sliding car and gave my father a chance to calm down. They did nothing, of course, for the long line of vehicles that quickly collected behind us, with drivers honking their horns and revving their engines. My father restarted the car and struggled to get the car to move forward. Shudder, stall. Shudder, stall. Finally one kind fellow traveler got out of his car and walked up to tell my father that despite the fact that the transmission was automatic, he needed to use the low gear to climb the mountain. With that reassurance, my father restarted the Rambler, put it in "L," and eased off the brake, and we crept forward.

During our time in the Rockies we camped, poked around little cowboy and mining museums, and visited tourist traps. We bought cowboy hats and rode horses and got our pictures taken with mountains rising in the distance. Our home base, the trailer, was moved from campground to campground. We fished, hiked in the forests, and swam in isolated lakes. Much of this was done while dodging rain showers, but we had so much fun we did not care. During the evenings, Rahm, Ari, and I would take "sink" baths near our camper and run around the campsite naked screaming at one another. At night we bundled up in blankets on the makeshift beds in the little trailer.

When we started the return trip home the temperature gauge on the Rambler dashboard began moving upward. My father stopped to fill the radiator with water, but this fix didn't last long. With the needle rising again he pulled into a gas station and popped the hood. An attendant found a tiny hole in the radiator, where steam was escaping, and recommended a new radiator. The only alternative, he said, would be to plug the hole with something like chewing gum and pray for it to hold. Ever the cheapskate, my father purchased a few packs of gum.

For three kids who were used to being denied access to gum and every other bad-for-you confection, this was the opportunity of a lifetime. We packed our mouths with Juicy Fruit and Doublemint, and, just when the sugar was depleted, announced we had some more ready for the radiator. He pulled over to the shoulder and we spit our nice juicy wad into our father's hands. He popped the hood and pressed the mass against the hole and we drove off. The repair lasted about twenty minutes until it fell off, and when the needle began to move again my father pulled over, took more well-masticated gum from our mouths, and made another plug. That lasted a few hours. Finally, we reached the next real town, where he found a local mechanic who had access to a used but intact radiator, which he swapped for our bad one. The next morning we were on the road again.

On the last day of the trip we had just passed through the center of an Illinois farm town called Pontiac, which is about 150 miles southwest of Chicago, when the sky darkened and the wind began to howl. The cars and trucks on Route 66 slowed to a crawl. Suddenly the wind gained even more force and a funnel cloud that had formed just to the west touched down behind us.

Stuck in the line of slow-moving traffic, there was nothing my father could do as the tornado roared down the highway, blackening the sky. From his seat, where the rearview mirrors gave him a full view of the approaching storm, the feelings of helplessness as well as fear must have been hard to endure. With telltale shrieking panic in his voice he ordered my mother to make sure that Rahm and Ari were buckled tightly in their car seats and told us all to hold on tight.

When it finally arrived, the twister slammed into the trailer and our car with the force of 100 mph winds. With a shudder and then a sudden lurch we careened to the left and then were tipped over and over onto the grassy median. The car blankets, pillows, maps, toys, and sandwiches flew everywhere. I found myself pressed against the rear driver's-side door of the car, unhurt but shocked by what had happened.

For a moment, the sound of the tornado made it impossible to hear anything. But then, just as suddenly, the wind died and silence fell over us. As the black cloud turned to gray I could hear my brothers crying and my mother asking if we were all right. She struggled to help us and my grandmother, who was suspended in midair by her seat belt.

With my mother's help we all crawled up and out of the windows on the passenger side of the car. On the highway, we saw other drivers who had gotten out of their cars and trucks come rushing to see what they might do to help. It was then that we realized that my father was still in the car.

Having seen the tornado bearing down on us, my father had focused on trying to keep the wheels of the car pointed down the highway. He hadn't rolled up his window and somehow, when the car tipped on its side, his left hand got trapped between the door frame and the ground. Although he was in excruciating pain, he was able to explain why he was stuck and in a few minutes a group of men, mostly truck drivers, organized to free him. First they managed to detach the trailer from the car. Next they actually lifted the car off my father's hand, righted it, and helped him out of the driver's seat. By the time they accomplished this, police cars, fire trucks, and an ambulance had arrived. The ambulance brought my father to a local community hospital.

That night, while my mother's older sister Shirley and her husband, Ernie, raced south to get us, the doctors in Pontiac studied X-rays of my father's hand and, noting that every bone was crushed and he was losing a lot of blood, recommended amputation. This was a horrific idea. First of all, my father is a lefty; this was his dominant hand, the one he used for writing and every other task that required both strength and fine motor skills. Second, he was a doctor who used his hands every day to conduct examinations, offer reassurance, and play with his young patients.

In those days most people, including physicians who were patients, followed a doctor's orders. My father considered his injury and the odds of a good recovery and agreed to let them operate. At this point my mother, who never accepted authority, put her foot down. She understood that the doctors in Pontiac were general practitioners, not orthopedists or hand surgeons. She did not think they had the experience to know for certain that the hand could not be saved. She asked them if my father could make it to Chicago safely.

None of the doctors, including her husband, thought this was a great idea; there was still blood accumulating in the hand and my father was in tremendous pain. But because my mother could be an overwhelming force when her mind was made up, they reluctantly agreed that with a tight bandage and enough painkillers he might reach Chicago without suffering irreversible injury. When Shirley and Ernie arrived, they piled blankets and pillows on the floor of their car and helped my father to lie down there; we all crowded in around him.

With the painkillers gradually wearing off, the drive from Pontiac to Chicago may have been the longest three hours of my father's life. When they got to the city Ernie drove directly to Mount Sinai Hospital, where two top surgeons, the Miller brothers, examined him. These doctors agreed that there was no surgery that could be done to make an effective repair. But they did not think amputation was necessary, either. They believed if the swelling could be controlled, his hand might heal on its own. They could not assure my parents that it would recover completely. In fact, the odds were against it. But with the right care in the short term and a commitment to physical therapy over the long term, my father might get most of his normal functioning back.

The initial treatment regime would require my father to keep his hand immobilized, and to plunge it into hot paraffin wax several times per day. The wax baths, which were intended to stimulate blood flow and healing, were quite painful. They were also effective—or an amazing placebo. Within a few weeks, my father had healed enough to begin an aggressive physical therapy routine that consisted mostly of squeezing rubber balls over and over again. Determined, he stuck to the routine religiously. He would never get full use of his hand. Today, he still cannot make his left thumb and pinky finger come together. However, the treatment was enough to make his hand almost normal. He could use it for writing, with the same old terrible penmanship, and for conducting physical exams. For us Emanuel boys, watching him work through a serious and painful injury with such gritty determination gave us one more lesson in how to approach life.

By late summer, my father and mother were back to their routines. He went to work every day and took his turn being "on call" every other night and weekend. She prepared to participate in the March on Washington for Jobs and Freedom, which was being organized by James Farmer, Martin Luther King Jr., and A. Philip Randolph, head of the sleeping car porters union. In the weeks leading up to the march, the backlash against civil rights protesters had grown more violent. The Big Bangah tried to talk my mother out of going to Washington but she held firm, again denying his claim to authority and asserting herself as an adult.

On August 28, 1963, my mother was one of 250,000 Americans who gathered in front of the Washington Monument and then marched to the Lincoln Memorial, where they listened to performances by Marian Anderson, Joan Baez, and others and heard a series of addresses capped by Dr. King's "I Have a Dream" address. The speech, broadcast live on television, would soon be hailed as the moment when the modern civil rights movement cohered into an unstoppable historical force. She came home filled with energy and stayed up late into the night talking with my father about what she had seen and heard. I was so young that I could not possibly understand all the reasons for her excitement. Nor could I fully grasp the historical significance of the events she had joined. What I would recall mainly was that what Dr. King had done had brought true happiness to our home.

Five

INTO THE WORLD

"And Jonathan, what's your father's name?"

Mrs. Lazan, my first-grade teacher, was checking her records. After confirming my new address she had noticed that my father's first name was missing from her book. She asked me what it was and then I said, "Benjamin."

"Can you spell that for me?"

I may have written a hundred notes and dedicated a thousand crayon drawings to "Daddy" but I had never addressed anything to Benjamin Emanuel.

I began, saying, "B-E-N," but then stopped and murmured, with some embarrassment, "I don't know the rest."

After all, it wasn't my name and I had no reason to know how to spell it. It was probably my first encounter with public failure in the classroom and I did not like it at all. My face flushed red and hot and I could not sit down fast enough. I would always remember the experience and it made me even more determined to avoid getting tripped up on facts I should know.

My parents chose Anshe Emet school—the words mean "people of truth"—mainly because it provided an hour and a half of Hebrew les-

sons to every child each day. They thought that when we moved back
to Israel, knowing Hebrew would be essential. When Rahm and I
moved back to Chicago in the late 1990s, we both ended up sending
our children to the same school. Walking my children through the
school for the very first time, I couldn't help notice that the rooms
looked pretty much the same, and to the annoyance and embarrassment of my girls, I insisted on pointing out which room housed each
of my classes, and reminiscing about my classmates and some of our
shenanigans. I also noticed that while the school still seemed small
and very communal—the principal still knew the name and family of
every student—there were now sixty children in three classes per grade
whereas we had just one class with the same peers year in and year out.
And the sociodemographics and politics of the families had changed.
When we boys were at Anshe Emet, the families were very middle-
class. While there were a few rich families, our family was the norm.
No one ever was teased for wearing Sears jeans or hand-me-down
coats; we didn't know that designer clothes existed. When my daughters were enrolled, despite being a two-doctor family, we found ourselves at the lower end of the income distribution. With children of
much wealthier stockbrokers and commodity traders, the feel of the
school changed to be more entitled and snobby, and there were even a
few Republicans, which would have been unheard-of when we walked
the halls in the 1960s.

The school was affiliated with Anshe Emet Synagogue. The temple
was Chicago's largest conservative congregation, but it was best
known for a public forum series that had been started in the late 1920s
by a famous rabbi named Solomon Goldman. The forum attracted
an astonishing lineup of speakers—including Eleanor Roosevelt, Carl
Sandburg, and Clarence Darrow—who addressed big issues like war
and peace and social justice.

Jewish regard for education is so widely recognized that it is hard
to discuss without lapsing into caricature. But what many people miss
when they consider the Jewish commitment to scholarship is that education is a pathway both to material success and to a happy, fulfilled

life that includes giving back to the community—one version of the American dream.

For the kids at Anshe Emet Day School in the 1960s, preparation for the good life in America took place in relatively small classes—nineteen to twenty-two kids each—where it was easy for teachers to foster a family-like atmosphere. We got lots of individual attention and heavy doses of art, music, and theater. Every year the fifth grade put on *Macbeth* under the direction of principal Morton Reisman, who knew nothing about stage direction but adored Shakespeare and put on a hell of a show. His enthusiasm was shared by most of the staff, including one of our Hebrew teachers, Mrs. Dubavick. A sturdy, middle-aged woman with a serious demeanor and heavy Eastern European accent, Mrs. Dubavick had a huge, bulbous nose and piercing eyes. Between classes she would sit by the open window in her classroom, smoking the European cigarettes that had turned her fingers yellow and made her voice gravelly and dramatic.

"This year we're going to read Exodus in Hebrew," she announced in September to my fourth-grade class. "I want you to understand there is violence in it. There's blood and guts and some sex. If there's anyone here who cannot handle it, I want to know now."

Of course we could handle it. In fact, the warning guaranteed she would receive our rapt attention for every lesson. The Hebrew we learned at the small school was rather formal, the type you would use to read religious texts, and not the fast, slangy language you hear on the streets of Tel Aviv. This would not matter to most students, who would never visit Israel, let alone live there. In fact, mastery of the spoken language was probably not the main point of the class anyway. In Mrs. Dubavick's lessons, and our religious studies, we discovered a shared ancient heritage that made us feel proud, secure, and part of something bigger than ourselves.

In the rest of our studies, we were held to high standards for both performance and effort. In fifth-grade math, for example, our teacher, Miss Hacker, required that all students score 100 percent on a weekly multiplication test before the class could stop taking them. Every week she called out twenty problems; we worked over them in silence and then handed our answer sheets to our designated partners across the aisle. Mine was Joanne Finkelstein. Over the weeks, we all became invested in the perfect class score, and chastised the student or students who missed one question. When we all scored perfects in March, we screamed for joy.

This multiplication exercise was typical of the way our teachers fostered both competition and group cohesion. The school was so small that as the one classroom full of kids moved together through the years, we came to feel almost as close as family members. In addition to the strict academic program, Anshe Emet gave us a community that supported achievement. Almost every child came from a family that put a high value on education. Most Anshe Emet kids were also second- or third-generation Americans. For them, the story of immigration and struggling for acceptance was a fading memory. Their parents had high expectations for their offspring. We, in turn, pushed one another, and just as athletes improve as they play against tougher opponents, we got better.

The competition was especially good for a kid like me. Inside our family, I was the undisputed academic champ. One of my advantages was temperament. I was slightly less hyperactive and better at studying than my brothers. I also benefited from my status as firstborn. As the eldest, I was always ahead of my brothers in reading, vocabulary, and conversation and was welcomed into adult-style interactions with my parents and their friends. But though I was a pretty smart boy at home, I was, fortunately, not the smartest kid in my class at school. That title, for as long as I attended Anshe Emet, belonged to a scrawny kid with reddish brown hair whose name was Spencer Waller.

Spencer Waller was a lot like me. My father was a doctor. His was a dentist. We both talked too much. Like me, Spencer had scuffled with the kids from Appalachia whom he met on the streets and in the parks, and like me he had been taunted with anti-Semitic slurs. Indeed, we were so much alike that in first grade I just *had* to stick out my foot and trip him when he was hurrying past me. Spencer fell on his face and bit his tongue so hard that he was rushed to a doctor for stitches. Considering my own accident with the radiator and the sucker, and Rahm's almost-severed fingers, Spencer's injury made me think, for a moment, that I might be a dangerous kid to hang around with.

Fortunately, I wasn't often so aggressive or hostile at school. For the most part I was an eager, albeit loud and occasionally obnoxious, kid who was desperate to seize the top spot in my class, a goal that Spencer Waller always denied me. Week after week (and eventually year after year), Spencer would score just a point or two higher than me on most tests, quizzes, and homework assignments. I would try to make up ground with higher scores on homework and special projects, but here again he usually prevailed. A good example of this competition was the special Greek history assignment we were given in fourth grade. I put in extra effort, and handed in a report on the story of the Trojan War, complete with a model of the famous wooden horse. I was sure my project would get an A. It did. But Spencer's project got an A-plus.

I became obsessed with beating Spencer Waller—indeed, for better or worse, part of me still is to this day—and this became a topic of regular conversation in our home. My father had dealt with his own academic nemesis in medical school and knew what it was like to finish second in his med school class. But though my parents sympathized, they never said or did anything to try to placate my hunger to overcome my rivals. In their view, you must work hard, tirelessly, using all the gifts God gave you, in order to succeed. Big achievements might be noted and celebrated in some modest way, but by the next morning life went back to normal and you were supposed to train your sights on the next goal. If we had a problem with the way things were handled we could ask for a family meeting—sometimes these were called powwows—and say whatever was on our minds.

.....

Under the rules of the powwow, which usually took place around the kitchen table, no topic was off-limits. Sometimes these discussions got quite raucous, and as my brothers and I got older, the vocabulary permitted around the table—and in our regular interactions—became more colorful. Yiddish, formal English, and cursing were all mixed up. In one burst of conversation you might be called a meshugenah, a moron, and an ass, all in rapid succession.

There was nothing personal in these words. It was the family style to include a little insult—"You're an idiot and here's why"—with whatever point you wanted to make. Also, you were expected to talk loud, and fast, and if you waited politely for your turn to speak you were lost. Our kitchen was a crowded deli at lunchtime, not a tearoom at 4 P.M.

My mother liked these powwows because they gave her a chance to see inside our hearts and minds. If we used a family meeting to complain about her, it was generally because we were upset over those moments when she ran out of patience and abandoned us both physically and emotionally. She would throw up her hands and say something like "I hate all of you equally," then retreat to the bathroom, which was the one place where she could find peace behind a locked door, flipping through a book or magazine and smoking a cigarette or two. For our sake I would pray that Rahm hadn't made pinholes in her cigarettes, which was something he did every once in a while to protest her smoking.

Depending on the severity of the episode our mother would either emerge from the bathroom and life would return to normal, or she would freeze us out emotionally for hours or even days. The worst inevitably came on Mother's Day, or her birthday. What she wanted was one day of special treatment—a nice breakfast, a thoughtful gift, and relief from her usual homemaking obligations. We usually failed to deliver.

It wasn't that our mother made a mystery out of what pleased her. We all knew that she liked flowers and hoped for gifts that showed someone had considered her as an individual and not some generic "mother" or "wife." However, our dad hated giving flowers; they were so ephemeral, dying after a day or two, and therefore wasteful. And he never had the insight for meaningful gift giving. Most of the time he didn't buy one. If he did, it would be some impersonal household item, or a utilitarian sweater. Without a great role model, we boys tried, but invariably fell short. We didn't have lots of money and couldn't coax him to cooperate. Also, we were not terribly good at planning either. The Big Day would arrive and we would have to scramble. Disappointed and angry, our mother would cry, "You don't care! I work hard all year long and it means nothing to you!"

Sometimes the screaming could go on for hours. Other times she would go silent—which was even worse. For kids who were accustomed to a generous amount of attention and a loud house, this freezing silence was excruciating. We all felt the loss of conversation, affection, and energy in a way that grew more painful as time passed. Indeed, whenever the freeze lasted more than a day the family fell into a sort of situational depression, marked by anxiety and the fear that things might never get back to normal.

We responded by gathering on Rahm's bed, the bottom bunk, to whisper ideas about how to get back into our mom's good graces.

"We should make dinner tonight."

"What can we make? Maybe we should ask Dad to take the family out."

"Dad, take us out? No way. Plus it would be one of those silent dinners. With Mom still angry and not allowing anyone to say anything."

"What's your big idea?"

"I don't have one. You know we just have to wait."

"Let's clean up the family room and make sure not to fight tonight."

Over the years we tried various approaches. Cleaning the house. Straightening our room. Cooking Sunday breakfast of lox, bagels, and eggs. In all cases, we offered an abject apology and dish-cleaning service usually performed by Rahm. At the next family powwow someone, usually brave Ari, would remind my mother of how upsetting these episodes were and complain that they lasted way too long. To her credit, my mother would explain why she did what she did. But though our mother eagerly sought our opinions and seemed to enjoy hearing what was on our minds, she did not always give us what we asked for, emotionally.

Perhaps because he sensed better than us the limits of conversation, our father was not terribly enthusiastic about these family meetings. If things went on too long, or we pressed a point too hard, he would flee the kitchen for a book or the television, leaving my mother to handle things by herself. At other times he would use his status as the father to assert his authority in a way that violated the Emanuel philosophy. During one of these moments I complained loudly.

"That's not fair!"

"Who told you it was a democracy?" answered my father.

"Well then what is it?"

"A theocracy."

"So you're God?" I shot back.

Across the table I could see Ari's face light up. He got the shovav look.

"I guess," he blurted, "that makes Mommy the god-ass!"

.....

When you come from a family that is temperamentally outspoken and viscerally antagonistic to power, you carry a kind of injustice radar with you at all times. This device, which is always switched on, detects arrogance and the abuse of power with exquisite precision. You then have the choice to act or acquiesce. I faced this choice in third-grade gym class with Mr. Kerr.

Physical education for boys at Anshe Emet was everything you would imagine in a gym class of the 1960s. Think skinny eight-year-olds—some hyperactive, some with undiagnosed attention deficit disorder, many woefully uncoordinated—playing dodgeball, tumbling on mats, and climbing ropes under the punishing gaze of a thirtyish male teacher dressed in a T-shirt, khaki pants, and sneakers.

No doubt Mr. Kerr had his hands full with my class. Some of us may have had minimal athletic ability, but we were really talented at talking and arguing. With our many questions, opinions, and suggestions we could drive any gym teacher crazy. Nevertheless, he should have known better than to draw the line he did one winter morning when the chattering and disorder got the best of him.

"All right!" he screamed. "Everyone line up! Now!"

I cannot recall now whether we had been treating our gym teacher with any extra disrespect on that day but he launched into a tirade that ended with the kind of question that reveals a commander who is afraid that he is losing his grip.

"From now on everyone is going to call me 'sir' at all times. Got that?"

Mr. Kerr paused for what seemed like ages, then asked, "Does anyone disagree with this? If you do, then step forward across this line."

Granted, this was elementary school, not the USS *Caine*, and Mr. Kerr wasn't Captain Queeg. But it was the third-grade equivalent of a moral showdown. Without hesitation I stepped forward and across the line.

I am not sure anyone noticed me at first. When he finally did, Mr. Kerr had to ask me if I had stepped out of line on purpose. I told him yes, and explained that the respect that comes with the title "sir" is something you earn. And by demanding it, he had shown himself to be someone who did not deserve it.

"Go to Mr. Reisman's office. Now."

Like all good private school principals, Morton Reisman was one part educator, one part administrator, and one part diplomat. A tall, balding, bespectacled man, he wore a tailored suit and tie to work every day. He knew the name of every child in the school and was so versatile and intelligent that he could serve as a substitute teacher for any class, including Hebrew. Sometimes, when he was under stress, he suffered from facial tics. He would suddenly twitch two or three times in the middle of speaking. He was so respected—loved, really—that no one seemed to notice or said a word about it.

When I arrived at the school office I explained what had happened and was told to wait while my mother was called. She walked the blocks to school in what seemed like just a few minutes and, after stopping to reassure me, went right into Mr. Reisman's office. When I was finally escorted into the office I could see that she and my principal were getting along just fine. They asked me to explain again what had happened and I did, doing my best to articulate my belief that respect can be earned, but never commanded.

My mother said she had raised me to hold this belief and that she agreed with me. Mr. Reisman studied us both and saw that we meant what we said. He then said he would handle it and told me to return to my classroom. I was never punished. In fact, at home I was praised for standing up to a bully. I never found out what happened between the principal and the gym teacher, but Mr. Kerr left Anshe Emet a few years later.

.....

At the time, I didn't know that many other parents would have handled my showdown with Mr. Kerr quite differently. More than a few would have sided with any adult who held authority, no matter what, in order to teach a child to be a law-abiding citizen. When these parents are called to school by the principal they begin by asking their kid, "What did you do wrong?"

My mother practiced what she preached when it came to equality and justice and that meant that we were innocent until proven guilty. She also trusted us, especially when we were little and more or less guileless, to be honest with her. If I said that Mr. Kerr was impatient and disrespectful, she believed me. If we stood up for ourselves, she supported us.

This high level of trust was balanced with responsibilities. The most important one, in my case, involved getting my brothers home from school safely. Because my mother did not drive we used city buses to get back and forth. I started going home alone when I was in first grade, and Rahm was all of four and enrolled in nursery school.

At the end of school, I met my brother and led him outside to the sidewalk, where we turned north on Pine Grove Street. We then navigated Chicago's traffic, crossing Sheridan Road, one of the busier four-lane streets in the city, until we arrived at a sign marking a stop on the 151 and 153 Chicago Transit Authority routes. Eventually a bus would glide to a halt and the driver would open the door. I'd boost Rahm up the steps of the bus and deposit the fare—eighteen cents for the two of us—in the box. If there were seats available we would take them, but sometimes the bus was so packed we had to stand and hold on to one of the steel poles. Fortunately, the ride to the stop around the corner from our apartment took only a few minutes.

Looking back from the perspective of a twenty-first-century father, it's hard to believe that allowing kids so young to cross busy city streets and travel alone on public transportation did not constitute parental neglect or child endangerment. Of course, those were different times, and as I recall I never complained or said I was anxious about the responsibility. Perhaps this was because I had figured out a way to profit from the arrangement. My unwitting co-conspirator was the mother of my classmate Michelle Lowe. Mrs. Lowe had a car, which she used to ferry Michelle back and forth to Anshe Emet from their home. On rainy days, or if she just took pity on us, Mrs. Lowe would offer us a ride home, which was a few blocks farther north than the Lowes' apartment. We always eagerly accepted. I would keep the unspent bus fare. I got Rahm to keep quiet by promising to spend the money with him.

The scheme worked until the day that Mrs. Lowe encountered my mother at some parent-teacher event. She asked, with a hint of irritation, why my mom had never thanked her for the occasional cab service she provided for the Emanuel family. After my mother and Mrs. Lowe figured out what had happened, and stopped laughing over my ingenuity, I was confronted about the pennies, nickels, and dimes I had taken. When my mother demanded their return I explained that it was "used car fare" and Rahm and I had already spent nearly all of it on candy or used books.

To their credit, my brothers behaved well enough that we made the trip to school and back hundreds of times without incident. They were not so accommodating at home. Whether we were arguing over who got to pick a TV show or who won at Risk, Monopoly, or some other board game, we shed blood almost every day. More often than not the battle line was drawn between me and the other two, who banded together out of shared resentment for a stronger big brother. I may have protected them at school or around the neighborhood but at home the competition between us was intense. As the eldest in this survival-of-the-fittest environment I benefited from being bigger and stronger. Though younger, Ari quickly grew to be taller than Rahm, which put Rahm in the awkward position of being outmuscled by the baby of the family.

.....

My best friend during the Anshe Emet years was a boy named Skippy Shein. Compared to us, the Sheins were the Rockefellers. They lived in a four-story town house located a block north of Oak Street, which is Chicago's version of Madison Avenue. They gave their only child the best of everything and he always seemed to have plenty of money in his pockets. His parents ran a family business from the basement of their house, which meant they were often too busy to watch us closely. We got into plenty of mischief. Once we collected a bunch of the nitroglycerin pills that Skippy's father Max took for a heart condition and spent the afternoon smashing them in the misinformed hope that we could cause an explosion. Early one Saturday morning Skippy suggested we get breakfast at a little restaurant on Oak Street called Eli's, where his father kept a tab with the manager. When the waitress asked us what we wanted, we ordered one of almost everything on the breakfast menu—French toast, pancakes, omelets, bagels, two big orange juices, bacon, sausage, muffins. The plates arrived and we nibbled a bit from each one, then the bill arrived. It was something like eleven dollars—a fortune for us. Skippy told them to put it on his father's account. When Max Shein got the bill, he hit the roof. After yelling at us about our misplaced sense of entitlement, he required us to do yard work in order to pay our debt. Our hands were blistered by the rakes and clippers we used but we learned a lesson about those magical words, "Put it on the tab."

Although sometimes I paid a price, the freedom that let me get into trouble with Skippy Shein was a gift from my parents. I also benefited from their somewhat unconventional views on chores and allowance.

My parents never established a routine that required us to perform specific chores in exchange for their approval or an allowance. Instead they heard out our requests for money and if they thought a purchase made sense—and we were keeping up with school—they gave us the cash. This was always an easy bargain for me, but not necessarily for my brothers.

Rahm did well enough in school, but he always heard from teachers that they expected the same straight-A performance they got from me. Though fiercely intelligent, especially when it came to sizing people up and assessing a social situation, Rahm was not naturally inclined to sit at a desk and put in extra effort to turn a B into an A. As my father often said, without noting that the phrase applied to himself at that same age, "Rahm always tries to get the maximum for the minimum." As if it is genetically wired, Rahm's son seems to have the same view of grades, which, of course, drives Rahm as a parent as mad as it did my father.

The fact was, Rahm was not interested in becoming a copy of his older brother. When teachers mentioned my grades or our parents posted our report cards on the refrigerator, he was neither envious nor motivated to match me. Instead, he resented being compared and became determined to find a way to succeed on his own terms. In the meantime he would do whatever was necessary to get under my skin as often as possible.

On many nights, Rahm got his revenge by lying in bed and whistling a long, complicated melody while keeping time by snapping his fingers. Since I could neither whistle nor snap my fingers, this little show was a good way to annoy me. When we lived on Buena Avenue, and he bunked over me, I would try to stop him by kicking his mattress from below so hard he had to hang on like a cowboy on a bronco to keep from being thrown onto the floor. When we lived on Winona and he shared the bunk beds with Ari, who laughed as Rahm trilled away, I'd bomb him with pillows or wrestle him to the floor to get him to stop.

Ari seemed to be born unafraid of competition and conflict, especially physical battle. Sympathetic to the underdog, he usually took

Rahm's side when the fight became physical and as he quickly grew to be bigger and stronger, their little team became quite powerful. More than anything, Ari seemed to enjoy inciting us whenever things got too quiet. With mischief in his eyes and a grin on his face, Ari would needle and annoy until someone lashed out. The instant you moved to swat him, he would dash off so quickly that it was almost impossible to catch him. All the while Ari would laugh with excitement because he had made something happen.

Inside the family, Ari's modus operandi fell squarely in the range of normal. We all liked to test and challenge and any hard feelings that arose during our fights faded faster than the bruises. He was also accepted by the Glass brothers and other friends in the neighborhood because of his fearlessness. But when he got to school, his restlessness became a problem. Ari was highly verbal, incredibly alert—he had a great memory and learned certain things very quickly—and very charming, yet when it came to reading and writing, he ran into a wall.

While other kids wrote out letters, Ari struggled to translate what he saw on the blackboard to the paper on his desk. He wrote individual letters backward and reversed the order of letters in words. *Dog* became *bog* and *boy* became *yod*. Born into a home filled with books, and now settled into a school where scholarship equaled success, Ari fell further and further behind his brothers and his classmates. Worse, he had trouble sitting still long enough to complete a lesson, and it was practically impossible for him to spend extra time studying. He had too much energy, and was too easily distracted.

Today, a boy like Ari would be diagnosed with dyslexia and would be given help from specially trained teachers, extra time to complete assignments, and a way to think about himself that would spare him from feeling like a failure. In the mid-1960s, dyslexia and attention deficit disorder were just beginning to gain attention among physicians and educators. Like most kids with learning difficulties, Ari was lectured and given extra drills in the belief that he just needed to pay attention and practice a little more. In the eyes of the adults charged with his education, Ari's problem wasn't developmental or neurological. Despite the obvious evidence to the contrary, they seemed to think that his problem was a lack of effort.

Ari could not make others understand that he was trying as hard as he could. Nor could he explain that to him, the letters and words he wrote on his paper matched what he saw on the blackboard or in his workbook assignments. Eventually he began to fear that his inability to read was caused by a character defect or a basic lack of intelligence. He did not share these feelings openly. In fact, he buried them so deeply that they only came out in bursts of aggression or anger. He argued and got into fights that showed he was upset, but Ari never explained his motives. Then, in an unexpected moment, the truth would bubble to the surface.

One day, he and my mother walked to the park with our dog Andele. It was the end of August and Ari, age seven, was thinking about the school year that lay ahead. As they walked he searched the ground for sticks that he then threw for the dog to fetch. "Look, Mommy!" he shouted as he wound up and threw a stick so far that it landed beyond the glow of the streetlight.

"Wow, Ari, you've got quite an arm," said my mother.

"Yeah," he replied, "I can throw but I still can't read."

Other kids had mastered reading and writing simple sentences, complete with proper punctuation, while Ari was still struggling to transcribe single letters properly. The humiliation he experienced every time he was called on to read aloud was so unbearable that even during the summer break, he was thinking about the failure that awaited him in September as adults again demanded that he "buckle down" and try harder. All his effort produced no real gain.

My mother understood Ari's predicament and tried to compensate by giving him extra attention when he did homework. She also pressed him by making sure he understood that he was expected to give it his best whenever he did anything. On his own, Ari would look for different ways to show his intelligence and talent. He became highly skilled at social relationships and adept at both charming and manipulating adults. Not surprisingly, his methods were least effective at home, where my parents understood Ari's techniques and generally refused to be charmed. When it came to measuring both our effort and our achievement, they maintained very high standards. It was a tough kind of love, and Ari often resented it.

Decades later, it would not take much prodding to get Ari to recall the burning sense of shame he felt as he tried to overcome his problem in full view of his classmates and brothers. "Do you have any idea what kind of torture it was like to sit there every day?" he would ask Rahm and me. "It was hard enough for me to sit still, and even if I could do that it was almost impossible for me to do what the teachers expected."

In fact, Rahm and I did know something of what Ari felt. As brothers we may have teased and tortured him on other matters but we did not try to embarrass him when it came to reading and writing. Ari's struggles were so painful to him that we would have been especially cruel to torment him about it. Also, he was a tough little guy, which meant that he could respond to our teasing with the kind of physical attack that more than paid you back for whatever psychic pain you might inflict on him. Fundamentally, though, it was easy for us to understand how it felt to be on the hot seat, sensing the pressure of our mother's expectations and fearing that you might not measure up.

This was the downside of life as a child of purposeful parents. Sometimes all the focus and devotion my mother gave us veered into the realm of excessive pressure. This was certainly true where Ari and reading were concerned. Rahm and I pitied him for the amount of attention he received as my mothered tried, sometimes with nothing more than demands and the force of will, to help him overcome his disability. But as we all would discover, lots of kids would have given anything to be part of a family where they received so much attention, even if it was sometimes hard to take.

Six

A FAMILY, EXTENDED

In 1965, Jeffrey Wacker was a soft, pudgy, pale boy of about six who knew the batting averages for every player on the Chicago Cubs but was so uncoordinated he had trouble tossing a ball across the alley in a way that gave you any chance of catching it. On any given day, he would miss at least one loop as he put on his belt, and his zipper was as likely to be open as it was to be closed, but you might not notice because his shirt was untucked and hanging down to his knees.

We met Jeffrey when his parents brought him to a service we attended at the famous Unity Temple in Oak Park. A center of support for the civil rights movement, this Unitarian church was a place where people of every type of belief or nonbelief came together for services and support. A Frank Lloyd Wright masterpiece, the building is a modern version of a Greek temple, with thick concrete columns and a series of flat roofs. Filled with light, the interior is both inspiring and peaceful.

Not that any of us boys, including Jeffrey Wacker, found it easy to be at peace, anywhere. Rahm, Ari, and I struggled to be quiet and Jeffrey was just as fidgety and distracted. His parents, who were brilliant but generally unable to cope with everyday life, had not taught Jeffrey much about how to fit into social situations or to moderate his behavior out of consideration for others. Individually they both struggled with psychiatric diagnoses that were much more serious than garden-variety neurosis. Mrs. Wacker had had multiple admissions to psychiatry wards. Mr. Wacker, who was a whiz in math but socially inept, worked only sporadically and vacillated between joy and despair. Together, they made a marriage that always seemed to teeter on the edge of disaster.

Raised in an insecure and unstable home, Jeffrey suffered and his parents knew it. Finally, on a day when Mrs. Wacker was once again admitted to the hospital, her husband showed up at our apartment with his son and asked if the boy could stay. My father the pediatrician and my mother—the woman who always tried to do the right thing—said yes. An extra place was set at the table and a bed was purchased and placed at the foot of mine. Jeffrey was enrolled at Brennemann Elementary, our neighborhood public school. My mother found a psychotherapist who would treat him, and we all tried to help him get accustomed to the routine of life with the Emanuels.

Life was not easy for Jeffrey. In a hyperverbal household where quick retorts and arguments were the main currency of conversation, he rarely found a way to fit in. Although he was incredibly intelligent, he was socially tone-deaf and struggled to follow a fast-paced conversation. Most of the time he was two beats behind the flow, responding to points that had already been made and settled, with statements that were non sequiturs. These statements would either stop the conversation cold for a few uncomfortable moments, or be greeted with a response from Rahm along the lines of "You don't know what the hell you are talking about, Jeffrey."

What made it worse was that Jeffrey had no sense of his own deficiencies. He assumed he knew things he did not know, or had talents and skills he never possessed, and just dove into every situation.

The best example of Jeffrey's unnerving, almost fantastic way of thinking arose when we all went to a swimming pool. Having been taught to swim when we were toddlers, Ari, Rahm, and I dove in and glided to the surface like a trio of dolphins. Jeffrey followed, hurling himself into the deep end and sinking like a stone. Having learned to expect anything from this boy, I watched him carefully and noticed he was in trouble. I raced to him and managed to push him to the surface and over to the side of the pool. Once he got hold of the wall of the pool and caught his breath he gasped, "Wow, that was fun. Let's do it again!"

We did not "do it again." In fact, Jeffrey was consigned to the shallow end of the pool for the rest of the day. In the weeks and months that followed, we all paid close attention to him, for safety's sake, even though he was often irritating. "A tough kid to love," was how my mother put it.

Our initial adventure with Jeffrey lasted for about a year. In that time we tried to treat him like the fourth brother. He joined us when we attacked my dad on the dining room floor and he was welcomed onto my parent's bed for story time. He was even covered under our all-for-one/one-for-all rule for back alley fighting, which meant that when he was attacked, we all came to his aid. Soon enough Jeffrey came to abuse this power by goading kids into a scrap and then depending on Ari, who was becoming a rather dominant fighter, to step in, which he always did.

Because loyalty and sticking up for the underdog were hallmark Emanuel values, we never let Jeffrey down no matter how annoyed we got about the crowding in the bedroom, the fights he instigated, and his strange way of talking. Then one day his parents returned, collected his belongings, and took him away. It was not the last we would see of Jeffrey and his parents. For the next ten years, they stayed in touch and every so often his mother or father would show up at the door asking if we could take him in again.

My mother knew that things sometimes got rough and even dangerous at the Wacker home so she always said yes, and Jeffrey would rejoin our household for a few days, weeks, or months. Once she even tried to delay Mrs. Wacker when she came to retrieve her son because she could see that Mrs. Wacker was not psychologically stable and ready to resume her duties as a mother. We helped see Jeffrey through his parents' separation and divorce. My dad became Jeffrey's only true father figure when Mr. Wacker went to live in an old mining town somewhere out west.

Eventually Jeffrey would graduate from high school, leave Chicago, marry, and settle in California. We could hope that in his time with us he learned something about family and the positive possibilities of socialization. We learned we were fortunate to have been born to parents who could give us so much, and that the suffering of others (something my parents often discussed) wasn't something abstract and distant. Unable to care for himself, Jeffrey had truly paid a price for something completely beyond his control and he had only been helped when someone cared enough to act. The fact that the "someone" was my mother reinforced for us the idea that you should not stand with your hands in your pockets waiting for others to make the sacrifice that matters. If you can do the right thing to make a person's life better, you do it.

.....

Jeffrey wasn't the last extra Emanuel brother and, technically speaking, he wasn't the first, either. Years before Jeffrey moved in with the three of us, my father brought home a baby boy named Boaz and announced to my mother that she was going to take care of him, along with me and Rahm, who was only a few months old. The baby belonged to another resident doctor at Mount Sinai Hospital and his wife, who was a nurse. All my father would say about them is that they were good people, and fellow Israelis, who were having problems and needed help.

Boaz got the same care, feeding, and cuddling as Rahm and me and he was part of everything we did, from visits to the park to shopping trips. On some weekends his mother came and took him away for a few days. On others, his father appeared for extended visits. After a few months passed, Boaz went back with his parents.

Along with Jeffrey Wacker, Boaz set a pattern that would be repeated, many times. My parents would offer their help to a friend or relative and suddenly our nuclear family would include a new member. The arrangements were made out of our view. All we knew was that suddenly a new boy or young man would appear at the dinner table. Some, like our cousin Gary, came for a few months, returned to their parents, and then came back for a second or even third stay with us. Another cousin, Teddy, was well into his teen years when he came to stay with us. An alienated and lonely adolescent, Teddy had exhausted his parents' patience. At our house, he found a refuge where there was always something to do, and my mother was always willing to talk and, more important, listen.

My mother seemed a sort of expert nurturer, a woman who could make any child feel safe, secure, and valued. She was a highly intelligent, energetic, and motivated woman who was denied other careers, and motherhood was her profession. At the time it was a logical and productive way to channel her energies. I suspect that millions of other mothers in these pre-women's-liberation days did the same.

Besides receiving my mother's attention, the older boys like Teddy and, later, Ralph Feldstein and Jack Skayan, got to be big brothers to the three of us. This role got them out of focusing on their own problems and into the pleasure of helping someone else. Ralph taught us how to swing a hammer and wield an electric saw when my parents allowed him to build a fairly elaborate wall unit in our family room. The end product was not exactly professional quality, but it was a cheap and sturdy piece of furniture that, more than forty years later, still supports a television and piles of books in my parents' basement.

Still, of all the visitors to our home, it was our grandfather Herman who had the most influence on our lives. He stopped by often and lived with us for almost two years in the early 1970s. During this time, he would commandeer the kitchen on Saturday mornings and set to work making toast, slicing bagels, scrambling eggs, and frying steaks. He did all this while dressed in his white boxer shorts and a sleeveless T-shirt and pausing, every now and then, to slurp orange juice from a big open carton and burp loudly.

Although the smells coming from the kitchen alerted us to the banquet that awaited, he wouldn't call us until everything was just about ready. We took our seats as he put plates on the table. In the process he might playfully smack the back of Rahm's head or call Ari "a good-for-nothin' *momser*," which is Yiddish for "bastard." But as rough as he was, we knew he was trying to connect with us. As Rahm would later say, "I don't think he knew anything else to say" to a bunch of verbally endowed but scrawny young kids.

When breakfast was over we went off to rest our swollen bellies or followed the Big Bangah out to his station wagon for a ride. For as long as I knew him the Big Bangah sold imported Scandinavian foods— cheeses, bacon, ham, butter cookies, candies, and other products— which he often delivered to stores and restaurants himself. On many Saturdays he made the rounds of his customers to deliver items that were piled in the back of the station wagon. On these days we would crisscross Chicago, or dash up to small towns in Wisconsin, at break-neck speed, weaving in and out of traffic and treating stop signs and red lights as if they were recommendations.

Although my mother was vigilant about seat belts, her father was not and we bounced around in the back of his huge Ford station wagon like boy-sized salamis. Wherever we stopped we followed him inside, lugging boxes and tins loaded with delicacies. Once we set the goods down, we got to watch him schmooze with his customers like they were close friends.

It did not matter whether we were in Polishtown, the South Side, or in some town in Wisconsin; Herman always acted like he belonged. His customers welcomed him with loud greetings and implored him to gossip about their competitors or commiserate about the state of business, which was never quite good enough. He was, for these shop-keepers, like the traveling storytellers of old who kept people apprised of the news from abroad.

In exchange for his information and stories, Herman took the kind of liberties reserved for family, grabbing Cokes or cookies for us with-out ever asking. I'll never forget how he reached right into the oven at one bagel shop on Kedzie Avenue and pulled out a handful of hot mini-bagels and gave them to us. I don't know which was more im-pressive, the exquisite taste of a bagel so perfectly fresh and hot, or my grandfather's pain-defying reach into the oven. For me, a skinny kid, the sight of those huge callused mitts plunging into the oven was the very picture of toughness. The only way we could hold on to our treats was to juggle them from hand to hand while they cooled.

Often gruff and intimidating with adults at home, Herman was usually energetic, confident, and generous with us boys. He gave Gary and me tickets for the one and only pro football game I ever saw, at a frigid Wrigley Field. (The Bears moved to Soldier Field in 1971.) During a trip to some general store in the hinterlands, he sprang for my first wristwatch. I was six or seven years old but he did not buy me a kid's model with Mickey Mouse or some other playful image on the face. Instead he got me a serious grown-up timepiece with a big white dial and black hands that pointed to numerals stamped on the face in blocky black type. My wrist was so skinny that he had to get a woman's model and he asked the store owner to punch two extra holes in the leather strap so it would stay on. However, it was a real watch and Herman knew that when I wore it I felt one step closer to adulthood.

In most cases, days spent driving around with my grandfather were about adventure and involved a lot of raucous interactions. His big, meaty hands made the steering wheel look small and delicate and his booming voice—"Shut up back there already!"—practically shook the windows of the car. On one occasion, when Ari and Rahm went out with him, the Big Bangah actually followed through on a threat we had always considered idle. For years he'd warned, "I'll put you out of this car and leave you here!" but we never believed him. On this trip he got so fed up with Ari and Rahm that he actually pulled over on some isolated roadside in rural Wisconsin and ordered them out. They were about seven and nine years old and could not believe that Herman would actually drive away, but he did.

Ornery as they could be, Rahm and Ari were also little boys and as they watched the station wagon disappear they became worried, anxious, and then truly upset. Rural Wisconsin may as well have been Zamboanga to them and they soon began to panic. They thought about finding a pay phone to call for help but realized that they did not know which way to walk in order to find civilization and that even if they did find a phone they did not have any money to pay for a call. In their telling of the story they were stuck there for an hour before

Herman came back, muttered something about hoping they had learned a lesson, and let them into the car. For all I know they had only been alone for a few minutes or so.

Fortunately, Herman rarely acted on his threats. Instead he took pains to instruct us on how to be his kind of man. At mealtimes he might take us into a diner, or roadside café, and generously urge us to order what we wanted, including foods that were never in the refrigerator at home, like cherry Cokes and orange pop. Watching him move so confidently as he interacted with shopkeepers, countermen, cooks, and bakers was like watching a veteran pol work a precinct meeting. He flashed a huge smile, talked sports and current events, slapped backs, and busted chops. Despite our current reputation, my brothers and I were cautious and even a little shy back then whenever we entered unfamiliar settings or encountered new people. We would each develop strategies to overcome this social anxiety to a certain extent, but Ari and I will never be as comfortable as Rahm, who was destined to become a professional politician and nearly Herman's equal when it came to small talk and jokes.

Between stops, the Big Bangah told us stories about how he had managed to make it in a world that wasn't always friendly to a Russian Jewish immigrant with hardly any formal education. The world he described, where powerful people and institutions rejected him because of his religion and nationality, led him to develop his tough, masculine personality. It was not the world we knew, but hearing about it helped us understand and appreciate him even if we could not emulate him.

A different, but equally impressive view of Herman's life came into focus when we attended services at the storefront synagogue he had helped to build. Located in the old Jewish neighborhood of Albany Park, the shul was home to about a hundred congregants, all middle-aged and older, including my family. We were the only children who ever attended the services. My brothers and I resisted and complained about getting dressed up and schlepping to the synagogue but once we got there we were proud to see how much people respected our grandfather. All during services he would wander the aisles, and whisper to various congregants. And he would invariably be the one who supplied the food for the Yom Kippur break fast or Saturday kiddushes. Most important, when something needed to be done—someone driven home after services, food delivered to someone who had just come home from the hospital, or an electric light fixed—Big Bangah just did it without the need to be asked or thanked. We basked in the reflected glory and, since we were the only children who attended services there, we came in for lots of cheek-pinching attention.

Services at the temple were conducted entirely in Hebrew, but if someone made impromptu remarks, they were made in Yiddish. Attendance varied depending on the time of year, but high holy day services were always quite crowded. They frequently got too loud for anyone to hear the actual prayer service. And then Herman would raise his enormous mitt of a right hand and bang it down on the counter, instantly bringing order to the old ladies gossiping and other loud murmurings.

On Yom Kippur we also watched as the congregation raised the money to fund the shul for the coming year. Conducted during a pause in the service, this collection began with an announcement. A few thousand dollars were required to pay the utilities and repairs, and members were asked to say, out loud, how much they were willing to contribute. Offers of ten to twenty dollars were voiced and usually the action stopped a few hundred dollars short of the goal. Everyone would look toward my father. He would smile and nod, which was the signal that Dr. Emanuel would fill the gap.

After services people stayed to mingle over honey cake, tea, and kosher wine. Many but not all of the people who went to that temple kept kosher households, either out of religious conviction or because the practice was part of their Jewish identity. When it came to theology the people at the Albany temple, like Jews in general, were all over the map.

In my family, we expressed our Judaism through our commitment to Israel, attending Jewish day school, and a devotion to the Friday night dinners. In keeping with tradition my mother lit candles and did the blessing, my father did the wine blessing, and one of us kids blessed the challah. My parents were not so religious that we did the handwashing, blessing of the children, or grace after meals that my children and I now include. Attendance at these dinners was mandatory and only a medical emergency would keep my father away. The meal was never fancy, but the table was set with a white tablecloth and cloth napkins, and the menu invariably included a roast chicken, vegetables, and salad.

If ever peace reigned in our home it was on these Friday nights when the TV and radio were switched off and no one answered the telephone. We still indulged in lively conversation and debate, but we made more of an effort to show respect for one another as we affirmed our Jewish identity.

In our family, the God of the burning bush was a concept that served a purpose when it was devised in ancient times but was not a matter of literal truth. Sure, there were references to God in our everyday conversations, especially from my mother, but in truth she was agnostic, and my father, if pressed, would say he's an atheist. But this would not be a deeply considered answer. It would be a way to brush off the question, which he wouldn't consider seriously. My father was never the type to be seriously bothered by a metaphysical question. He had neither a scientist's nor a theologian's interest in the origins of the universe or the nature of morality. Instead he was interested in watching and interacting with people, and thrilled at both the variety and the creativity in human expression.

For our mother, who was more concerned about us attending synagogue, religion was a matter of us being authentically and culturally Jewish. Going to synagogue was a matter of Jewish identity in the America of the 1960s, which was overwhelmingly Christian in fact and spirit. In Israel, attending synagogue doesn't mean the same thing. In a land that is Jewish, you never feel any pressure to attend religious services because you don't have to prove your membership. You are Jewish by birthright, conversion, and location and that settles it. In the America of our childhood, attendance at Friday night or Saturday services signaled your commitment to your Jewishness and the Jewish community. It was a way of showing, to yourself and the world, who you were.

Given our household, none of us brothers became believers in God, but we are all deeply Jewish and take the practices seriously. Our children have gone to Jewish day school; each of us still makes Friday night dinners special and says all the requisite prayers. Interestingly, two of my children and one of Rahm's are strictly kosher. More important, we never saw a contradiction in practicing Judaism and yet not believing in God. For us Judaism is a religion without a supreme authority like the pope. Instead it offers a tradition in which sages offer various interpretations and arguments about the meaning of every passage of the Bible. As a result we became imbued with the Jewish ethos of constantly challenging authority, asking questions, and examining every aspect of life.

The fact that my parents did not believe in a man-in-the-sky kind of God and ate some nonkosher foods did not make them any less accepted in the shul or the community. They were loved and accepted because of their generosity of spirit. They always made an extra effort to include you in their circle.

.....

My father's openness meant that once you got to know him, almost anything could happen. A young single woman who became his office assistant told him soon after she was hired that she had never seen a baby born and was eager to do so. This was the 1960s, a time when delivery rooms were off-limits to everyone but medical personnel and mothers, most of whom were drugged and would never recall what went on. Ignoring prevailing custom, my father took his assistant to a hospital where he had privileges, got her into scrubs and a mask, and all but shoved her into a delivery room, where he explained that she was in training for something and would like to observe. The doctors and nurses simply nodded and let her watch for as long as she cared to stay there.

Diane Fisher, who married and became Diane Ianiro, would say that this experience changed her life forever. The birth she witnessed dispelled the mystery if not the fear around an experience she was quite certain she would have in the future. More important, the respect my father had shown her by admitting her to a sort of secret society and assuming she could handle it gave her a sense of self-confidence and made her feel like she was Dr. Emanuel's colleague and not an employee. Diane, who was so pretty that all three of us developed crushes on her, spent her entire career in my father's practice and became a close family friend.

Over time, many friends, colleagues, neighbors, and allies in various political battles found acceptance and comfort inside the family orbit. In turn, Rahm, Ari, and I would bring our friends, classmates, and even our teachers around. Some would sample the raucous enthusiasm they found in our home and feel so overwhelmed they never came back. Others felt warmed by the affection and liberated by the way they were invited to speak their minds.

The longest-running family friendship has been with the Glasses, who met my parents soon after they returned to Chicago from Israel. From the day when I asked Carol Glass to peel that orange, she and my mother have been steady friends, as close as sisters. Bill Glass was as much an uncle as any blood relative and his sons were the boys we knew best from the time we were toddlers until we went to college.

It would be hard to exaggerate the amount of time we spent with the Glasses and the importance they played in our childhood. Like us the sons were three Jewish boys growing up in middle-class Chicago. But unlike us they attended public school and were not subject to nearly as much pressure when it came to academic success. Less focused than my parents when it came to educational enrichment, Bill and Carol did not take their sons on regular outings to museums, the ballet, and the theater. Bill Glass was more of an all-American dad, the type who trekked with his sons (and occasionally an Emanuel boy) to his alma mater, Michigan State, for football games. He also loved to indulge us at roadside restaurants. Every time Bill drove us to their Michiana cottage, on the lakeshore sand dunes at the Indiana-Michigan border, we stopped at the famous Phil Smidt's restaurant in

Hammond, Indiana, to fill our bellies on fried lake perch, coleslaw, and french fries.

For eight or nine years, we might as well have been six brothers with two sets of parents. The experience taught us that we could be close to people outside our family and that common ground isn't hard to find.

Seven

RIGHT AND WRONG AND GOOD AND EVIL

In 1966 television was relatively new, so it was a big deal to see someone you recognized on the screen. Rarer still was the chance to actually be invited to be on TV. When one of the Chicago stations sent a truck plastered with its call letters down our block it instantly attracted attention. When it stopped in front of our building and the crew rang the buzzer for our apartment the sound created a wave of excitement through our family.

Although we had been instructed to "behave and be quiet," we were not barred from the living room, where the crew set up a film camera on a tripod and placed their lights on telescoping stands on either side of it. After the reporter positioned my parents on the sofa he sat down beside them with a big microphone in his hand and began asking questions. The subject was the lead paint that had been used in thousands of Chicago apartments and the danger it posed to young children.

As my father explained for the camera, and all of the station's viewers, babies and toddlers will pick up almost anything and put it in their mouths. In older, poorly maintained buildings—like the one we lived in on Broadway—crawling kids could find lots of peeling and chipped-off bits of paint that were as colorful and chewy as gumballs. It only took a little lead to do a lot of damage to their bodies. Chronic low-level exposure causes gradual kidney damage, neurological deficits, and hearing loss. Swallowing larger amounts could lead to sudden organ failure and death.

Every year thousands of American kids were injured, and hundreds died, from poisoning that occurred when they chewed on chips of paint they either picked off deteriorating walls or found loose in substandard housing. Even greater numbers suffered from lowered intelligence and learning disabilities that would never be recognized or connected with the lead contamination. Many of these kids also came from poor Hispanic and African-American households, which meant they began life two steps behind kids who did not have to deal with poverty or prejudice. Lead could add a burden they might never overcome.

Never the policy maker, always the doctor, my father viewed the threat posed by lead paint not as a matter of statistics but as a matter of his patients. He had seen kids suffering from lead poisoning and administered chelation therapy to get the lead out of their bodies. As he answered the reporter's questions I noticed the pride on my mother's face. Rahm, Ari, and I were awestruck by the fact that our father was the focus of so much attention and technology. We got the same feeling on the night the interview was broadcast, right along with the rest of the important news of the day, and Benjamin Emanuel, MD, was identified as a medical expert.

At age nine, I was old enough to understand that my father was standing up for children in his practice and across the city. I also knew he was sticking his neck out a bit as he blamed city slumlords who were maiming infants and children as they refused to maintain their buildings. In calling them out, he was making it clear that they were bad guys, and that good people had no choice but to stand against them. It's not that he made himself out to be a hero. The way he explained it was: "When you have a choice, you do the right thing. Every time. Even if it makes you uncomfortable."

.....

Because our parents got directly involved, it seemed perfectly normal to us that the issues covered on the nightly news and in the magazines that came to our home—*Newsweek, The New Republic,* and *Ramparts*—were active subjects of everyday conversation. We assumed that everyone took great personal interest in civil rights, the needs of the poor, and the growing American involvement in Vietnam. These were not abstractions to us but, rather, personal concerns. Positive news, like the passage of LBJ's Great Society programs, made us feel inspired. Troubling developments, like the violent backlash against the civil rights campaign, were a real worry especially for our mother, who had to think more carefully about what she did on behalf of the cause. When members of the Chicago movement decided to send people to march from Selma to Montgomery, Alabama, in 1965, my mother contributed money but did not go herself. Her fears were confirmed when a white marcher and mother of three from Detroit named Viola Liuzzo was murdered days after the Selma march.

Because my mother had children, she declined the more dangerous forms of activism. But as a protofeminist she chafed at the ways that she occasionally found her options limited. Despite some advances, women were still expected to sacrifice more than men in order to serve their families, and when they considered questions of "right and wrong" they were expected to give more weight to the needs of others. Men, on the other hand, had much more leeway to follow their own dreams and desires. Occasionally the inequity caused real friction between my mother and my father.

In one instance, my father objected when she wanted to accept an invitation to attend Lyndon Johnson's presidential inauguration in January 1965. At first the issue was framed as a matter of money. My father said we just could not afford to send my mother to Washington, D.C., for three or four days. When she questioned my father's math—in fact they did have the money to send her—he then said that attending that type of celebration, though an honor, did not really count as doing something of value that would benefit anyone. With this point, my father pushed the argument in a moral direction. Here again, he was wrong. The trip may not have accomplished anything for suffering people in need, but it would have benefited my mother. She would have seen a new corner of the world and, perhaps, would have encountered new people and ideas that could help her grow stronger, more experienced, and more competent. But it was hard for her to say this without seeming selfish.

When it came time to decide about the inauguration, my mother weighed my father's objections and actually considered taking the trip against his wishes. Ultimately, she stayed in Chicago, but she would never be completely comfortable with the choice. She believed that a man in her position would have found a way to attend the inauguration and that no one would have thought he was selfish for doing so.

The unfairness my mother experienced around the inauguration echoed her experience as a girl, when her father asked her to give up her dream of college simply because she was female. It also reminded her of the sacrifices she had made when she accepted the traditional role of full-time mother. Her life revolved around caring for three wild kids while her husband went to work earning the money that supported the family and the social prestige, achievement, and satisfaction that come with a career in medicine.

During the years when she did not work, and cut back on her activism, my mother was fully devoted to raising us boys. In exchange she assumed almost full authority over domestic affairs. Even though her husband was a pediatrician, she was the expert on child development, nutrition, discipline, education, and enrichment. My father seemed happy to let her take this leading role, and for the most part they functioned well as a parenting team. Occasionally they might argue about money, especially when my cheapskate father was flipping through his checkbook on Sunday mornings, trying to balance it and determine where all the money was going. But for the most part they agreed, and they shared the same fundamental priorities for spending. How you spend money says a lot about your values.

To begin with, neither one of our parents ever cared much about stylish clothes, or getting fancy stuff for the apartment. In my friends' homes, the living room was the best place to hide during a game of hide-and-seek because no one was supposed to go in there. There was no "stay out of the living room" in our home because my parents did not believe in buying expensive furniture or carpets, or anything else that needed to be protected from children (except for my dad's stereo). Instead they filled our house with ordinary things that they expected would suffer scratches, dents, and stains.

The money they saved on stuff was used to pay our tuition at Anshe Emet, which was important to my parents. They were also willing to spend on anything that would make us boys a bit more educated, worldly, and cultured. For a trio of antsy little boys, we spent an extraordinary amount of time squirming around in the nosebleed seats at the ballet or Chicago Symphony. Ironically, on those trips I looked around and learned to appreciate the architectural beauty of the stunning Auditorium Theatre and Symphony Hall more than the actual dance or classical music. We spent many of our other Sunday afternoons at free concerts in Grant Park or viewing exhibits at the Field Museum or the Art Institute of Chicago. When the musical *Hair* came to Chicago, we not only attended dressed in striped bell-bottom pants and white turtleneck sweaters but we got up on stage to dance when the audience was invited to join the finale.

Our parents also took us with them to clubs where we could hear live music. Often we were the only kids in sight at places like Amazing Grace and the Old Town School of Folk Music, where Pete Seeger, the Weavers, Joan Baez, and every other important folk act of the era played to packed crowds. They took us to hear music when we traveled, too. On a West Coast road trip in 1965 we saw Janis Joplin at a little place in the Haight-Ashbury district of San Francisco.

It was an unusual thing for American kids to accompany their parents to clubs and coffeehouses, especially when these outings lasted into the late hours of the night. Even as a kid I knew this was true because none of my friends and classmates even knew about these places. (My buddy Skippy Shein's weekend outings revolved around sitting in the boxes on the first-base line at White Sox games at the old Comiskey Park.) We knew nothing else. So it seemed perfectly normal to go to these clubs, especially since the music was infused with political and moral values and the people in attendance talked about the same issues we debated at home.

.....

The one thing my parents disagreed about when it came to money was my father's desire to buy a house in the suburbs. To him, owning his own suburban home represented both status and security and, most important, fulfillment of the American dream. To her, a house in the suburbs meant death. Moving into a whites-only, middle-class fantasyland was the antithesis of the vibrant city life in which my mother found it easy to make friends and find outlets for her liberal political views. Suburbia meant selling out and was, therefore, unthinkable. "Go ahead," she would say to him. "You'll live there by yourself."

The disagreement over the suburbs revealed one of the flaws in the unstated agreement that governed my parents' marriage. They both talked about equality of the sexes and when it came to respect and honor my mother was supposed to get an equal share. But as the so-called breadwinner, my father harbored the belief that in the end, the big financial decisions were his to make. This meant he never gave up on his dream of a house in the suburbs and every once in a while he tried to deliver some sort of edict on spending. I suspect this was because he was secretly saving up for a down payment.

Deep down, my father understood that my mother worked very hard and made plenty of sacrifices to keep our household running. Unlike most wives and mothers, her burden also included caring for a darkly judgmental mother-in-law and the occasional extra boy, who needed to be fed and decently clothed. Given her limited budget, my mother was forever stitching up rips in our shirts and ironing in patches on the knees of our pants. She also devoted an extraordinary amount of time to purchasing and preparing food, which we consumed so voraciously that my father would call us "the locusts." It was my mother's careful shopping that enabled my parents to fill us up with the type of wholesome foods—lots of fresh fruits, vegetables, and salads—that cost more and were supplanted, in many homes, with stuff that was canned or frozen. "You could not keep them in clothes and feed them decent food with what I have to spend," she would say during their disputes over spending.

While it may have seemed that they were arguing about money, the struggle was also about power and respect and all the little things that build up over time with any married couple. If my mother did not get the respect she felt she deserved—she was an adult, after all—she would then go out for a little spiteful shopping. But she had trouble following through. Where another woman might buy piles of expensive clothes for herself at Marshall Field's or Saks, Marsha Emanuel would buy clothes for us or maybe something practical for herself. It just wasn't in her to spend recklessly or self-indulgently. Shopping was not, for her, a form of self-expression or an antidote to depression. She preferred to express herself in action and she got a chance to do this when her hero, Martin Luther King Jr., came to Chicago.

Having won the Nobel Peace Prize in 1963 for his nonviolent campaign for civil rights, Dr. King reached the height of his fame and influence in the spring of 1966. In our city he began an almost messianic effort to end a system of segregation in housing that had been in place since the reconstruction that followed the Great Fire of 1871.

Unfortunately, many whites in Chicago had not seen the problems in the black community firsthand and they responded negatively to the pressure from King and his supporters. Angry crowds met every march, sit-in, and protest and as the summer heated up, the crowds got bigger and their taunts were accompanied by hurled bottles, rocks, and bricks. Mixed in with the crowds were young men who wore Nazi-style helmets and displayed swastikas; the insults shouted from the sidewalks included plenty of anti-Semitic rants along with racist insults. By midsummer my mother decided to join members of CORE and other groups that were going to march behind Dr. King on a three-mile route that took them through the South Side communities of Chicago Lawn and Gage Park, where real estate companies, rental agents, and landlords refused to do business with blacks.

On a hot, sunny Thursday my mother gave us lunch, packed up some sandwiches, fruits, and drinks, and got us out the door by two o'clock. A fellow activist met us with a car and we drove from our North Side neighborhood south past the Loop and then through the all-white neighborhood of Bridgeport, where the mayor lived. By the time we reached Marquette Park in Chicago Lawn my mother had gone through her instructions—"Hold hands, stay close to me, never wander off by yourselves"—at least a dozen times. She had also told us that a lot of people who could not understand what we were doing might turn out to shout about it. Some of what these people might say would be hard to hear and they might even throw things to try to stop the march. If this happened we should listen to her instructions, and follow her lead.

By the time we got to Marquette Park, hundreds of whites, most of them teenagers, were already there to heckle and threaten the marchers. They milled around on a small hillside overlooking the spot where we were supposed to muster and chanted slogans. "Two, four, six, eight, we don't want to integrate!" they shouted. Then they sang a song to the tune of the Oscar Mayer hot dog jingle.

I wish I were an Alabama trooper.
That is what I'd really like to be.
For if I were an Alabama trooper,
I could hang a nigger legally.

To accent this performance one of the singers swung a rope that had been tied into a huge noose.

While police in the South were likely to harass and attack civil rights marchers, a sizable contingent of Chicago's finest came to protect us. With blue riot helmets on their heads and batons in their hands they stood between the angry whites and the growing number of people arriving to participate in the march. Most of these people were black, but at least 10 percent were white. Included in this group were some Catholic priests and nuns and a good number of Jews.

As the marching group grew to more than six hundred and the stepping-off time of four o'clock came and went, local men who had gotten off from work joined the teenage hecklers and the ranks of the hostile onlookers grew to more than two thousand, as the next day's papers would report. Glass pop bottles, eggs, tomatoes, rocks, and the occasional cherry bomb flew over the police line to land near us and we began to hear shouts of "Cannibals! Savages!" and "Go home, niggers!" Hewing to the rules of nonviolence, none of the marchers responded in kind.

When Dr. King finally arrived by car, about two dozen police formed a wall to protect him from a hail of projectiles. Despite their efforts a rock struck him in the head over his right ear. He stumbled but caught his balance and quickly reassured everyone that he was all right and ready to walk. Reporters surrounded him and asked questions that were later broadcast on TV:

REPORTER: Did you get hit?

KING: Yes, but I've been hit so many times I'm immune to it.

REPORTER: How do you feel about this reception?

KING: Well, this is a terrible thing. I've been in many
    demonstrations all across the South but can say that I have
    never seen even in Mississippi and Alabama or New
    Orleans a reception as hate-filled as I've seen in Chicago.

REPORTER: Are you still going to march?

KING: Oh definitely, we cannot stop the march. We're going to
    go on in a few minutes.

REPORTER: Do you feel you are in a closed society here in
    southwest Chicago?

KING: Oh yes, it's definitely a closed society, but we're going to
    make it an open society. And we have to do it this way in
    order to bring the evil out into the open.

Ari, Rahm, and I watched King's arrival from a relatively safe distance as my mother kept us on the edge of the marching group. We had participated in other marches and demonstrations, but none of them had been met with this level of anger. In my mind flashed images I had seen on TV and in magazines of high-pressure fire hoses, attack dogs, and billy clubs used against civil rights marchers in the South.

All three of us were nervous about what might happen here. But we could see that the police were on *our* side, and we knew that when we began walking we would be surrounded by friends and allies.

Our group benefited from organization and experience. The mob that gathered to oppose us had no preset plan, but in the long wait for Dr. King's arrival they did devise a mocking kind of strategy. Borrowing from the techniques CORE had used to disrupt traffic in the Loop, about fifty of them sat in the road in front of the marchers and refused to be moved. They didn't last very long. Once the police began using their batons to rap on their knees and ankles, the sit-down boys immediately stood up.

A phalanx of police officers led us out of the park and down Kedzie Avenue. Deep inside the ranks of the marchers, my mother held our hands and did her best to look and act unafraid. As we walked, people sang—"We Shall Overcome" and "We Shall Not Be Moved"—and at some moments the eggs and tomatoes that flew at us seemed to land in rhythm with our voices. In the lulls we heard people screaming "Nigger lovers!" at the police and some shouted out a call for one of the priests in the march to be hanged. "God, I hate niggers and nigger lovers!" yelled a woman who, by her gray hair, looked like she could be someone's grandmother.

The worst of it came when we reached Sixtieth Street, a point that was just ten blocks east from the Airport Homes, where my mother, then just a girl, had witnessed this kind of conflict for the first time. Here a group of men and women brought out an effigy of Dr. King, which they proceeded to stab and kick and rip to shreds. Small bands of men broke the windows on the cars that trailed the march and were driven by blacks. As police officers ran to protect these drivers, the sound of glass breaking and the voices of so many angry adults who literally screamed with rage because we dared to march against bigotry sent shivers through us.

The march ended at a Baptist church, which we entered along with other marchers. Dr. King took to the pulpit.

Decades later I cannot recall what Dr. King said in the church that night, but I do recall that I felt like I was bearing witness to something important. Those who were with him in private meetings after he preached would report that a fierce debate had broken out among the leaders of the movement, some of whom wanted to attend the next march "holstered up." Reverend King listened and then pressed them with a question. "How do you put out a fire?" He then explained that fire won't extinguish a fire, but water will, and nonviolence is the water that would put out the fire of hatred.

While the leaders of the movement struggled over the best way to respond to what they had experienced, my mother found a driver whose car was available to take us home. It was dark and well past our bedtime when we finally got to our block. Ari, who could always fall asleep anywhere the instant he had burned all of his energy for the day, had to be carried inside the apartment. The next morning the newspapers would report that twenty-eight people, including three police officers, had been sent to hospitals for injuries suffered during the march. Of the hundreds of people apprehended while attacking the marchers, only forty were formally arrested and charged with crimes. The rest were let go.

It would be hard to exaggerate the impact my brothers and I felt from our direct experience at the march and from learning of what happened after we left. Being part of a mass display of courage made us believe that a great many people in the world are good and decent. We learned to draw strength from a group of like-minded souls and to stay cool under pressure and resolute in our convictions. Most important, we came away with the sense that even the biggest problem should be confronted and that we could be part of the solution. Today each of us has tried to be part of the solution to society's biggest problems, whether it is me working on improving end-of-life care and health-care reform, Rahm trying to rebuild Chicago's infrastructure and education system, or Ari's efforts on the environment and speaking out on learning disabilities.

After Gage Park, a great debate arose within the local civil rights movement. Many members of CORE wanted a more confrontational approach, to force Mayor Daley to do more than talk. They proposed a march through the all-white suburb of Cicero, where many people were outspoken in their opposition to the civil rights movement. My mother sided with King and decided not to go to Cicero. When the march took place the governor of Illinois sent two thousand National Guard troops and the city marshaled five hundred police officers to keep the peace.

The Cicero march probably accelerated the flight to the suburbs by middle-class whites who saw in the chaos and anger—on both sides—a frightening future for the city. In our own circle of friends, the Glass family decided to move to the northern suburb of Glencoe. Bill Glass would say that he was looking for financial security, more living space, and better public schools for his sons, and all of this was true. But Carol Glass would forever recall that for her the decision was made when her son Jerry was mugged at knifepoint in a local park. As her friend packed and left, my mother felt sorry for her, certain that she herself would remain in the great city for the rest of her life and never stop trying to make it better for all of us.

Eight

CITY KIDS

Skippy Shein had a fast five-speed bike with easy-rolling one-inch tires. He also owned a Schwinn Sting-Ray with a banana seat and high handlebars. My bike was a one-speed clunker that my mom had bought for five dollars from a man who lived a few blocks away and sold reconditioned bikes out of his darkened basement.

On many Friday afternoons Skippy's mom picked us up at Anshe Emet and took us to the Shein home, where I would spend the weekend. I loved getting the chance to explore the Sheins' big house—reading Skippy's entire collection of Tom Swift books, or playing with his pool table. I especially liked riding his bikes.

The inevitable happened on a Saturday morning when we decided, against explicit parental edicts, to pedal from his house on Bellevue Place to my home on Winona, seven miles to the north. The route took us along the trails on Lake Michigan and then onto the trails that passed through the twelve hundred acres of Lincoln Park, near the zoo. Flat as the Midwest may be, at one point on the route we hit an incline and thought we could make better progress by hopping off our bikes and pushing. Suddenly a couple of high school guys jumped out of the bushes that lined the path and grabbed our bikes. One held a knife to my neck and demanded we empty our pockets.

Then Skippy began to cry and begged them to not take the bikes. They preferred cash, so they told us that if we emptied our pockets we could keep our wheels. As usual, mine were empty, but Skippy had around fifteen dollars in bills and change, which he handed over. The muggers took off.

We found two police officers in a patrol car and reported what had happened. One of the officers reached for his radio to broadcast an alert. Soon another patrol car rolled up. Inside sat a couple of young black men. The officers asked us if these were our muggers but we saw that they were at least four or five years older than the teenagers who had jumped us. As the minutes passed and the crime got cold, it became obvious that the muggers would get away.

Later that day our family conversation about this incident included what we all knew about race and poverty and how two black teenagers might think it would be a good idea to go to Lincoln Park, find some white kids on fancy bikes, and rob them. Nothing excused the specific crime perpetrated by those particular young men. But it was easy to understand why they might be angry and resentful enough to mug a couple of boys who looked like they had it good. The police response was also instructive. How would it feel, I wondered, to be plucked off the street and treated like a suspect based solely on your skin color and a police officer's assumptions?

We understood we belonged to a minority that had suffered in the past and was still subject to discrimination and exclusion. However, change was coming fast. Jews were quickly becoming accepted into the white majority and our parents taught us that nothing that really mattered was beyond our reach and we had little to fear as we moved through the world. We were safe in this assumption except, ironically enough, when Rahm was "black."

While I had inherited my father's complexion—so fair that I easily burned before developing a tan—Rahm and Ari had my mother's skin coloring. Both of them needed just a few days in the sun to turn the color of café au lait. By the end of the summer the two of them were almost chestnut brown. With curly black hair and a broad, flat nose, Rahm could easily pass for an African American.

We got most of our ultraviolet rays at Foster Avenue Beach, which became our regular summer hangout. In yet another demonstration of her confidence (today it might be called child neglect), our mother would send us off alone to spend entire summer days playing in the lake and on the sand. I led the troop down Winona, through the Foster Avenue underpass that let us safely cross Lake Shore Drive, and then into the park, where the beach stretched northward for a quarter mile or so.

In this time before cellphones, our mother did not need to hear from us every half hour to be reassured that we were okay. As the hours passed, she somehow assumed we were fine, and for the most part, her confidence in us and the city was well-placed. Less crowded than most city beaches, the strand at Foster Avenue was patrolled by lifeguards who kept watch as we built complex sand castles, dove into waves, and engaged in brotherly fights. Exceptions arose when some stranger decided to call Rahm and Ari "niggers" and demand that we get off the beach.

Although legally open to anyone, in the 1960s Foster Beach was segregated by custom and practice. Certain people—mostly white males between the ages of ten and fifteen—made it their business to enforce the unwritten whites-only rule. When they called my brothers niggers and tried to bully us off the beach, we—naturally—refused to move. Instead one of us would answer with some defiance—"You can't make me leave." The other two would stand to support him. The argument would quickly escalate to threats and sometimes punches.

Usually these confrontations ended quickly because we presented a united front and we would create enough commotion to attract the attention of the lifeguards and others. When shouting wouldn't work and we had to fight, we remembered the stories the Big Bangah told us about union organizing. In every case we would return to the beach the next day because the beach was at the heart of our summer routine and we wanted to make sure these bullies knew they could not scare us away.

As a parent reflecting on these days at the beach, I am flabbergasted by my mother's behavior. I certainly would never have let my daughters spend the whole day at the beach unaccompanied, especially when they were under ten. But there must be something unspoken that passes from generation to generation, because my children have ended up spending a lot of time in Africa and Israel, and they would frequently go to dangerous places, such as displaced persons' camps near battle zones. They would never tell me beforehand, even though I could do nothing about their trips. They would only call me after they returned safely.

.....

Similar incidents happened to Rahm, Ari, and me on sidewalks, and in playgrounds and alleyways. On a few occasions passing remarks led to fights. It may seem paradoxical that boys raised by a pacifist in a house where plastic squirt guns were banned were so willing to throw punches. But we felt no inner conflict. We were not pacifists. When we were at the beach or walking the streets, we were city kids, not civil rights activists. If we wanted to move freely and safely around our neighborhood, we had to prove we could not be pushed around. The cuts, bruises, and torn clothes that came in the bargain were a small price to pay for the feelings of confidence and pride that come with standing up for yourself. I don't remember our parents ever scolding us for these fights, nor did they call the police or search for the parents of the kids who gave us a hard time. Instead they appreciated the way that city life, which naturally included a bit of scrapping with bullies, helped us to become more assertive and independent.

Our strength was reinforced by the bond of brotherhood that grew every time we confronted bullies as a team. In the heat of the battle we always knew we had each other. At night, when we settled into the room we three shared, we sorted through the day's events. Exhausted from his hyperactivity, Ari would say a few words but then fall asleep holding on to a favorite blanket that he kept well into grade school. Rahm and I might play catch with the stuffed elephant that was my version of a teddy bear. As the elephant flew across the room Rahm might say something like "Weren't you afraid those guys were going to kill us?" Tossing it back, I would confess my fears but also repeat what our parents had taught us. "You can't run away. If you do, then you'll be more scared the next time."

During these conversations and the endless hours we spent playing games, we resolved our insecurities and tested the limits of competitiveness. Cheating at Monopoly? That's normal, so everyone had to keep a close eye on the banker. Arm-twisting during a wrestling match? It's okay until the other guy starts to cry. Sitting on someone's chest and tickling him? Well, what else are brothers for? Moment by moment, through contests, conflicts, and confessions, we figured out the limits of behavior and forged an unbreakable alliance. As the eldest, I learned to go easy on my brothers in order to avoid causing serious injuries. As the youngest, Ari pushed things far beyond the point where Rahm and I would have stopped, and exploited his cuteness, appealing grin, and charm to get away with it.

The extra patience my parents reserved for Ari could bother me and Rahm. However, rough equality—with the emphasis on the word *rough*—is about all you can hope for in a family where three very energetic kids are constantly competing for attention, comparing the results, and calling the smallest inconsistencies tragic injustices. My parents were tolerant of our minor infractions, reserving serious disapproval for those times when we were genuinely cruel or disrespectful to others. The sin was doubly serious when it was committed against one of our brothers.

Fortunately, the competition for attention was usually suspended on our birthdays, when, as Rahm recalled, we each benefited from special status. "Mom would take you on the L to the State Street Marshall Field's for lunch. We'd take the escalators all the way up to the seventh floor to the Walnut Room, where you could sit by the fountain and get their special turkey sandwich. It came with a huge amount of lettuce on it and drowned in Thousand Island dressing. After lunch you'd get to pick something out for a present. I once got Hush Puppy shoes. Then you went across the street to Goldblatt's and sat at the fountain where Aunt Gittie [our grandmother's youngest sister] would serve you a sundae or a banana split."

By making sure we each got special treatment on our birthdays, and requiring us to offer respect when it was not our turn, my mother made it easier for her sons to get along. This doesn't mean we avoided jealousy and competition. Indeed, we had plenty of arguments about who "Mom loves the most." But the truth was we all got equal treatment. And this equality inside the family bred solidarity as we faced the outside world.

.....

If the family was a tightly knit unit, this togetherness was balanced by the freedom we were granted to explore first the streets around our apartment and, later, the city itself. Chicago was full of places to explore, including movie theaters, libraries, museums, the Lincoln Park Zoo, and shops that sold everything a boy could want. One of my most frequent haunts was a used-book store about two miles from our apartment called Shake, Rattle and Read. It occupied a twelve-foot-wide storefront right next to the Uptown Theater on Broadway between Ainslie Street and Lawrence Avenue.

Built in the Roaring Twenties, the Uptown was an ornate movie palace that occasionally hosted *Queen for a Day,* a TV program that invited so-called housewives literally to compete by telling sob stories in order to be crowned and covered in a velvet robe while receiving a pile of gifts—appliances, silverware, clothes—that symbolized her elevation to the middle class.

While would-be queens cried real tears at the Uptown, Rahm and I worked slowly up and down the aisles at Shake, Rattle and Read. Since the used paperback books cost between ten and thirty-five cents apiece, our unused-carfare stash went a long way. Fortunately, we did not have to depend only on coins acquired on the sly. My parents never hesitated to give us money for books, and we bought them by the armful. I started with biographies—the life stories of Sam Houston,

Daniel Boone, and Thomas Jefferson were early favorites—but my interest quickly widened to include American and world history, with a special emphasis on World War II. To this day, Rahm and I exchange recommendations on history books on a regular basis. Like most boys who read avidly, I was captivated by heroes and adventure and people who overcame adversity. My taste in fiction ran toward the Tom Swift series, which was the boys' version of Nancy Drew. My friend Skippy had a complete set of the hardbacks and he was generous about lending them to me.

When a particular book was not available at Shake, Rattle and Read I often found it at the local branch of the public library. As the eldest, I was also trusted to trek to the main library in the downtown Loop to read or borrow whatever I wanted. I just loved that library on Michigan and Washington (now the Chicago Cultural Center). The librarians were always patient, and thoughtful in helping me pick out interesting books. But I think what captivated me the most—or at least what I remember to this day—was the architecture of the building and its views. The huge winding marble stairs, the ornate ceiling, the mosaics, the Tiffany stained-glass dome, all enchanted me. And when I tired of reading, I would walk over to the huge windows of the children's room facing east, and just stare out at the traffic below, the park, and in the distance the Buckingham Fountain. I often wonder if my frequent visits to this magnificent building taught me to appreciate architecture. Again my mother showed extraordinary trust as she let me travel alone to downtown Chicago and be gone for the better part of the day.

It would be hard to overstate the effect that the city, and the freedom we had to explore it, had on us when we were young. It may have been totally irresponsible for our mother to let us wander the city alone, but the experience bred in us a sense of independent self-reliance that never went away. City life was so exciting that even the idea of a sleepaway summer camp filled with outdoorsy adventures held absolutely no appeal.

Of course, other kids and their parents spoke glowingly of camp experiences and one year my parents actually arranged for me to attend one in rural Wisconsin. My mother and one of her friends drove me north to the camp and stayed around for the orientation and tour. As soon as I was assigned to a cabin group I began to feel uncomfortable. No doubt part of this was my intense anxiety about being in new social situations and having to make friends from total strangers. I just hated to have to walk into a cabin or cafeteria without knowing anyone. Another part was that in my family, in my school, and even in my religious education, I had been encouraged to be an independent thinker. I also had acquired a certain wariness about groups organized to follow the orders of a leader. This did not mean I thought that every time people sit together around a campfire a mob mentality takes over. However, I was aware of how people can lose some of their identity in groups. In the interest of harmony, or because of peer pressure, some might go along with choices they might not make on their own. Everyone in my family felt the same when it came to maintaining a sense of independence and individual responsibility and rejecting uniformity and groupthink.

At camp, I lingered long enough to determine that I would constantly be thrust into new social situations and that there was a regimented program, moving groups of kids from one organized activity to the next. I quickly concluded this wasn't for me. I preferred my freelance, self-designed summer of beaches, books, and parks instead of weeks of structured play. When I explained this to my mom she was not immediately sympathetic. As a girl she would have given anything to get out of the city and attend a summer camp. But after I insisted and explained how I felt—and she saw my anxiety—she let me come home with her.

.....

By the fall of 1966, I was a fourth grader, Rahm was in second, and Ari was starting kindergarten. In my social studies class, we were required to pick a topic and follow it in the newspaper. While other students focused on the space program or the Chicago Cubs, I studied the war in Vietnam. Every week I brought clippings into class for discussion and when it was my turn to make an oral report I gave a lengthy talk on the numbers of American military deaths, which rose almost four-fold between 1965 and 1966. By the end of the school year the annual death rate had almost doubled again, to more than eleven thousand.

My concern about the war was driven in part by the conversations at our dinner table and the articles I read in the magazines that were piled in the rack in our bathroom. Pictures from the war made a deep impression on me. One of these photos was the February 11, 1965, *Life* magazine cover shot that showed two wounded GIs, their heads wrapped in bandages, waiting for help in a foxhole. More disturbing was a widely published image of a Buddhist monk who had set himself on fire in Saigon in 1963 to protest the war and the corruption of the American-backed leaders of South Vietnam.

The emotions stirred by what I read and saw made me deeply skeptical about the justifications voiced by those who got our country involved and kept raising the stakes. No one in my family accepted Lyndon Johnson's assurance about the war being necessary simply because he was the president. Born and raised to question authority, I prodded my classmates with questions about just what America hoped to accomplish as it waged war at an ever-higher price in a small country with little or no previous relationship to ours.

These discussions seemed natural and normal to me, but many of the kids in my class struggled with the idea that America might be losing a "bad" war. Many adults were also reluctant to see the tragic folly of Vietnam. On Winona Street, our upstairs neighbor John Downs had terrible difficulty reconciling his own experience in the army and his brothers' service during World War II with the critiques of the military he heard from my mother. In time he would come to agree with her view that America's leaders had led the country astray in Vietnam. But at the start of the war, and even as it escalated, John was firm in his support for the direction our leaders had taken. He felt uncomfortable as he listened to my mother talk about the corruption of the regime we were backing, the unfairness of a draft system, and the shaky rationale underpinning the whole enterprise.

Fortunately, liberal Anshe Emet was not the kind of school where they forced you to stop talking when other people became uncomfortable, so I was not discouraged from addressing a controversial subject, even in the fourth grade. However, I was guided by my teacher to tone down my arguments, which no doubt sounded shrill in my squeaky voice, and give the kids who did not have the benefit of getting dinner table lessons in debate a chance to make themselves heard.

.....

In the sixties it often seemed like the political issues that dominated the front pages were played out in our daily lives. I think this was true for many families as the draft brought almost two million sons, neighbors, and friends into the service for the war in Vietnam, and the raging debate over civil rights made it impossible for people of different races to interact without being aware of the ways that minorities had been mistreated over the generations. For us, the arrival of Vern Henry brought both of these crises—the war and the struggle over racial equality—directly into our lives.

All of five feet tall, and perhaps a hundred and thirty pounds, Vern Henry was a black woman whom my parents paid to come to our home to help out with cleaning, cooking, and other chores. Though she worked for our family, we were taught from the day we met her to call her "Mrs. Henry" and to treat her with the utmost respect. Indeed, we cared so much about her that we actually cleaned our room ourselves because it was so messy we thought it would be unfair to have her even cross the threshold.

Mrs. Henry wore a maid's uniform on her first visit to our apartment, but my mother immediately put an end to that, insisting that she dress for comfort, not status. She became so comfortable around us that when she had an earache she showed up with cotton stuffed in her ear canal and a toothpick, for easy extraction, hanging out of it.

We boys looked forward to Mrs. Henry's visits. She told us stories and fed us southern foods like fried chicken and greens, which she prepared with consummate finesse. She also taught us skills that would last a lifetime. When she set up the ironing board in the corner of the dining room but within sight of the television, we actually fought over who would be allowed to help her first. She was an expert at steaming, pressing, and starching and under her guidance we became quite expert ourselves. There was something exciting about having charge of a tool that blazed hot enough to burn the skin and belched great clouds of steam. We all became quite proficient, but what we liked best was being close to Mrs. Henry.

This relationship between Vern and our family was first and foremost a friendship. Vern got kisses and hugs from us when she arrived and departed and we frequently visited at her home. She lived in an apartment in an old triple-decker house on the West Side, which was the heart of the city's black community.

We went to the Henrys' once every month or two. We often ate Sunday dinner, which might include a few dishes like chitlins and okra, which we considered exotic. The crowd around the table included Vern's two younger sons and, if he wasn't working, her husband, a bus driver. Before dinner Rahm, Ari, and I played with the neighborhood kids in the back alley and the street. As the only whites in a crowd of black kids, we may have felt a little like racial outsiders but we were readily accepted. At Christmas we brought presents to them and got a glimpse, through their eyes, of what the holiday meant.

When Mrs. Henry's son Rodney was drafted into the army my father tried to get him a medical deferment. He felt justified doing this on moral grounds. After all, young men from middle- and upper-class families received routine deferrals on the basis of minor medical problems or because they enrolled in college and, afterward, in graduate schools. Dick Cheney, future vice president of the United States and super-hawk, received four educational deferrals and avoided service altogether. Rush Limbaugh, the similarly hawkish radio commentator, got a medical deferment for a "pilonidal cyst," which is a fancy medical term for a small, painful abscess on the area of the tailbone right between the butt cheeks. Hardly a serious medical condition.

While millions of sons of privilege (most of them white) were being excused from service on the basis of college studies and medical problems, blacks entered the military at a much higher rate, eventually making up 23 percent of the combat troops in Vietnam. This was more than twice their representation in the population as a whole. My father was keenly aware of this disparity and tried to identify a serious medical justification for a deferment. When he could not come up with something, Rodney was drafted. A lovely, caring young man, he went through basic training, shipped out to Vietnam for combat duty, and returned a heroin addict.

Mrs. Henry would be a fixture of our lives for about five years. My parents talked to her often about Rodney, and when Martin Luther King was assassinated we validated her grief with our own deep feelings of sadness. My mother gave us black armbands to wear to Anshe Emet for the next few days. Although we attracted stares and questions at school, we understood the statement we were making.

Of course, the fight for equality wasn't just about symbols and marching. It was also our responsibility to act whenever possible. With constant urging from my mother, who also paid the tuition, Mrs. Henry added school to her work schedule and eventually got her certification to be a licensed practical nurse. She soon found a job that paid well, had fringe benefits, and allowed her to work plenty of hours. When she stopped coming to our house to work we missed her warmth, wisdom, and attention. She remained a family friend and we would continue to see her for the occasional chicken dinner, but we all felt her absence in our home.

.....

Vern Henry's departure wasn't the only big change that required some adjustment. While my brothers and I were focused on school and neighborhood adventures and my mother was busy caring for us and running the household, my father quietly put down a deposit on a split-level house in the North Shore suburb of Wilmette. Remarkably for a guy who was so thrifty he would haggle over the price of a pair of shoes, he paid the asking price and did not even attempt to negotiate on the biggest purchase of his life. After he put down a deposit he came home one night to announce, "I've bought a house." My mother, her voice dripping with sarcasm, replied, "Why didn't you buy two?"

The argument that ensued was more serious than any I heard before and since. My mother was a Chicago woman, through and through.

She thrived on the variety of people, ideas, and cultures she bumped up against in her daily life and was proud of her ability to move surely from neighborhood to neighborhood. A move to the suburbs would deny her everything that gave her an identity as a Chicagoan. She was adamant in her objection to moving, and furious with my father for making such a big decision, and a great financial commitment, all on his own.

This was not the kind of intense but brief conflict that we were accustomed to seeing from our parents. Instead the argument was joined, suspended, and resumed countless times over many months. For weeks my mother would not even go look at the actual house. When we finally drove out there we discovered a modest, four-bedroom split-level on Locust Road, a north-south path that ran through a grid of residential properties that were each about a quarter of an acre in size. Nearly all the houses were ranch/split-level hybrids of modest size. Each one was set back from the road about thirty feet and flanked by a strip of concrete that served as a driveway. Some had garages.

On Locust Road my father saw the ultimate emblem of American middle-class respectability, bringing with it an end to rent payments and a chance to accumulate some wealth in the form of appreciating real estate. There he could also escape private school tuition payments because the local public schools were excellent. What he did not say, but was understood, was that as my family bought into the real estate aspect of the American dream, the possibility that we might ever move to Israel became much less likely. My father had stayed in contact with colleagues in Israel and even visited several times to explore the potential opportunities for work. However, every time the jobs being offered to him were just a grade or two below what he had already achieved in the United States. And none offered the kind of potential that would make it worth giving up the medical practice and collegial relationships he had developed in America.

Somewhere in her heart, my mother surely understood that a house in the suburbs finally closed the door on returning to Israel. More important, she also saw isolation, boredom, and, for her, a kind of semiretirement at the tender age of thirty-five. This was not what she had planned for herself as she approached the ten-year mark in her career as a mother. She had been thinking that as we boys became more self-reliant, she would get more deeply involved in her own interests. Maybe she would go back to school, start working, or run for political office and stand against the corruption that defined political life in Chicago. The office of alderman sounded good to her and she had the energy, intelligence, charm, and stamina to make a great campaigner. "I wanted to be a thorn in Daley's side," she would later explain. This would be impossible if she had to abandon her status as a citizen of the city of Chicago and start a new life in suburban Wilmette.

In all their conversations about the house, my father listened to everything my mother had to say and, as was his style, hardly ever raised his voice or showed much feeling. He was, however, unmovable. To him a house in the suburbs was part of the good life, and an essential element of his plan to make our family financially secure. As the sole earner, my father could wield this last point, about financial security, as a kind of trump card. To be fair, he hardly ever threw it down. But when he did, my mother had no good defense against it. Not that she did not try. "What about schools?" she asked. "The boys are doing beautifully at Anshe Emet."

Here my father had done his homework. The small Wilmette district had excellent elementary and junior high schools and fed students to New Trier High, which was one of the best public high schools, if not the best, in the country. Local taxpayers routinely approved increased spending for the school system, which had just opened a $75 million (2011 dollars) high school—New Trier West—that adopted the same high standards for teachers and students as the original New Trier, where many courses were offered at a college level.

The public schools might be good, my mother allowed, but what about the social environment? For generations, Jews had been excluded from the North Shore suburbs. Some neighborhoods and private clubs still kept Jews out. How might that affect us?

My father had to admit that anti-Semitism had once been a big problem, and the older, eastern parts of Wilmette were still populated

almost exclusively by white, non-Jewish families. However, new sub-
divisions on the west side of town had become magnets for upwardly
mobile Jewish families. Doctors, lawyers, and businesspeople, many
of whom grew up on Chicago's Maxwell Street, in North Lawndale,
or Albany Park, made Wilmette the place where they declared themselves upper-middle-class homeowners. In the end there was nothing
my mother could say or do to stop our relocation. She ceased arguing
and reluctantly began to prepare for a new life.

As my mother contemplated all she would lose in the move, she got
one little bit of good news. Savta decided to return to Israel rather
than settle with us in the suburbs. But otherwise my mother faced a
grim prospect, forced to prepare for a life she did not want, in a place
she did not like.

This was the fate of millions of women in the 1960s. With limited
options for work they threw themselves into the roles of wife, mother,
homemaker, and community volunteer. These activities were worth-
while. But their lives revolved entirely around serving others. Most did
not enjoy the power to make big decisions and, by definition, their
jobs came with built-in obsolescence. Inevitably kids grow up. They
need you less and less, until the day they leave home. Your purpose in
life quite literally walks out the door. Then, there you are, with little
to no experience in the working world and few marketable skills.

.....

The first thing my mother did as she faced the prospect of suburban
life was to take driving lessons, acquire a learner's permit, and practice by motoring in our white Pontiac Bonneville from Winona Street
to Wilmette. On more than one of these trips my mother might get
temporarily lost and we'd watch as her mood, which was not good to
begin with, worsened. Once, when she decided to practice parking
at the Turnstyle shopping center, near our new house, I got out and
tried to direct her into a space that was big enough for two cars. Somehow she managed to wedge the Bonneville in at such an extreme angle
that she could not get out. We had to wait until someone arrived to
move the car in the spot next to ours. Only then was she able to back

out, and beat a hasty retreat to the city. On other occasions she tried to be calm when faced with impatient drivers who honked their horns or raced around us. In a bid to josh her out of her funk, Ari and Rahm scrambled into the backseat and held up signs they had made that said, Beware, New Driver and New Driver, Stay Away. She was enough of a good sport to laugh along.

Our mother shouldered almost all of the responsibility for the family's big move from city to suburb. Our job was to stay out of the way, which we were never very good at. We were curious, after all, and wanted to be "helpful." As moving day got closer, we could feel our mother getting more and more tense. Whenever we noticed her sliding into this kind of mood, we tried to think of something we could do that might please her. The solution was for us to "surprise" her by helping out. Since we were under strict orders to leave things alone, we picked an out-of-the-way spot—the walk-through closet connecting our study and the bathroom—and tried to save her the chore of packing some of our stuff.

The walls of the closet held built-in chests of drawers topped with a clothes rod and then shelves. The shelves were piled with puzzles and board games like Parcheesi, Monopoly, checkers, and chess. Of course, the cardboard boxes that held them were squashed and broken, which meant that all of the pieces inside were only loosely contained. Ignoring my mother's orders, I climbed onto one of the chests and began pulling down games with one hand, which I then passed down to Rahm, who was supposed to collect them in neat stacks in the hallway outside the door.

As I handed each game down from the shelves I asked, "Are you being careful to stack them neatly?" He said "Yes, yes" as he stretched to take the games out of my hands and simply piled them on the floor, letting some of their contents spill out.

I kept asking him if he was being neat.

Exasperated, he shouted back, "Shut up! I'm trying!"

Before I could shush him so that my mother wouldn't catch us, Rahm lost control of a box holding a game with umpteen pieces inside it. They tumbled out, making a sound like a plastic waterfall.

In Rahm's defense it must be said that no one could have made an orderly stack out of those battered and out-of-square game boxes. And as a hyperactive eight-and-a-half-year-old he was never the kind of kid who did anything in a neat and systematic way. (His youthful messiness is in complete contrast to the fact that today he never leaves a piece of paper on his desk at the end of the day.) Of course, these details did not matter to my mother, who suddenly appeared out of nowhere. Already sweaty and dirty from packing, she looked at the mess on the floor and at me balancing on the chest in the closet and her face flushed red with all the anger and frustration that had been building inside her ever since my father announced he had bought the house in Wilmette.

"Get down, Jonny!"

"But we're helping," I said.

"I told you not to."

I should have noticed that her voice sounded more serious than usual but when it came to this kind of nuance—judging mood, temper, impatience—I was pretty tone-deaf. While Rahm recognized that something bad was about to happen and backed away, I did what I always did. I argued and defended my position.

In almost any other circumstance my mother might have indulged a little debate and sass from me. In this moment she completely lost control. Although the words she uttered were soon forgotten, her anger became a permanent memory as she reached for the nearest available weapon, a long stick that one of us boys, or perhaps our dog, had dragged home from the park. She swung to whack me on the rear end but I moved. The stick caught my back and broke in two, which made more of an impression on me than the burning red welt caused by the blow. I scampered away, suddenly cognizant of the fact that it was possible to go too far, and that even my pacifist mother might be moved to violence under duress.

She ordered us to go to our room while she straightened up the mess we had made. We stayed in the room in scared silence, shocked by what had happened. My mother was shocked, too, and nothing was ever said about it.

When moving day finally arrived, our cousin Teddy was engaged to occupy us away from the apartment. Teddy was one of the few people up to the task. He took us by bus down to the Lincoln Park Zoo, where he thought we should be able to kill several hours. We were so filled with excitement about the move that we did not have the patience for observing elephants, monkeys, and bears. We raced through the place and then looked at him as if to say, "Now what?"

Regarding us as the wild animals that we were, Teddy decided to wear us out by having us walk all the way home. Five miles separated the zoo from 931 Winona Street. Teddy made the time pass by telling us lots of jokes and stories, inventing complicated steps for us to copy as we leaped over cracks in the sidewalk, and letting us stop for ice cream. By the time we reached Winona Street the moving truck was fully loaded and my parents were about ready for us to pile into the car. Despite our somewhat prickly exteriors, Emanuels are sentimentalists who cherish relationships and cry easily. Hoping to avoid sloppy good-byes, we did not seek out friends and neighbors for farewells. We told ourselves that Wilmette was only a half hour away by car and so of course we would be seeing them all again soon. As Rahm, Ari, and I crowded into the backseat of the car and wiggled and pushed one another for space, we could not begin to imagine the life that awaited us.

.....

The deal my parents made allowed my father to move us to Wilmette in the spring of 1968, only if we would continue to attend classes at Anshe Emet until the end of the school year. This arrangement required that he drop us off every morning at North Pine Grove Street. We got home with the aid of two teachers, Mrs. Dubavick and Ms. Goldstein, who lived in Skokie, not far from our home in Wilmette, and drove us every afternoon.

For kids accustomed to living in the city, Wilmette seemed more like a vast and underpopulated prairie than a human community. The town still claimed one operating farm, and everything was so spread out that instead of blocks, distances were measured in miles. The town had no buses, and while a commuter train and the Chicago L ended at Linden Street in Wilmette, the stations were on the east side of the town, miles from our home. Given the lack of public transportation, a kid who wanted to go anywhere would either catch a car ride courtesy of some adult or pedal his bike for at least a half hour.

Fortunately our block was home to lots of families with kids. If you stood in our front yard you could throw a rock to four houses that were home to boys who would be in my grade at Romona Elementary, which would become my school in the fall. They all played Little League baseball, which was a very big deal in Wilmette. Raised by a father who did not know the difference between a ground ball and a curveball, Rahm, Ari, and I would never don uniforms and play. However, we would ride our bikes over to watch the games, serve as bat-boys, and work in the concession stand. But where this one bastion of middle-class America was concerned, we would always be outsiders.

We did, however, find other ways to connect with the kids in our neighborhood. Here my mother's laid-back style came in very handy. The boys who lived on our block loved hanging out in a place where nobody got uptight about noise, or mess, or how much food you ate. My mother also made kids feel comfortable by letting them speak their minds and listening when they opened up. She was happy to be a sounding board for kids with problems that might not be taken seriously by other adults. Eventually she too would make connections and find outlets for her passions in the strange new land of suburbia. But it would take time. First we had to make a long summer trip to Israel, where we would renew our relationships with friends, family, and a country we had come to know under unexpected circumstances the previous year.

Nine

ISRAEL

Before sunrise on June 5, 1967, I heard whispering and wandered out of our room to find my parents on their knees in the darkened family room, their faces aglow from the flickering light of our black-and-white TV. The sound was turned down low, and they were both listening and watching intently. Israel was at war with Egypt, Syria, and Jordan.

The fighting was not unexpected. Neighboring countries, officially committed to its destruction, had harassed and threatened Israel ever since its creation. In the weeks before the war, Egypt cut off Israel's access to the Red Sea and completed a military alliance with Jordan and Syria. All three countries began positioning arms and men on their borders with Israel, and Arab sentiment shifted decidedly in favor of armed conflict. The rest of the world feared the United States entering the conflict on Israel's side and the Soviet Union joining the Arabs. After negotiations failed, Israel's leaders had decided that the best defense would be offense. This was a tactic my father favored in life as well as war.

The scale of the attack far exceeded anything that outside military experts expected from the Israeli Defense Forces, and in the early hours of the war reporters struggled to provide information. No one watching television or listening to the radio could be certain about what was happening. Still my parents craved information and remained in front of the television. They knew scores of people who lived in Israel and all were within range of enemy warplanes and artillery. They also understood that the IDF was vastly outnumbered as the enemy fielded twice as many troops and three times as many aircraft and tanks.

I stayed with my parents while the sun rose. Ari and Rahm got up and we went to Anshe Emet, where the atmosphere was filled with apprehension. By the middle of the day the news reports said that Israel had overwhelmed its enemies with the almost flawless execution of a brilliant strategy. On June 10, as the fighting ended, Israel held the Sinai Peninsula, the entire city of Jerusalem, the West Bank of the Jordan River, and the strategically vital Golan Heights, where Syria had located guns that had shelled the Galilee region of Israel, including a kibbutz where one of our cousins worked.

As stories of heroism and victory poured in from the battlefield, military experts around the world marveled at the IDF's proficiency. Israeli planes had all but destroyed the much larger Egyptian air force. Counterattacks made by Jordan, Iraq, and Syria were repulsed. It seemed as if in an instant, Israel had become mature, muscular, and feared, and this recognition by the world community made Jews around the world feel exceedingly proud. As international Jewish organizations and Israeli agencies appealed for support, millions of people sent donations. My mother and father decided to send us.

.....

Considering the fact that gunshots could still be heard in border towns and terrorists still living within Israel could attack anywhere in the country, it may have seemed a strange—even irresponsible—moment for my mother to haul her three sons from Chicago to Tel Aviv. But the decision to send us there, in this time of emergency and danger, was not made lightly. My parents read everything they could find on conditions on the ground in Israel and my father called friends, who reported that life was quickly returning to normal. After concluding that common sense and a little extra vigilance would keep us safe, my parents considered the import of the moment in history and decided that it was the perfect time for us to learn more about our heritage, not to mention the country that we, as Jews, could claim as our own.

Once the question of safety was resolved, the big challenge of this trip would be maintaining our sanity during the six-thousand-mile journey. My mother brought snacks for us, plus an armload of little games, books, *Highlights* magazines, and word puzzle books. The books, puzzles, and magazines helped Rahm and me pass the time but were of little interest to a dyslexic kid like Ari. Unable to stay in his seat, Ari, who was just six years old, roamed the Boeing 707 aircraft and became the darling of the economy-class cabin, accepting treats and engaging in long conversations with the other passengers. He prodded us to play with him and tried to burn off energy by marching up and down the aisle. My mother spent so much time exploring the plane with Ari to make sure he did not annoy people too much, she said, "I walked all the way from Chicago to Israel."

Between 1967 and 1970 we would make four of these long summer trips to Israel. Each one lasted the entire summer and was financed in part by my father's shrewd investment in the stock of a company called McDonald's. These were not so much vacations as a chance to live, for a season, as Israelis. We ate the local cuisine, played on the beaches, swam in the sea, shopped in the markets, and practiced our Hebrew.

On our first trip Ari, Rahm, and I fought with one another to see who would be the first to scuttle down the stairs that were brought up to the tail of the plane and stand on Israeli soil. I won, and after I put my feet down on the ground I also bent down to touch the oily tarmac with my hands. All around me people were doing the same thing, making direct contact with the land that represented acceptance, dignity, and, should he or she need it, a safe haven for every Jew in the world. Even at age nine I understood the seriousness of history and the pride and joy represented by a Jewish state. And it did not seem strange to me that some of my fellow passengers cried as they stood beside the plane.

The military presence in Israel made a big impression on us. The recent war had heightened security concerns and led the authorities to put even more troops in the streets. As boys, we were in awe of the soldiers. Whenever we were in a car and saw them hitchhiking we urged whoever was driving to offer them a ride and then seized the chance to examine their rifles and pepper them with questions.

Except for the many soldiers we saw, Israel circa 1967 struck us as a place where the climate and the pace of life were relaxed and comfortable—more Mediterranean than American. The place was much poorer, in material terms, than America. There was no television and very few people had phones in their homes. And compared to the United States, where we were accustomed to seeing roads and highways jammed with private cars, most Israelis rode buses, walked, or pedaled bikes.

Tel Aviv was a city of smaller, low-rise buildings set along streets lined with palms, cacti, and flowering poinciana trees. Designed by Jewish architects of the Bauhaus era who had fled Nazi Germany, hundreds of these buildings were distinctly modern, with plain lines, flat roofs, airy balconies, and unadorned façades. Many were built around courtyards with ground-floor day-care centers, tiny grocery shops, and other amenities for the residents.

Our aunt Esty—a heavyset, potato-shaped woman with a loud voice and sarcastic demeanor—lived on Mapu Street in one of these typical Tel Aviv apartment houses, located three blocks from the Mediterranean beaches. Her place, on the third floor, was just two rooms with a small kitchen and a balcony but she welcomed us to stay with her for more than six weeks. If you included her two hairless, rat-like Chihuahuas, the population of that little apartment totaled seven, including us three hyperactive boys.

Life at Esty's was a mix of challenges and delights. The tiny space, which required that Ari, Rahm, and I sleep on thin mats on the "living room" floor, forced us to become more patient and flexible, a positive development. In fact, when we were in Israel very few brotherly arguments ever escalated beyond a few angry words. Away from our home and our friends we depended on one another for fun and companionship. We spent many lazy hours on the beach reading, swimming, making sand castles, and soaking up the sun.

When I think of it now, these four summers might be the single most important factor in cementing our brotherly bond. For weeks on end, we spent every waking moment as a threesome. We slept together. We walked to the beach together. We swam, bodysurfed, built sand castles, and lay in the sun together. We went shopping at little groceries together. We made and shot rubber band guns at the neighborhood cats together. There was nothing we did not do together. And it wasn't just being in physical proximity. While we could speak some Hebrew, we were more comfortable in English and this led us to rely more on one another for companionship and fun. Even when we got angry with one another, it never lasted for long because the next day it was just the three of us together. Years of this togetherness—along with sharing a bedroom for so many years—forged an inseparable bond.

Rahm would have fond memories of riding horses on the beach with some girls we met one summer at camp and less fond recollections of touring the country with our mother. "We went to Sinai, Jericho, Nablus, and Jerusalem. She would take us all over the countryside in 110-degree heat and we'd say, 'Mom, can't we get some water?' and she wouldn't want to stop. We had to go to see some cemetery somewhere or we would have to hurry to get back before Shabbat."

My mother used the bus system for most of these tourist outings and we learned to take the bus ourselves. Sometimes we'd grab our fishing poles, hop on a bus, and ride to the stop near where the Hayarkon River empties into the Mediterranean Sea. Once a free-flowing stream, the poor Hayarkon had been reduced by diversions to a brackish trickle. However, it did support a few tiny fish. On our most successful expedition we caught about fifteen of these little swimmers and brought them home. For a scientifically minded kid, learning the not-so-fine art of gutting and skinning our catch—and a chance to examine eyes, gills, and intestines—was fascinating. And of course there was the pleasure of filling our bellies with the panfried fillets we had caught.

On other bus trips we went to parks and markets. When crowds were light and there was room to breathe, we often fell into conversation with Israeli adults. They were quite surprised to encounter three American boys who dressed and looked like Israelis and were adventuring on their own in Tel Aviv. We were more outgoing than typical Israeli kids and open to conversation. Communicating in a mixture of Hebrew and English we'd manage to explain that we were from Chicago. Half the people responded immediately by fashioning their hands into the shape of a handgun and saying the name Al Capone.

We were a curiosity and an amusement for adults who considered us precocious and who would either test our Hebrew or try out their English on us. Sometimes the buses were too crowded for conversation, though, with rush hour passengers who filled every seat and stood toe-to-toe in the aisles. On one of these trips Rahm's small stature served him quite well. I'll never forget the expression of devilish delight on his nine-year-old face when he was wedged between two riders in a way that left his head nestled in the bosom of a buxom woman. The woman in question did not seem to care about providing support and a bit of a thrill for my brother. She even let Rahm remain close after the crowd thinned out.

Life in Tel Aviv was so different from what we knew at home, even the most ordinary activities could seem exotic. For example, like most people in Israel, Esty owned just a tiny refrigerator, so every day was a shopping day. Sometimes we took a bus with her to the Carmel Market, a large outdoor market where vendors sold fruits, vegetables, fish, cheese, meats, and everything else you could imagine. Indeed, Esty even knew a butcher shop that sold bacon—which at that time was not openly sold in Israel. Jammed with people who haggled over prices and debated the quality of the wares, the market was a much livelier place than any grocery store back in America.

On days when we did not troop to the Carmel Market, Esty would send us downstairs to the grocer on the first floor of her building, who had a limited but reliable supply of canned goods, bottled juices, fruits, bread, milk, and yogurt. We also listened for the men who sold fresh vegetables from old-fashioned carts pulled by tired and slow-moving donkeys or horses. Street vendors, who had long disappeared from Chicago, brought a bit of excitement to the neighborhood. When we heard the cry "Avah-tee-ach! Avah-tee-ach!" echo up from the street, we knew that the watermelon man was coming and raced down to meet him. We reacted with even more excitement when we heard "Ana-vim! Ana-vim!" because that meant we could buy a pound of sweet grapes that had been picked at the peak of ripeness just a few hours earlier. Thanks to the standoff between growers and farm labor leader César Chávez, our mom had banned California grapes from our house, which made the Israeli ones taste even more delicious.

When we ate outside the apartment, we might grab a shawarma sandwich of sliced roasted meat with onions or visit Café Gilda to get some pistachio or chocolate ice cream to enjoy as we walked the shopping district bisected by Dizengoff Street. Named after the first mayor of Tel Aviv, Dizengoff was then the equivalent of Fifth Avenue and Times Square put together.

The debates and storytelling heard on the sidewalks and in the shops of Tel Aviv were, to my mother, like jazz sessions where she was always welcomed to play along. Whether the topic was the Six-Day War (1967), the hijacking of El Al Flight 426 (1968), or the election of Golda Meir (1969), my mother was ready with an opinion. But what the Israelis really wanted to hear from her was news about America. The political assassinations, urban uprisings, and antiwar protests fascinated them because many of them had family and friends in the States and because America was both Israel's protector and the leader of the West in its Cold War standoff with communism.

We boys were also encouraged to offer our opinions on everything from the food at a particular café to the political torment of President Johnson. In 1968 a stranger's question—"So where are you from?"—would lead to a long discussion of the violence at the Democratic Party's nominating convention back in our hometown.

As the eldest and most talkative I would usually push my way to the front of these conversations, but as they got older Rahm and Ari managed to add their voices to mine. On most nights I was able to follow the flow of the conversation, even when it was laced with Hebrew, and the excitement kept me alert late into the evening. My brothers, especially little Ari, did not have the same stamina. By eight or nine o'clock at night he was liable to fall asleep right where he was sitting.

It was easy to understand why he might be worn-out. Although our days were not exactly demanding, they were full of play and relaxing doses of sunshine at the beach. Just a few blocks from Esty's apartment, Gordon Beach was a wide expanse of clean sand that occupied all the space between the street and the warm Mediterranean Sea. We would meander down the beach to a place where you could rent a few minutes on an in-ground trampoline to practice bouncing and doing flips. We also got pretty good at a paddleball sport they called *matkot,* and we made friends with the lifeguards who oversaw the beach from raised platforms and skimmed across the water on little boats they called *haseke*s (hah-seh-kahs), which looked a lot like oversize paddleboards that could hold five or six people.

Over the years we became quite friendly with three lifeguards in particular. Big, bronzed guys who seemed stronger and more athletic than anyone we had ever met before, David, Avraham, and Mickey chain-smoked cigarettes while they scanned the water for trouble and the beach for pretty girls. I think they were interested in us because we were Americans and because of our beautiful mother, whom they would chat up whenever she appeared to get some sun herself or to bring us back to Esty's apartment. From the distance of several decades I know, now, that they must have been attracted to my mother. Tall, slim, and to locals exotically foreign, she was prettier than most Israeli women of this era, who aged quickly under the hot sun and did not have access to the clothes and makeup that were available in Europe and the United States.

Our mother was never quite as charming as when she was in Israel with us. In this setting, she did not have to compete with my father, whose magnetic personality and social gifts usually made him the center of attention. Out from under his shadow, our mother enjoyed being the most interesting person at the table. She could also reconnect with people she had known when she lived there, and make some new friends.

Fortunately, Esty and my mother knew people who were happy to take us boys on adventures of different types around the city and in the countryside: Yaacov, a young lieutenant and navigator in the Israeli Air Force; Victor, a lieutenant colonel in the IDF who ran the jail in the West Bank city of Nablus; and Max, a retired British diplomat with white hair, a big handlebar mustache, and a convertible MG sports car who had served in Egypt and Nigeria.

Each of these men was a model of the kind of robust, action-oriented, risk-taking man who inhabited the history books and biographies I liked to read. Victor wore his uniform and gun almost all the time, even when he took us to the park or to see the sunset at the beach. He told us stories about the battles he had seen and reassured us whenever we had questions about moving safely round the country. He was so confident that he invited us to visit him on the West Bank even though Al Fatah terrorists were infiltrating from Jordan and conducting attacks.

On the day we went to Nablus, Victor picked us up in his own car, drove us from Tel Aviv to the jail, and then commandeered a military jeep that he used to take us all over the region. Riding in a military vehicle only increased the macho thrill we boys got as we toured battlefields as well as historical sites. He also took us through downtown Nablus to visit cafés and markets and out to see an old Arab sheepherder who measured us for sheepskin jackets, which turned out to be smelly and more fashionable for Lawrence of Arabia than for Chicago. We never wore them.

We were still in town after the last bus back to Tel Aviv departed. "No problem," said Victor as he invited us to stay at the jail. Built by the Turks, who ruled the region until 1917, the prison was an imposing concrete block surrounded by fences that were topped with barbed wire. Once operated by the British and then the Jordanians, it became one of the main processing centers for prisoners taken by the IDF during the war. After the fighting stopped, the prison became a detention center for terror suspects and convicted criminals. It was the site of many protests by local Arab citizens, and prisoners often went on hunger strikes and attempted riots.

On the night when we visited, the Nablus jail was overflowing with more than 350 convicts and detainees. For three boys from the United States the sight of the facility and the security search required as we passed through the gates were thoroughly sobering. We followed Victor through the complex and saw the bars on the windows and heard the sounds of men talking in Arabic and heavy metal doors opening and closing. Victor, who was originally from Iraq, spoke fluent Arabic and Hebrew and was learning English from Esty. He used all three in the course of interacting with us, the guards under his command, and the prisoners.

Exhausted from the day, we all fell asleep pretty quickly. Sometime later shelling and small-arms fire woke us up. We could hear men running and shouting outside and dogs barking. When the lights came on, we noticed that Ari was missing. Within minutes, as the commotion subsided, Victor showed up with eight-year-old Ari in his arms. He had crawled into Victor's bed. When the gunfire began he wet the bed. Victor reassured him, changed him into one of his own T-shirts, which hung down to Ari's knees, and let him spend the night with him.

In the morning Victor and our mother were so calm and matter-of-fact about the gunshots and fighting that we felt reassured enough to go out and play basketball with some of the prisoners. For Israelis, who had to deal with potential enemies and terrorists every day, this attitude was the only one that allowed them to live halfway normal lives. If you let yourself live in constant fear you might as well leave the country.

Most of the time, this live-and-let-live philosophy worked. But we never lost sight of the danger faced by Israelis who served in the military and were charged with patrolling the West Bank and other captured territories. This reality was brought home for us by a letter we received in Wilmette several months after our adventure with Victor.

In that letter, my mother's sister Esty reported that Victor was dead. He had been on patrol in the West Bank looking for Al Fatah terrorists. He and his soldiers went into a cave where they suspected armed men were hiding. Instead they came upon a woman who was breast-feeding a baby. Finding no fighters, they turned to leave. In that moment Victor was shot in the back and killed.

.....

Victor's death was a sharp reminder of Israel's status as a new and endangered country where conflicts over land and power were very real and everyone had a personal stake in both history and current events. Indeed, everywhere you went, and almost every time you opened your mouth, there was a chance that you would stumble upon an issue, person, or place that reverberated with political significance. History lay in every square inch of the Israeli soil.

For example, you only have to mention the King David Hotel to open a door to emotions ranging from pride to shame and from resignation to condemnation. The symbolism of the grand hotel that overlooks the Old City of Jerusalem looms large in the history of Israel. This is how it is in that country. The woman sitting across from you on the bus was a courier who carried secrets around the world. The family friend sitting beside you on a veranda was part of a team that bombed the King David Hotel and killed ninety-one people.

Born in Turkey but raised in Israel when it was part of the British Mandate of Palestine, Yoel Carmi was married to my father's childhood classmate and close friend Batya. With a big, round chest and full head of dark hair, he looked strong and full of life. But he also had developed a potbelly that spoke of his increasing comfort. Usually it was hard to get him to speak seriously for very long. His habit was to joke around, and play at switching from accent to accent. One second he would ask a question in the Queen's English. In the next he would answer in southern American drawl. Then it was on to Cockney or an Australian accent. His attitudes were as varied as his comic routines. Politically, he was rabidly right-wing and anti-Arab. But he also had a deep and warm appreciation for every culture in the world and almost everyone he met. This contradiction was evident in the bomb shelter he built at his house to withstand a poison gas attack. It was crammed with freeze-dried rations but every wall was lined with bookshelves carrying all the great Western classics of philosophy, literature, and history, from Plato to Bellow.

Yoel claimed to speak ten languages and I believe he did, because he did not need to exaggerate. His strengths and talents were obvious to anyone who met him and he was brutally honest and direct whenever he talked about his own life and the life of Israel. He was a Zionist with such firm convictions that he had no doubts about participating in one of the most controversial attacks ever, carried out by the Jewish underground paramilitary called the Irgun.

The year was 1946, Yoel recalled while sipping tea next to me and my mom on the King David veranda. The British—who controlled what is now Israel—were doing little to stop Arab attacks on Israeli civilians. At the same time, hundreds of Jews were rounded up and thrown in jail on suspicions of anti-British activity. In truth, all but a handful of Jews had come to settle the region with the specific goal of creating the state of Israel and that required getting the British to leave. The reality of the Holocaust had intensified their resolve. When the British raided Irgun offices and carted away truckloads of documents, the Jewish militants chose to strike back at the British military and police headquarters, which was housed in the King David.

Yoel, who worked for the British as a translator, says he did not plant the bomb. However, he was intimately involved with the plot. One of his tasks involved checking to see that the offices were cleared of Jews. The men who planted the bomb actually gathered hotel workers, held them at gunpoint, and then allowed them to flee before the bomb went off. Three separate calls were made to warn the British before the explosions. The officer in charge said something about "not taking orders from Jews." Then, at 12:37 on July 23, 1946, the explosives carried into the hotel in milk cans went off, collapsing the six-story wing of the hotel where the British kept their offices. While dozens inside were killed by the collapse, others outside died from the impact of flying debris. The passengers in a bus on the road outside the hotel were injured when the shock waves hit it.

The Jewish Agency and the National Council of Palestine Jews, the two main civilian Jewish authorities, immediately condemned the attack as a crime. Talk of shutting down the Irgun spread quickly. But as Yoel told the story, this public condemnation was a cover for the private support the Irgun received from almost every corner of Jewish society. They agreed with the American senator Guy Gillette, who immediately blamed pro-Arab British policies for the attack. This feeling intensified as five hundred Jews were rounded up in what the British called a "contempt" campaign.

The drama and danger in the story Yoel told was much more real and tangible than anything recorded in a book or recalled by the marker at some ancient battlefield. The fact that the place where the attack occurred was unchanged from that era, and I could sit with one of the bomb plotters and drink tea, made a profound impact on me. Yoel and the King David were solid, palpable proof that big, historic events were carried out by real people I knew, called upon to act, who were willing to live with the consequences.

Public opinion was, and may forever remain, divided on the point, but Yoel believed that time had shown that the attack on the King David had been justified. He was certain that the bombing was a legitimate attack on a military target and that it had hastened the birth of the state of Israel and saved countless Jewish lives. In Yoel's mind the casualties were the fault of the British officers who failed to heed the warnings.

The stories people told about these grave and powerful events were often spiced by the flavor of personal experiences and unexpected connections. Yoel could tell bawdy jokes and swear in many languages. One of his best tales recalled the time when he and Batya took me, still a baby, my parents, and Esty, all crammed into my parents' tiny Fiat, for a tour of the Negev Desert. The year was 1958 and thousands of Bedouins lived as nomads in the Negev, herding sheep and camels unmolested across Israel's borders with Jordan and Egypt. Yoel found his way to one of their camps, where everyone piled out of the car like the circus clowns and he began talking with the man in charge.

Yoel, whose Arabic was excellent, was such a friendly and gregarious fellow that the group was quickly invited inside one of the tents for lunch. Everyone sat on pillows and platters of food were served. The man in charge cast a romantic eye upon Esty, who, with her zaftig figure, represented the Bedouin feminine ideal.

In short order, Yoel, with my father's assistance, began negotiating with the sheikh over how much he would pay to make Esty one of his wives. After a great deal of bluffing and waving of hands, Yoel managed to get the price to six camels and a few goats. With my father roaring with laughter, Yoel decided to press his luck and ask what he might get if he added my mother, the tall, skinny one, to the deal.

"Two chickens," came the answer.

It was, in the long history of my mother's relationship with her sister, the only time she was deemed less desirable. The problem, of course, was that the sheikh was more than a little bit serious about adding Esty to his harem. As the sun set on the desert, Yoel had to do some fast talking to facilitate a peaceful exit and escape to Tel Aviv.

The Bedouins were direct reminders that Israel was home to ancient cultures as well as fast-paced modern development. We found it all fascinating and we almost never felt afraid or out of place. The main exception to this rule was our first visit to an Israeli sleepaway camp, in the summer of 1969.

The whole idea of the camp was for us to experience a bit of Israeli life on our own, away from our mother, and to give her and Esty a much-needed break. We hated the idea when it was first broached and hated it even more when we found ourselves alone at the camp with counselors who had decided to treat the Emanuels like they did all the other campers, by assigning us to cabins based on school grade. We all began to cry when each of us realized we would have to go alone to bunk with Israeli children our own age. Distressed by our show of emotion, the adults in charge of the camp quickly rearranged the rooms, letting the three of us bunk together in a four-man room.

Apparently that little episode of bawling and special treatment wasn't enough to make us pariahs. As the only Americans at the camp, we were the objects of much curiosity and our room became the in place to be. What we did and said was of great interest to the Israeli kids, but that did not stop them from teasing us when the moment

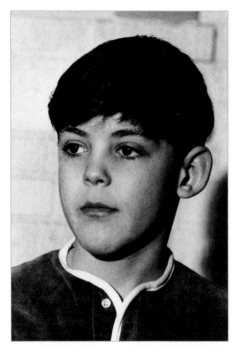

Serious Zeke.

Mischievous Ariel.

Quiet Rahm.

Benjamin with his parents, Penina and Ezekiel, in Israel.

Benjamin and Marsha
at their wedding, 1955.

Zeke with Marsha
and Benjamin, 1958.

A friend, Alan Dean, holding Rahm,
with Marsha, Zeke, and (far left) Alan's
son Michael, 1960.

Zeke sitting on a living room
chair, circa 1963.

The three Emanuel brothers with Penina.

Rahm with Big Bangah—maternal grandfather Herman Smulevitz.

Zeke with Big Bangah.

The entire Emanuel
family, circa 1963.

The Emanuel brothers hanging out on Ben Yehuda Street,
Tel Aviv, 1967.

The Emanuel brothers with Sheva, a paternal step-great-aunt, in Tel Aviv.

The Emanuel brothers with lifeguard David Malamud, Tel Aviv, 1967.

Big Bangah (maternal grandfather Herman Smulevitz) and Little Bangah (maternal grandmother Sophie Smulevitz) circa Zeke's bar mitzvah, 1970.

Long-haired Zeke at Rahm's
bar mitzvah, 1972.

Rahm at his bar mitzvah, 1972.

The entire Emanuel family at
Ariel's bar mitzvah, 1974.

Rahm on his way to high school, circa 1975.

Rahm, Benjamin, Ariel, and Zeke, early 1980s.

required it. One night they showed a movie in the open-air theater. When the movie ended and the lights came up, there was Ari, slumped in his chair, not moving, with his eyes open. The adults panicked, thinking something was wrong, maybe he had had a seizure or fainted. One of the men picked him up and, as the other camp counselors shouted, began running to the medical station. Rahm and I were perplexed by all the commotion. Because he burned so much energy, Ari regularly fell asleep suddenly and slept very deeply. And he frequently had his eyes open. We tried to explain that there was nothing wrong—this was normal. Eventually everyone calmed down and took the sleeping boy to his bed.

All the attention we received made our adjustment easier and in a matter of days we were actually able to enjoy the horseback riding, target shooting, pottery, and bonfires on the beach. Like so many kids, I got my first kiss at camp—from a beautiful brunette girl named Ronit. We also got to test ourselves in the end-of-camp sports competitions.

Ari was especially assertive, throwing himself into sports he had barely played before, such as soccer, and dominating simple contests like capture the flag. Watching him at camp, it was hard to deny that he was a fierce and fearless competitor. In part he was showing the effects of growing up with highly competitive brothers. But the sibling rivalry wasn't his only advantage. Ari was also driven by an intense desire to prove, despite his obvious problems with reading and focusing his attention, that he was as good as, if not better than, anyone else.

Combine Ari's drive with a setting like Israel, where everyone seemed to be striving and competing with a sense of life-or-death urgency, and you got a kid who won a handful of first prizes and also became one of the more popular boys in the camp. Pitted against kids his own age, instead of his older brothers, Ari found a level of success beyond what he had experienced at home and at school. Whether the competition involved swimming, basketball, or running, he loved winning.

Israelis admire a fellow who can get things done and none of them seemed to mind Ari's sharp-elbowed intensity. Courage and physical toughness were revered as traits of the pioneers and of those who were devoted to a "never again" response to the Holocaust. In a nation where every man and woman was required to serve in the military, you had to be willing to accept a challenge and give it your all.

Also, all the campers understood that what happened on the basketball court, or the soccer field, wasn't a matter of life and death. Some of the kids who attended were the sons and daughters of men and women who had been killed in the Six-Day War. The kids had paid a terrible price as their country struggled to survive in a hostile corner of the world, yet they threw themselves into camp life determined to be happy despite their terrible losses. This lesson in the Israeli way of life, taught to us by children our own age, was a strong reinforcement for the values my parents had tried to impart over the years.

Ten

WILMETTE

Nervous as hell whenever we entered new situations, my brothers and I were not our usual boisterous selves on the first day of school in Wilmette. Under normal circumstances we would have been anxious about leaving the family cocoon of Anshe Emet and enrolling at a big new school. However, our cheapskate father had made the situation even worse.

Families who returned to America from Israel or Europe paid a premium for flights that got them home by Labor Day, to start school on time. Consequently, after Labor Day airfares dropped substantially. Always wanting a bargain, my father booked us to fly after the holiday. This meant we were "new" students who appeared three days after the start of class. We needed special attention to be seated in our classrooms, obtain books, and get caught up on lessons and homework.

Unlike little Anshe Emet, where there was one class per grade, Romona had four or five for each grade level. As I took my seat I searched for my only friends in Wilmette. As luck would have it, all four of the boys from Locust Road had been assigned to different teachers. In another corner of the school, Rahm was quietly making his way through the day, adjusting to a new environment with his usual caution. Schoolboys used size and muscle to establish a pecking order, which inevitably put Rahm at a disadvantage. In time he would make up for his size by being funny and, if possible, cool. Unfortunately, because of my parents, cool often lay just out of reach. As he explained it, "I remember that what was cool then was brightly colored socks. The other kids had blue, red, yellow, and green and we had only black or white." There was no way Rahm could talk my parents into getting him different socks. They would say that "it built character" to go against the fads. Rahm would say it just made him less popular and a little less secure.

While Rahm worked hard at fitting in, Ari's first day of school included a fight with another second grader who called him "nigger" because his skin had been browned by the Israeli sun. He hit the boy so hard he broke his glasses. When summoned to the school, my mother stuck up for Ari and was so charming that Harold Smith, the principal, became an ally, not an enemy. They agreed that the year to come would be "interesting."

This sort of "interesting" continued for much of the year. When some boys grabbed Rahm's bike and said, "Niggers cannot ride here," Ari responded by pulling one of the boys off the seat and beating him so badly that Rahm had to intervene to protect the little bigot. Ari also managed to locate and challenge the reigning alpha male in his second-grade classroom. Ari and Michael Alter fought each other at first and then, after establishing a truce, engaged in a long campaign of mutual mischief.

.....

Soon after we settled in Wilmette our mother found some kindred spirits and discovered that she could carry on her civil rights work in a new and provocative way. Essentially all white and pretty much devoid of poor people, Wilmette wasn't the site of protests or marches for equal access to decent housing. However, it was the kind of place inhabited by the people who owned the substandard housing that was the subject of outrage in Chicago. When CORE activists checked Cook County records to discover the identities of the various slumlords who charged top-dollar rents for apartments in dilapidated buildings, one of the biggest offenders turned out to be a fellow named Braverman, who lived on Locust Road just four houses away from us.

Led by my mother and some other suburban liberals, CORE picketed the Bravermans' home several times in an attempt to bring the shame of the condition of his properties right to his doorstep. Among the pickets were some of Braverman's tenants, who demanded he make long-neglected repairs and bring his buildings up to city standards. The tactic wasn't original. CORE and other groups had marched on the home of Chicago school superintendent Willis many times. Wilmette, however, hadn't seen this kind of action before. Not surprisingly, Mr. Braverman did not appreciate having a neighbor lead a mixed-race group of sign-carrying, slogan-shouting protesters to the sidewalk in front of his house. He emerged from his house shouting and waving his arms and bellowed at the protesters to stay off his property "or else!" My mother and the others knew all the laws relating to protests and private property and when the police rolled by they discovered that the picketers were doing nothing illegal.

The "or else" shouted by Mr. Braverman wasn't specific, but we found out what he meant a few months after the picketing ceased. The ostensible provocation involved our harmless German shepherd, Andele, and their dog, which was a little hairy thing that yapped at anything that moved. During our daily walks when we reached our block I would let go of Andele's leash and let him run home free. One day I was running behind him when we encountered Mr. Braverman with his little dog. When Braverman barked at me to leash my dog I responded the way Emanuels always respond to self-appointed authorities: I ignored him. A dog-to-dog encounter ensued. After a little yelp, which may or may not have been prompted by Andele, Mr. Braverman accused Andele of biting his little precious. I walked away, ignoring his protestations.

Soon after I got home the house practically shook with the sound of someone pounding on our front door. My mother answered and I heard a deep voice raised in anger and heard her speaking in the kind of measured tone you use when faced with an angry and dangerous person. I came racing downstairs to discover my mother facing down Mr. Braverman, who was outraged about how I let our dog attack his defenseless darling.

Certain that nothing serious had happened with the dogs, I tried to stand beside my mother to argue with Mr. Braverman. The louder he shouted the more agitated I became in defense of myself, Andele, and the family honor. Then Mr. Braverman moved so his jacket came open and my mother could see the handle of a pistol he had tucked into the waistband of his trousers.

My mother, fearing that I would badger this man into doing something violent, began to tell me to shut up and step away, and by then Ari and Rahm came to find out what the commotion was all about. As they crowded around, Mr. Braverman's anger peaked and he said something like "You people have pushed me too far."

It was then that my mother turned, pushed us away from the door, and slammed it on our armed and possibly dangerous neighbor. Once she had us quieted, she explained that she had seen the gun and that sometimes it's better to back away from a fight.

Fortunately, Mr. Braverman and his family moved away from Locust Road a few months later. The tale of the dogs, the gun, and Mr. Braverman was quickly installed in the family legend under the heading "Stories About Zeke's Big Mouth."

.....

Mr. Braverman aside, the people we met in our new hometown shared many of the values we held, especially our focus on education. Wilmette's elementary and middle schools fed into the prestigious New Trier High School district, which rivaled the best East Coast prep schools in the quality of its program and the number of its graduates who went on to the Ivy League.

By the late 1960s there were two New Trier high schools and anyone who looked closely at the way enrollment in these schools was handled could see old-fashioned bigotry at work. The plan to separate Jewish newcomers from the children of old-line New Trier families was developed as the postwar influx of families filled the original New

Trier High to capacity. By the early 1960s plans were set to build a second high school, called New Trier West. Students would be assigned to the schools on the basis of geography. The line separating the districts was gerrymandered—sometimes on a house-by-house basis—to make sure that most of the Jewish students from the western side of town would attend the new high school while the original was reserved for the older white Anglo-Saxon Protestant communities near the lakeshore.

Eventually the North Shore would become so accepting that New Trier closed for the Jewish high holy days, something that seemed impossible when I attended. However, when we were young, the tension between Jewish newcomers and certain members of the established community required us to think about how we fit in. We identified with anyone and everyone who had to deal with exclusion or prejudice. Rahm, for example, became a close and protective friend to the Alanzo boy, the son of the first Mexican-American family to move into our neighborhood. The boy's father was a preacher and it was obvious that he struggled to support a large family on a pastor's salary. Jews and non-Jews alike picked on this kid until Rahm took him under his wing.

Fortunately, most of the teachers in Wilmette were sensitive to early signs of trouble among their students and worked hard to make the schools welcoming and safe. Typical was my sixth-grade homeroom and social studies teacher, a novice named Robert Zahniser, who was as excited as he was nervous to face his first classroom full of eager faces. I can still see him, a skinny guy with close-cropped hair, a fading chin that accentuated a prominent Adam's apple, desperately trying to bring order to the room by knocking on the desktop with his big Slippery Rock State College class ring. I was one of the overeager kids who always had their hands raised and called out "Oh, oh, oh!" to get his attention.

All through the fall I used discussion periods in social studies to start debates on the Vietnam War, presidential politics, and other issues in the news. While he was not a doctrinaire conservative, Mr. Zahniser had what I in my eleven-year-old wisdom considered to be an unhealthy respect for authority figures. Where Vietnam was concerned, he seemed to believe that if America's political leaders and foreign policy experts were convinced we needed to fight, we should trust them. I could tie him in knots with questions like: Why do so many middle- and upper-class whites get out of the draft? With the big body counts reported every week, why aren't we winning? Do the Vietnamese people really want us there?

Zahniser, who actually broke into a sweat during these debates, still appreciated the energy we brought to the classroom. "I was relieved to have some students who jumped into everything so completely," he said many years later. Zahniser saw the same quality of passionate, intense engagement in Ari, who showed up in his class when he was shifted from sixth grade to fourth.

Ari's hyperactivity and dyslexia continued to make schoolwork a torture, but he was relentless about doing his best. Zahniser went out of his way to encourage him. This effort included involving Ari in a summer-long psychology experiment that featured a collection of little white mice, a maze, and Pavlov's theory of stimulus response. Along with a few other kids, Ari got to care for and train a rodent troupe that learned to run through the maze in response to a sound that they associated with a treat at the other end. Like Pavlov's dogs, they responded even when no treat was to be found.

The psych experiment was a special project but not something out of the norm for schools in Wilmette. Teachers there routinely went beyond the call of duty to help kids in any way possible. In Ari's case, Robert Zahniser made sure to reward Ari's great social skills—he was the most popular boy in his grade—and to find activities that would allow him to succeed without much reading and writing.

"Ari," Robert remembers, "was in this class that happened to have a lot of boys in it and they were a pretty noisy and hyperactive group, which was why I, the only male teacher in the grade, got them. One day when everyone was talking all at once and I was losing control of the class Ari suddenly decided to take care of me. He stood up and shouted, 'Shut up and sit down!' and then he pounded his fist on the desk and they all did. Classic Emanuel. You put your heart into everything, one hundred percent. Of course later I had to take Ari aside and explain that while I appreciated his help, keeping order in the classroom is something I'll have to do by myself."

My youngest brother was incredibly sensitive to matters of fairness, especially when it came to kids who stood out as different in any way. Ari became a staunch defender of his friend Michael Alter's younger brother Harvey, who had profound learning disabilities and endured a lot of teasing.

Harvey was the kind of kid that bullies picked as a target. In one memorable instance a football player who had always rubbed Ari the wrong way decided to make fun of Harvey during lunch in the high school cafeteria. Ari, who was carrying a food tray and walking with Harvey, whacked the bully in the face with the tray and then threw himself at him, punching furiously.

Generally speaking, these fights required my mother to come to the school to hear what had happened and while she might defend Ari in front of a school official, she would always lecture him later. Here was a woman devoted to the antiwar movement and peaceful resistance, yet she was regularly required to come to school to deal with a violent and self-justifying kid who was quick to start throwing punches.

"There's always a better way to settle things than fighting," she would say. "What would the world be like if every time one country insulted another they had a war over it? What the world needs is more peacemakers, not people who lose their tempers." In the case of the bully football player, Ari soon forgot the blow-by-blow details. He had so many fights as a kid that they all ran together. But he would always remember how Harvey, Michael, and his mother appreciated what he did.

Harvey and Michael's mother, Laura, became something like a favorite aunt to Ari in part because she saw so much of him at her house and at the school. Michael and Ari got into trouble together so often that Laura Alter arrived at more than a few meetings in the principal's office only to find Marsha Emanuel already waiting.

What struck Mrs. Alter about these incidents, and about Ari in general, was that he was almost always able to charm his way out of trouble and, even if he could not escape punishment, he always managed to quickly rebuild any relationships he may have damaged. "Even when he was little he had this glibness, a way of talking that helped him get away with things."

As she got to know our entire family, Laura Alter saw that Ari's easy way with words, and his ability to disagree and even fight without breaking bonds, came directly from our family. The older we got, the more our dinner table conversation became like a round-robin debate with people taking various sides of an issue just for the sake of arguing. "You liked that movie? Well then, let me tell you why you're wrong."

Laura also got to hear, especially from my mother, a brand of politics and feminist values that reinforced ideals that Laura had nurtured for many years but had rarely expressed. When she did, her conservative husband complained that she was talking "like Marsha Emanuel."

.....

In the late 1960s the northern suburbs of Chicago were home to quite a few women who, like my mother, had a deep interest in social issues and were becoming more outspoken. Behind the picket fences and well-trimmed lawns, Wilmette was one of those places where many seemingly traditional men and women—especially women—were giving serious thought to what were then radical ideas about race, politics, gender, and the war in Vietnam. Consciousness-raising groups sprouted like dandelions and ideas voiced by radical thinkers began to get a hearing in sunken living rooms and breakfast nooks. Laura Alter was among those who were, for the lack of a better word, radicalized by what they read and what they heard in conversation with other women, like my mother.

Unlike ours, the Alter family was more conventional. Bill Alter firmly claimed the role of patriarch and made it clear he thought his views were superior. A real estate developer who became quite wealthy, he was on the conservative side when it came to politics and the roles of men and women. During a business trip to New York with her husband, Mrs. Alter visited a favorite great-aunt who had been a card-carrying communist. On the spur of the moment she joined an antiwar march on Fifth Avenue. By coincidence, Bill happened to get out of a cab at a spot where the parade was passing and saw his wife, who was dressed in a bright orange designer outfit. Later Bill Alter scolded her for making a spectacle of herself, but she stood proud. The moment marked the beginning of a new phase of life that would lead her to more activism, college, and then graduate school.

Laura Alter's move away from the life of the traditional home-maker and toward a renewed engagement with the world was repeated a thousand times over in Wilmette. More than a few men were able to see their wives' point of view, and liberalism, which included equal rights for women, opposition to the war, and a generalized distrust of authority, came into fashion. Wilmette was even a stop on Jane Fonda's fund-raising tour on behalf of veterans' groups opposed to the war.

Liberals in our community found both spiritual and social support at a synagogue called Am Yisrael, which was a hotbed of activism. The congregation was led by Rabbi William Frankel, who had been born in Vienna in 1923 and had lived under Nazi rule as a child. In 1966 he was one of three rabbis who marched with Dr. King in Chicago and invited him to speak at three suburban temples. The congregation's Friday night lectures became standing-room-only venues for politicians, writers, and others who talked about all the vital issues of the day.

Even though we were just kids, we were encouraged to attend the lectures and were welcomed to ask questions, like anyone else. The first time I tried this was when the archconservative Philip Crane was running in a special election for the House seat vacated by Donald Rumsfeld, who had been appointed to serve in the Nixon administration. We were studying ancient Greece in school so I asked Crane, who was a super-hawk on Vietnam, why he chose to act like a Spartan instead of a more enlightened Athenian. Although I don't recall it now,

Crane, who held a doctorate in history, probably gave me a pretty good answer. I do know that he went on to win the election and many more after that.

.....

Although I was already a bit of a nerd when I arrived in Wilmette, the feedback from teachers, other students, and parents in Wilmette fueled my obsessions. In fact, the whole educational endeavor in our new hometown seemed designed to supercharge ambitious kids with a continuous loop of educational challenges, support, and rewards. In my case the best early example of this process was my project for a class about the Middle Ages. I chose to create a replica of Harlech Castle in Wales.

My neighbor Mitch Cohen, who lived directly across the street, agreed to be my partner. I also got help from my mother's cousin Jack Skayan, who had come to live with us while recovering from hepatitis he contracted while traveling. Jack had studied some architecture in college and had an artistic streak. We commandeered the linoleum floor of our family room. At first Ari and Rahm teased me for being a nerd obsessed with creating a glorified dollhouse. They hung back while Jack, Mitch, and I glued the cardboard base, laid out the floor plan, and sketched the location of the outer walls, the four main towers, and all the buildings. Using X-Acto knives, pliable rulers, and surgical tools lent by my father, Jack, Mitch, and I scored hundreds of individual "bricks" on balsa wood, rounded pieces for turrets, and glued walls together. As they watched the castle take shape Ari and Rahm became interested enough to volunteer their help. They painted the "water" a deep blue and used our mom's hair dryer to heat up clay so it would be easily shaped to form the contours of the countryside.

Like most monumental building projects, the construction of the castle was plagued by cost overruns, accidents, and labor disputes. Misapplied clay slid off the cardboard base. Misplaced footsteps—some *purposely* misplaced by angry brothers—caused further damage, while arguments over tools and methods led to wrestling matches and stockouts of balsa wood at Tom Thumb crafts store delayed completion. Fortunately I was big enough to prevent my brothers from destroying the castle, and my parents, acting like some municipal bonding authority, happily covered the expense of repairs, alterations, and additions to the project.

When it was finished, the castle was eased into the back of the family station wagon and my mother drove it very slowly over to Romona School. Everyone was impressed as Mitch and I carried the castle into the school. The A-plus grade was satisfying but we felt especially proud when we were asked to put our project on display at a district learning center. For months we heard that people were inspecting the project with great care and admiration. The idea that you could get such recognition from the community for academic work was a major revelation for me. Equally inspiring, for all three of us, was the notion that anyone—including a kid—could conceive of something ambitious, marshal resources, and with a concentrated effort achieve some success.

After the castle project, Jack got the idea to build a rudimentary computer based on a plan he saw in *Scientific American*. A bit of delicate soldering was required, but the real work involved going to Radio Shack and hardware stores for the switches and other components. My mother was happy to accommodate us, and in short order we had the contraption built and running. Basically a set of switches and a battery glued to a board and connected by wires, the device was more like a humongous if crude calculator than a computer, but it was more sophisticated than anything we had ever seen.

As the family geek, I got the most out of projects like the calculator/computer, but when they found something they wanted to pursue Ari and Rahm got similar backing. In Rahm's case, his major interest was a bit surprising. He was keenly sensitive to any slights based on his height, age, or masculinity, which is why we were all taken aback when he decided to take up, in earnest, the art of the dance.

.....

It started with my mother's decision to make us all take ballet lessons. His 1960 bar mitzvah injury notwithstanding, our father was a terrific dancer, and our parents were always the dancing hit of any Jewish celebration. Our mother figured that it would be a good skill for us to possess, too. But for reasons that have been lost to time, she signed us up not for ballroom or modern dance, but for introductory ballet.

Our dance school occupied a big space above the Rexall drugstore at the Edens Plaza shopping center, which was about a mile and a half from our home. It was run by an enterprising male dance teacher who had outfitted it with a smooth wooden floor, mirrors, and ballet barres. He seemed to promise the parents of Wilmette that he could turn their children into stars. More like tumbling, biting bear cubs than fleet-footed antelopes, Ari, Rahm, and I would have preferred to study karate or jujitsu but there was no way we could escape the dance studio. To our relief, the three of us had a private lesson each week, which spared us from the judgment of other kids.

Ari would later confess that the dance lessons at Edens Plaza helped him in sports. I did not make enough progress to be considered coordinated or elegant, but I learned enough to enjoy myself at bar mitzvahs and parties through my high school years. But neither of us enjoyed going to those lessons. Quite the contrary. We hated the black tights and ballet shoes we were required to wear and dreaded being seen going in or out of the dance studio. Whenever we were spied by classmates or friends we had to endure their taunts. Once Ari chased a boy down the sidewalk and beat him until he cried for mercy after he asked if we had remembered to bring our tutus.

After a year devoted to learning the first through fifth positions and other moves, Ari and I had had enough and were permitted to quit. Rahm, to everyone's surprise, stuck with it.

For the next six years, Rahm endured teasing from friends and classmates and risked being spotted in his tights, in order to learn and master ever-more-challenging elements of dance. He progressed rather quickly, showing that he had the strength and natural athletic ability to perform impressive leaps and lifts and the discipline to accept criticism and endure the physical pain that comes with ballet. My mother loved that Rahm found something to pour himself into, something that helped him to distinguish himself. But she also reminded him that his ability "is a gift from God. It's not for you to keep, but to share" through performance.

As strong as he may have been, Rahm was still very small for his age. Ari and I made a point of watching out for trouble from anyone who even thought about making fun of him. This did not mean we foreswore teasing him ourselves, or even suggesting from time to time that he might be ready for a new tutu. What's a brother for? But where outsiders were concerned, we were extremely protective and made it clear that anyone who bothered him would have to deal with us.

When he outgrew the ballet school over the Rexall pharmacy, my parents transferred him to a studio in Evanston, where he could get more advanced coaching from a locally famous teacher named Gus Giordano. Working with Gus, Rahm developed strength, stamina, and a kind of grace that was evident even when he wasn't performing. The way he walked, and even the way he occupied space in a room, changed in ways that made him seem more substantial and more confident despite his relatively short stature. This was, no doubt, the benefit my parents were imagining as they supported the lessons and attended his performances. Ballet was an art form but it was also a way to build discipline and character.

By the time Rahm reached high school, he was good enough, and confident enough, to let anyone know that he was passionate about dance. With Ari helping to police the knuckleheads, he got much positive reinforcement for his efforts, and he did both choreography and performances in high school. Rahm's crowd of friends included lots of kids who were interested in theater, music, and dance, but he also enjoyed a brief stint as a soccer player. I think he gravitated toward the game because it was the one sport we had played with our dad.

Although Rahm wouldn't have a long run in varsity sports, he got all the family support he needed to make steady progress with Gus Giordano and make a lasting impression on the stage at school. I received similar backing for every interest I ever expressed. One example of this involved a cow heart, with lungs attached, that my grandfather Herman acquired somewhere in his wanderings through butcher shops and delivered to me wrapped in white, waxy butcher paper. My parents allowed me to dissect these organs on a card table that I set up in the family room and covered with plastic. Most of the time I performed this cardiac surgery with my friend Jerry Glass. We would make slices here and there and compare what we saw to anatomical drawings of the human heart and the plastic models that my father brought home from his office. But even though he gave us tools and anatomical aids, my father did not coach us through this work or even discuss it with us. He left it to us to find out how the valves worked, discover the artery opening, and trace the vessels that move blood to the lungs and back to the left atrium.

While I played surgeon and Rahm required frequent taxi service to rendezvous with beautiful ballerinas, Ari made very few requests for help with any of his interests. This was probably because he already spent more than enough time with my mother working on academic skills. Hyperactive to the point where he literally shook as he struggled to sit still, Ari nevertheless managed to wait as my mother spread flour on a silver tray she had received as a wedding gift and then took his hand in hers to trace the letters of the alphabet. An invention of her own design, the flour tray was intended to give my brother some physical sensation to match the appearance of the letters on paper.

The pressure Ari felt as my mother coached him was matched by the embarrassment he experienced whenever he was in a situation that required him to read out loud. When everyone at synagogue picked up their prayer books to read some passage in English, Ari stared at the page and hoped no one would notice that he couldn't participate. Sometimes he would attempt to recite, listening carefully and then voicing the words a split second after he heard them. I recall being perplexed by his struggle. No one in our family could spell worth a damn. I was always the first one out in spelling bees at school. But Ari couldn't read even a few sentences out loud. He had similar experiences in school. If a teacher ever told him he would have to read out loud the next day, he would spend hours practicing the night before, hoping to memorize the words so he wouldn't have to actually follow the text.

Dependent on others for extra help with academics, Ari made it a point to go it alone in many of his extracurricular pursuits, most of which involved moneymaking ventures. The first was probably the sale of our mother's cheesecake, which she prepared on a weekly basis and included in our school lunches. The cake was almost achingly good, but Ari had the discipline to be satisfied with the piece he had with dinner so that he could sell his next day's portion at school to the highest bidder. My mother did not have any idea this was going on until a neighbor telephoned to ask her to supply her with an entire cheesecake for a party. For a moment she thought this request was part of the suburban subculture—maybe she could ask Mrs. Grant for a pot roast—but then the caller asked her for a price.

"How much do I charge?" she asked incredulously. "What gave you the idea that I sell cheesecakes?"

Once the two women stopped laughing, my mother had to say she felt a bit encouraged by Ari's initiative. She also insisted on making one of her cakes and delivering it to our neighbor as a gift. Soon after this little retail adventure, Ari showed more entrepreneurial potential as he drafted Rahm and me and some other boys as laborers to do yard work while he kept a cut of the proceeds for himself. These little businesses required a degree of planning and organization that stood in stark relief to Ari's struggles at school and his many conflicts with our father.

No one would ever question our father's devotion or skill as a parent, but Ari, the youngest shavov, certainly challenged his patience. In some instances he deliberately tried to get my father's goat. At every restaurant, for instance, he would scan the menu to identify the most expensive appetizer, entrée, and dessert, and order them all. This habit was partly connected to his dyslexia. He had trouble reading menus and he found it easier just to look for the higher prices, which he anticipated were associated with the better dishes.

In other cases, Ari really could not help but be annoying. No matter what day of the week it happened to be, or whether school was in session or not, he was always awake by 5 a.m. Jittery and anxious, he could not stay in bed, and he would prowl around the house looking for something to occupy his mind and help him burn off excess energy.

Although he tried to be quiet, inevitably Ari would awaken Rahm, or me, or worse, my father on a morning when he was trying to recover some of the sleep he lost during a busy workweek. To his credit, our father understood that Ari was just too energized to control himself. He was less sanguine about the harassment and goofing around that Ari practiced as he got older and learned the fine art of persistent and intentional irritation.

Typically these elaborate episodes involved something as mundane as a television-channel-changing contest. These began with my father, home after a long, hard day at work, descending into the family room and stretching out on the sofa to watch something on channel 11, Chicago's public television station. Ari would waltz into the family room and change the channel. In these days before remote controls, my father would have to command Ari to restore his program of choice, or else would have to get up from the sofa, walk across the room, and do it himself.

One day Ari switched the TV to *All Star Wrestling* on channel 32. My father got up and flipped the channel back to 11. Just as my father sat down on the sofa, Ari reached up from his spot on the floor and flipped it back to channel 32. My father then got up and changed it back to channel 11. Ari waited again and as my father sat he flipped the channel.

Thirty-two.

Eleven.

Thirty-two.

Eleven.

Seated nearby, Rahm the peacemaker laughed nervously to encourage my father to see the humor in the situation, all the while praying that his little brother would stop before he crossed that imaginary line and reached my father's breaking point.

As Ari continued to defy him, my father finally warned, "You better stop it now!"

Ari should have known better than to risk one more flip. He did not. "Gudt-dammit!" my father cried, and leaped off the sofa. Ari dashed up the stairs to the kitchen. My father gave chase. Rahm followed. Hearing the commotion, I came out of my room just in time to see our father chasing Ari through the kitchen, where my dad picked up a large carving knife and shouted something about how Ari better not let himself get caught.

My brother raced to the kitchen and through the formal living room, putting enough distance between himself and our father so that when he dashed up the steps to his bedroom Rahm and I could fill the space in the stairway and slow down his knife-wielding pursuer. We grabbed our father and, though we knew in our hearts he would never hurt Ari, we used all our strength to hold him back until we heard the door to Ari's room slam shut. At this point my father gave up and, having spent most of the energy that powered his outrage, he simply dropped the matter and walked away.

This was generally how things worked with my dad. You could needle and bother and argue with him a hundred different times and he would manage to keep his cool. When he did finally lose his temper, the outrage was volcanic but always short-lived. And if his pique included some threat of physical violence it was always a threat, and nothing more.

Consider, for example, the winter day when he rose early for his breakfast, went out to the garage, opened the big door, and got into the Pontiac Grand Prix (white with a black vinyl roof) for the commute to work. Ari stared out the back door as my father started the engine and revved it to get it warm. While my father waited for the engine to fall into a reliable rhythm Ari came outside and ran around like some meshugenah elf.

Remember, it was early morning. Dad was probably a little groggy and reluctant to shout or honk the horn for fear of waking the neighbors. Hyper as always, Ari was thrilled to at last have something to do after waiting so long for someone, anyone, to awaken in the house. When the car was finally ready my father slipped it into reverse gear, looked in the rearview mirror, and saw my brother still dancing on the driveway.

Getting out of the garage was tough because you had to back up a little, then turn the wheel and drive forward a few feet to get the car on the proper angle to roll down the driveway. My father made the first move, all right, but when he put it in drive to ease it forward, the rear wheel hit a patch of ice. He tapped the accelerator a bit, and before he realized what was happening, the car had lurched forward and smashed into the back wall of the garage. The car did not stop until the wall had been knocked off the concrete slab foundation.

Once he made sure that the garage was not going to collapse, my father grabbed a short piece of two-by-four lumber and chased Ari, shouting mortal threats. The accident may not have been Ari's fault, but his antics had distracted my father, and his hyperactivity was always a trip wire for my father's tension. Once again, Ari escaped any real physical punishment, but he did get the kind of lecture that passed for punishment in our house.

If you transgressed inside the family you were supposed to own up to it, take responsibility, and acknowledge the harm you had done to another person. As young children, we brothers were also required to literally kiss and make up after any grievous conflict. We generally hated doing this, and put a lot of effort into finding ways to say we were sorry, which satisfied our mother, but communicated that we really did not mean it.

.....

The thing that bothered us the most was losing esteem in the eyes of our mother and father. Having a parent say something like "I'm so disappointed in you" is a big deal in a close family that counts character as the highest value. We were never "grounded" or punished by having money withheld. Still, my parents had their limits, especially when outside authorities were involved, and they eventually reached the point where they believed a little suffering might do us some good.

Consider what happened to Ari on a summer night in 1974 when he and his friends rode their bikes to the Turnstyle shopping center. A little context helps. At the time the nation was being swept by the "streaking" fad, which involved individuals or groups of people—usually they were college students—running naked through public places, like the Yale library. Maybe people were blowing off steam after a decade or so of serious political strife or perhaps it was just one of those quirky, unexplainable crazes like swallowing goldfish that began with a few isolated events and then spread across the country. Whatever the cause, exposing oneself was *the* thing to do. The trouble was that the driver Ari decided to bless with the sight of his naked ass was a plainclothes police officer in an unmarked car. He promptly took Ari into custody, along with his bicycle, and brought him to the village police department.

By the time the cops called our house my father was in bed. He grabbed the phone when it rang, and listened while the officer on the other end of the line explained the situation. My father coolly replied, "You can keep him."

His reaction wasn't just pure emotion. After countless little conflicts with his youngest, Ben Emanuel thought it might be a good idea for Ari to discover that his charm wouldn't always get him out of trouble in the real world. Eventually my parents went to bail out their wayward mooner, but not until they made him wait a while.

Although Ari was more rambunctious, I don't want to leave the impression that Rahm and I were significantly more restrained. From a very young age Rahm was notorious for testing adults, but he tended to practice this risk-taking with friends and family. The Glass brothers, whom we visited often, would marvel at the way Rahm responded to their father. Bill Glass loved to quiz us on geography and show off how much he knew. He also pestered us with half-serious comments about how women should stay in the kitchen and Nixon was a hero. Rahm would eventually say, "Fuck you, Uncle Bill" and launch into a tirade about how Mr. Glass was Archie Bunker come to life.

Rahm's use of swearwords began in earnest when he was twelve or thirteen. My mother would chastise him, but so inconsistently that it never had much effect. By the time he was in high school, he was fluent in both English and Yiddish cursing and could have held his own in the navy or at a construction site.

"One of his favorite words was *schmuck*," recalled Bruce Glass. "Rahm would always say, 'Oy, what a schmuck,' and that would get everyone arguing."

Burned into the memory of Bruce's brother Michael is a summer afternoon when his father ordered the six of us out onto his lawn to pick weeds and mow with the care and concern of the grounds crew at Wrigley Field. "He wanted us to mow twice, on the diagonal, and to get every dandelion and leaf of crabgrass out," explained Michael. "Rahm would protest, saying, 'I'm not your kid. I don't work for you!' He would do a sit-in at the house, saying he wouldn't work on a non-union job site and that my father was practicing taxation without representation."

The Emanuel family's loose regard for authority helps explain my own adolescent run-in with the police at the park. The pavilion at Ravinia, a few suburbs north of Wilmette, accommodates more than three thousand people. Some pay for stadium-style seats, which are arranged in a semicircle before the stage. Behind these seats, separated by a low fence, a big lawn dotted with trees offers space for people like the Emanuels, who were happy to spread out a blanket to eat a picnic dinner and hear the music for a few bucks apiece.

Ravinia is beautifully landscaped. The trees that border the picnic grounds twinkle with white lights during evening events. They also offer a terrific view of the stage, which is why I climbed one of them on a night our parents brought us to see Joni Mitchell.

Naturally, the security staff was not too keen on adolescents climbing the trees. When a police officer ordered me down I first ignored him and then protested his order rather loudly. From my adult perspective I can see that my resistance was juvenile but also completely characteristic. My brothers and I naturally pushed limits and challenged the powerful even when in the wrong. I knew that the local police would be reluctant to arrest a white kid from the suburbs. But as cocky and obnoxious as I was, I eventually bowed to my parents' impatience and the officer's discomfort, and climbed down.

Eleven

TIME OF TURMOIL

"We don't hire your type."

Out in the world we discovered the exceptions to the Emanuel rules. This happened one summer afternoon when Arnie Grant and I hopped on our bicycles and rode to the Indian Hill Country Club. As the crow flies, the club was less than two miles from our Locust Road house. In terms of culture, tradition, and status it was on another planet.

We had heard that a kid might earn as much as five dollars per round working as a caddie there. Of course, neither Arnie nor I knew the first thing about golf, but as an Emanuel brother, I did not think this lack of experience mattered.

When we reached the imposing whitewashed clubhouse we were met by a tanned, square-shouldered man in a golfer's uniform of plaid pants and a short-sleeved, cotton piqué shirt. We rolled to a stop and in our most formal and eager voices, asked if the club might need some new boys to be caddies for the summer.

"There are no openings," he said.

When we asked if there was a waiting list he said, "We don't hire your type."

By "type" he meant Jews.

Although it was hidden, anti-Semitism was at that time standard operating procedure at the Indian Hill Country Club. This was the time when many people did not consider Jews to be equal American citizens. A significant percentage of Americans in all social strata felt comfortable spouting all sorts of bigotry. This point was clearly illustrated when historians released tapes of then-president Nixon disparaging black, Irish, Italian, and Jewish Americans. He considered Jews to be a people with "a very aggressive and abrasive and obnoxious personality." The recordings were made in early 1973, after Arnie and I were rejected by the Indian Hill club.

Was the guardian of decorum who turned us away a true anti-Semite? It's hard to say. What I do know is that he was paid to maintain a status quo that made the members feel at ease, which meant not having to rub shoulders with Jews and not having to worry about making a racist joke or comment. He did his job well, dismissing us with a look that made us speed away and never try again.

The painful reality of discrimination at Indian Hill was, for me, a lesson in the limits of my ability to get what I wanted based on merit, and of my rights as an American. Then, as now, private clubs could discriminate against those they considered to be the wrong "type," however it's defined. Although I could regard this as a sign of ignorance and immorality, it was not illegal. Indeed, American history is, in part, the story of one new "type" after another—Jews, Irish, Italians, Asians, Hispanics, gays—suffering exclusion and rejection but eventually gaining acceptance by the majority culture.

As the Big Bangah and my mother showed us through example, politics was one place where America offered a chance for almost anyone to play a role. Once we were old enough to walk door-to-door without complaining too much about getting tired, our mother began bringing us with her to ring doorbells and hand out literature.

At the start of 1968 our mother's main political concern was the Vietnam War, which President Johnson seemed unable to win on the battlefield. More than twenty thousand Americans had died in the fighting and every male over the age of eighteen was subject to the draft. The first presidential candidate to say he would immediately negotiate an end to the war was Minnesota senator Eugene McCarthy. The promise won my mother's support and mobilized great numbers of people who helped him win a stunning 42 percent of the vote in conservative New Hampshire's first-in-the-nation Democratic Party primary. Robert Kennedy then jumped into the race, which split the anti-LBJ forces in half.

With the Wisconsin primary next we went north with our mother for another lesson in democracy. We pinned McCarthy buttons to our coats and joined groups of students who went door-to-door distributing literature. Few people can say they actually enjoy receiving canvassers at their door. But the presence of a child or two can impose an extra level of civility on these encounters or break the ice to start a conversation, and we understood that we were there mainly to serve as props. Our labor also meant that a few hundred packets of paper could be hung on doorknobs each day and there were times when we actually had fun running from house to house.

Then, on Sunday, March 31, all the television networks suspended their normal broadcasts to air a speech by the president. We sat with our parents to hear President Johnson announce that he would not seek reelection. As he spoke, the weary, long-faced LBJ seemed the picture of a defeated leader.

McCarthy won in Wisconsin and for a moment it seemed like he would fight Kennedy one-on-one. Then Vice President Hubert Humphrey offered himself as a sort of compromise candidate. After Robert Kennedy was assassinated in June on the night of the California primary, which he won, it became apparent that the nomination would be decided in August in the smoke-filled rooms of the national convention in Chicago. In June, we went to Israel and read about the historic debacle in *Newsweek*.

During the convention, antiwar protesters, young men and women with long hair, staged legal rallies where they were attacked by elements of an eighteen-thousand-man force, which Mayor Daley had mobilized for security. An independent commission later established that police had provoked the ensuing battle, which it described as a "police riot." The commission concluded that officers had beaten scores of peaceful citizens and had specifically targeted journalists for assault. With the world watching on television, all that troubled the country was visible in stark relief.

In Tel Aviv, Israelis asked us questions about the level of political strife in our country and the conduct of the Chicago police, as if we were experts in these topics. We were home in plenty of time to witness Nixon's narrow defeat of Humphrey in the general election.

The aftermath of the convention included a kind of show trial in which a group of defendants who came to be known as "the Chicago Seven" were prosecuted in federal court on charges including conspiracy and crossing state lines to incite a riot. Among the defendants were Abbie Hoffman, Jerry Rubin, and Tom Hayden. The judge in the case, Julius Hoffman, struggled to keep order in the court as the accused continually disrupted the proceedings with shouts of "bullshit" and insults directed at the judge and prosecutor. He overreacted by issuing extra-long contempt-of-court sentences against all of the defendants and their lawyers.

Our friend and former neighbor, the newspaperman John Downs, covered the trial and considered it such a travesty of justice that he was finally won over to my mother's critique of the American political system. A six-month proceeding ended in a mixed verdict and all the convictions were eventually overturned on appeal. Through it all we received insider details from Downs, and pored over press reports. But even when the defendants were convicted on some of the counts we never felt like the cause we shared with them—calling out injustice and the abuse of power—was truly lost.

It may seem strange to read of boys who were ten, eleven, and thirteen acting out of conscience, but given our parents we did think of ourselves as actors, albeit part of the supporting cast, in a huge national political drama. My first published letter to the editor, which appeared in the *Chicago Tribune* in early 1970, dealt with what were then alleged atrocities perpetrated by U.S. troops at a Vietnamese village called My Lai. I was thirteen years old.

In our family, politics and current events were the subject of constant conversation and, more important, action, which is why Rahm was able to hold his own with Bill Glass when the latter went into Archie Bunker mode. It also explains how we all knew, immediately, that the killing of four protesters in early May 1970 by Ohio National Guardsmen at Kent State University was a watershed moment.

Kent State made something snap inside many Americans, who decided they had to do something to protest. For us it meant joining our mother as she drove to Evanston to participate for four days in what would become a historic protest that shut down Northwestern University.

When we got to the campus students had already voted to strike and built four mock graves, with headstones, to call attention to the four students slain at Kent State. They had also barricaded Sheridan Road, which cut through the campus and was the main north/south route linking the wealthy North Shore suburbs to Chicago's downtown and financial center. If nothing else, the barricades would force the powerful lawyers, executives, and bankers who commuted on Sheridan to recognize the protesters' outrage over the Kent State killings, the Vietnam War, and the imperial presidency of Richard Nixon.

News reporters were working the barricades when my mother, Rahm, Ari, and I arrived to spend the better part of twenty-four hours, which included naps on the university lawn, standing with the students who sang songs, waving flags decorated with peace symbols, and blocking traffic in both directions. A bonfire was lit, and from time to time someone threw something symbolic into the flames. This was the era of burned draft cards, so this routine was almost to be expected. According to the *Chicago Tribune,* one young man from our village of Wilmette tossed in his New Trier High School diploma and his Boy Scout cap.

After we left, the Northwestern protest continued with performances of protest songs and a memorial service for the Kent State dead. The hard-core protesters, who wore red armbands and waved red flags, manned the blockade for about a week. We visited the blockade from time to time and noticed the crowd and enthusiasm dwindling, although the fortifications were improved by young men who used pickaxes and shovels to dig up asphalt and concrete and add it to the pile. On the other hand, the commuters who were inconvenienced got a little more upset every day. Evanston City Hall was flooded with complaints and every so often someone would drive up to the barricade, get out of his or her car, and try to argue for an end to the protest and a return to normal traffic flow.

These encounters marked some of the few moments when regular citizens on both sides of the debate over issues like Vietnam met face-to-face. One especially poignant exchange was reported in the *Tribune* by a young journalist named Philip Caputo, who had served in Vietnam as a marine and would become famous in 1977 with the publication of a memoir called *Rumors of War.* In 1970 Caputo reported what happened when "a burly man in working clothes" climbed on the barricade and tried to wrest an American flag out of the hands of a younger man whose long hair was "blowing in the wind."

In the encounter that unfolded the older man was pushed aside as he explained that he had "fought for" the flag and insisted that the protesters had "no right to it." They fell into a heated discussion in which the students tried to persuade him to join their movement because he was oppressed by the powers that be in ways that he did not understand. "I came to resist your movement!" he shouted at them. When someone in the crowd said, "You can't talk to him," the man seemed to give up. With his parting shot, however, he revealed a more personal element of his anger. As Caputo reported, he said, "And I can't talk to you. All I can see is a lot of kids blowing the chance I never had."

The idea that the student protesters did not appreciate what they had thanks to the American system they criticized so fiercely was emotionally resonant with a vast number of people who saw a generation blessed with more wealth and opportunity than any in history. The great paradox of this time of turmoil was that those who resented the long-haired strikers were correct, and so too were the protesting students. We were all living in an era of unprecedented wealth and freedom and optimism when minorities, the young, the old, and women were gaining rights and great access to power, and when there was a war on poverty. Where else would so much protest and criticism be tolerated and even sanctioned by many members of the elite? We were lucky to be living in a country that allowed us the comparative luxury of both education and free speech even as we waged a hot war in Vietnam and a Cold War against the ideology of communism.

But it was also true that change was coming too slowly for many, and that the radical critiques of our government and society often rang true. Too many people had suffered for too long as second-class citizens and blind patriotism wasn't helpful to young men in their teens and twenties who faced the prospect of being drafted to fight a war that had been losing public support at an alarming rate. In 1965 a Gallup poll found that 61 percent supported the United States sending troops to Southeast Asia. By April 1970, this number was 34 percent. Clearly a lot of mothers and fathers agreed with their children who were marching in the streets.

While these antiwar protests polarized the country and there was a significant "silent majority," as Nixon put it, who dissented, the protests activated many more people than even Occupy Wall Street has. For all the ease of today's social media, the protests of the late 1960s and early 1970s were far larger. Maybe in part this was because the relative wealth made it easier. In part it could also be that people felt much more in control of their circumstances and secure about their future. In part, it could also be that the various Web outlets—blogs, Twitter, and the like—that provide a way to virtually protest drain away the felt need to physically protest.

For us Emanuels, engaging in protests seemed a natural and reasonable option regardless of whether our side won or lost, or whether any change was even possible. Ari was so inspired by the power of the people that he and Michael Alter called for a student strike against the lunchroom at Romona Elementary School. The little agitators organized a boycott that held until their demands for lower milk prices and the addition of bagels to the menu were met. With the perspective of time it seems likely that the adults involved were very purposeful in their response. As educators they saw something to be gained in rewarding the courage and organizational skills displayed by Ari and Michael. By negotiating with kids on the basis of mutual respect, they showed themselves to be gifted and understanding teachers, and proved that our generation truly was being given, as the man at the barricades said, "a chance that I never had."

Twelve

CULTURAL STUDIES

For my father, travel was not a luxury. It was, he believed, absolutely necessary for an understanding of the world, and of oneself. When he went to Europe as a young student he discovered many things about himself—his ability to learn languages, his intellectual abilities, which had been well hidden, his leadership skills, and a remarkable capacity for adaptation and growth. With every border he crossed and every new idea he absorbed, he found himself dreaming bigger dreams—and happier. He wanted us to have the same experiences; my mother agreed. The only point of contention on the issue was Germany.

As a Jew who came of age during the Holocaust, my mother was uncomfortable with anything German, whether it was a kitchen knife or a Volkswagen car. The sound of the German language made her cringe and when travel to Europe was considered she made it clear that she would "never set foot" in Germany. My father, on the other hand, saw nothing wrong with passing through Germany on the way to Denmark if doing so saved you more than a thousand dollars on airfare to Europe.

The year was 1971 and my parents had decided that instead of going back to Israel for the summer we should see Scandinavia, particularly Denmark and Norway, countries no one in the family had been to. The cheapest way to cross the Atlantic was on Icelandair's flights to Luxemburg. Every other option to fly a family of five would have cost a fortune. Of course Germany lies between Luxemburg and Denmark, and so the only way to get from point A to point B involved a car ride across the land of my mother's nightmares.

The argument about this problem raged for days and weeks. In the end, my father offered a compromise. We would fly at cut-rate prices, rent a car at the Luxemburg airport, load it with food and drink, and speed for the Danish border, which was roughly 360 miles away. If her bladder held, Marsha Emanuel's feet would never touch German soil.

All went according to plan on the flight and after clearing customs we went to the rental car agency, where we picked up a four-door, pastel green Opel and zipped away in search of supplies. We crossed into Germany without a hitch.

Although we proceeded in silence, because of my mother's anger, the first few hours of the drive went better than expected. Near Bremen my father announced he needed to pee, stretch his legs, and eat lunch. As he slowed the car and steered to a roadside rest area, he said we could have something to eat. We four males got out of the car. Our father opened a tin of sardines, cut up some tomatoes, cucumber, cheese, and bread, and we ate.

In the front passenger seat my mother looked out the window in stony silence. When the meal ended we got back into the car. Our father told us to buckle our seat belts and reached for the ignition key. He twisted it to the start position, and nothing happened. No revving. No clickety-clack. Nothing.

He turned the key off and then switched it to the start position again. This time he pumped his foot a bit on the accelerator. Again, silence. The engine did not turn over. After some muttering about flooding the engine and a long, pregnant pause, the third attempt brought the same: nothing. As is his tendency when mechanical things go awry, Benjamin Emanuel, MD, became a shrill, flustered, panicky guy who believed that somehow the car would respond to curses and threats.

My father had absolutely no aptitude for anything related to machines of any sort. When he opened the hood of a car, he saw an incomprehensible jumble of metal, rubber, and plastic. It was an odd kind of incompetence, given his acuity in making medical diagnoses. Like human beings, cars have systems for breathing, heating, and cooling, and even a nervous system that distributes electrical signals. My father recognized none of this.

Fortunately a roadside assistance phone was available and my father managed to summon a tow truck. The mechanic diagnosed a broken starter and determined that the car would have to be towed to the nearest city, Hamburg. By the time we got there the hour was late and we were told no mechanic would be available until the morning. We would have to stay overnight. The grand compromise on foot-setting in Germany was completely abrogated.

Finding ourselves in the center of the city, there was nothing for us to do but find someplace to sleep. Holding Rahm's hand, my slightly panicked father led the rest of us to check out some of the nearby hotels. He led Rahm inside one, as my mother fumed outside with Ari and me standing near her. Inside, as Rahm would recall, a man who seemed to be a desk clerk emerged from a back room and my father immediately asked about accommodations. Rahm gazed into the bar off the lobby and noticed it was populated by several women who wore a whole lot of makeup and very little fabric. My father told the desk clerk he wanted "zwei Zimmer"—two rooms. The man behind the counter raised his eyebrows. Rahm began tugging at my father's sleeve. Anxious and frustrated, my father shushed him and explained to the clerk that one of the rooms was for "der Kinder," which meant the children. But before he agreed to pay for them, he said he wanted to check them out to see if they were suitable.

Listening to my father's strange-sounding mix of Yiddish and German, the proprietor could not make sense of my father's request. Whatever the desk man thought, he eventually decided that he was not going to accommodate my father, no matter what he asked. My father, hearing nothing but "Nein!" began to get a little panicky and impatient.

"Dad?" said Rahm again.

"Be quiet," said my father.

"But Dad!" said Rahm, more forcefully.

"I said quiet!" shouted my dad.

Finally, with Rahm again tugging at his sleeve and his eyes adjusted to the light, my father could see that he had been trying to arrange for family accommodations at a bordello. He quickly turned and steered Rahm to the door. When they returned Rahm was grinning with sheer delight and my father, knowing that my mother was already severely irritated, struggled to deflect inquiries into his faux pas.

Once we settled into a hotel, we went in search of dinner. My father always taught us that in European cities the place to purchase the maximum amount of calories for the lowest possible cost was the main train station. The Hamburg station was an elegant old hall with a second-floor dining room overlooking the concourse. But we noticed none of it as we navigated the hall. Furious, my mother was silent and so were we. Eventually a waiter dressed in a black suit and white shirt brought us menus. My father used his pidgin German to order for us.

Sometime in the middle of the meal, a voice came over the loudspeaker to announce a train departure. "Achtung! Achtung!" My mother's face turned white. In unison we dropped our forks, rose from our chairs, and hustled out of the station restaurant. Our collective reaction, more a reflex than anything conscious, reminded me how deep this anti-German feeling had been instilled in us.

Indeed, I didn't return to Germany until the mid-1990s, when I was invited to present to a medical ethics conference and my rabbi at Harvard Hillel, himself a Holocaust survivor, insisted that I go to contribute to the flourishing of humanistic thought in Germany. There I was pleasantly surprised to find many people, from the middle-aged academics to graduate students, more open and apologetic about the Holocaust, and genuinely interested in my views as a Jew. In my experience—and to their credit—the Germans had engaged in a serious and reflective engagement with their culpability for my people's deaths.

After an uneasy night in the hotel we picked up the car, which had been repaired with a new starter, and drove the short distance to the border with Denmark. There, at the crossing, Ari, Rahm, and I took special note of the many garishly decorated Danish sex shops with neon signs that invited travelers arriving from staid old Germany to come in for a good time.

.....

In the summer of 1972 my mom, Rahm, and Ari went to Israel, mainly to see the Big Bangah and Sophie, our grandmother, who had, at last, managed to emigrate and settle south of Tel Aviv in a relatively poor neighborhood of Bat Yam. I got the "privilege" of living at home with my father for most of the summer while I did high school biology during summer school. Once the course ended, my father and I would take a trip together to Europe, just the two of us.

In Wilmette my father and I became like *The Odd Couple*. As Felix to his Oscar, I did most of the cleaning and cooking, becoming quite proficient in the art of backyard grilling. For his part my dad enjoyed the peace and quiet of nights free from the sound of boys fighting, and delighted in having full control over the TV.

When all the dissection and tests of my biology course ended, my father and I flew to Luxemburg and headed for Zurich, Switzerland. Our first stop would be at the home of Albert Richter, a physician my dad had known during his residency at Mount Sinai in Chicago. A religious Jew, Albert had depended on my dad to cover for him on Saturdays. This little arrangement helped them become close friends. In the late 1950s, Dr. Richter, a pediatrician, had returned to his home country to practice.

Following my father's method, we traveled without a detailed plan and instead just stopped to take in interesting sights. As the sun began to go down we looked for a room with breakfast. My father always asked for just one bed, which we shared. He would call me "the propeller" because of my constant tossing and turning, which interrupted his slumber. Mind you, he was never bothered enough to pay for two beds.

Naturally, Oscar and Felix got on each other's nerves from time to time. We bickered for hours during a drive from the French Riviera to Milan, where my father insisted we go see the great Gothic cathedral. Luck allowed us to reach the center of the city and park right next to the cathedral. My father ordered me to grab the camera and we hopped out of the car, locked our doors, and slammed them shut. In an instant my dad realized that he had left the keys in the ignition switch—with the car running. Since we had just topped-off the tank before entering Milan it could probably idle like that for half a day or more.

"Watch the camera!" my father shouted at me, his voice rising with panic.

He dashed across a wide boulevard and into a nearby department store, where the clerks were closing for their lunch break and afternoon naps. Crazed, my father grabbed two clothes hangers and ran out without paying for them. When he returned to the curb he paused for a moment to catch his breath and then proceeded, in his clumsy way, to fashion one of them into a long hook that might be snaked through the rubber gasket that sealed the car door.

Unfortunately the car was very well sealed and the wire was too thick and inflexible. As he struggled, my father—in his semi-panic and buried annoyance at himself—alternately explained what he was doing and shouted at me to find some way to help him.

Not surprisingly, my mechanically challenged father was not able to negotiate the hanger trick. Nevertheless, his antics did attract a veritable United Nations of onlookers, including Italians, Germans, French, North Africans, Swiss, and even an Israeli couple. Each one of these observers offered advice encapsulating their national character. For instance, the Italian fellow kept gesturing in a way that said, "Just smash the front window." The Frenchman just slowly walked around the car examining it for a possible opportunity but never offering a useful suggestion.

After about an hour and a half, the serious German guy loosened the rubber around the vent window on the driver's-side door. I was then able to snake my thin left arm inside to unlock the door. With the crowd laughing and applauding my father shouted at me, "Get in!"

When we were both seated in the car he turned the key to the off position and silenced the motor. He then started the car again and put it in gear and hastily pulled out of the treasured parking spot.

"Where are we going?" I inquired in a puzzled way, since we had not entered the cathedral.

"Lake Como," he said, making it clear we weren't going to see the inside of the Milan cathedral no matter how majestic it was.

.....

About that name—Jonny. It wasn't until I saw the invitations my parents prepared for my bar mitzvah that I discovered my full name. As my mother explained, the name Ezekiel had belonged to my father's father, who died two years before I was born. She also told me that she did not like the sound of Ezekiel as a baby's name and that she had called me Jonny to spare me unnecessary teasing in America.

This explanation made sense on some levels, but was incoherent on others. For one thing, she wasn't at all concerned about teasing when she sent us to ballet lessons. Moreover, she had named her subsequent kids Rahm and Ariel—hardly sparing them teasing because of their unusual names. Rahm especially encountered problems as people would pronounce it Ram or Ron and, after being corrected, derisively ask, "What kind of name is *that*?" What became obvious to me was that the paramount consideration had always been her personal preference. She always loved the name Jonathan, and Ezekiel represented the tense relationship with her mother-in-law. But now I had the power to decide for myself.

The Ezekiel of the Bible was a prophet to the Israelites in exile in Babylon. He had railed against sin, called his people to faith, and predicted the rise of a new Jerusalem. This was inspiring, but my decision was also guided by the rebelliousness of adolescence. It would be Ezekiel. Understanding that everyone in Wilmette knew me as Jon or Jonny, I wasn't going to ask everyone to immediately call me something else. Instead I registered for high school classes using the name Ezekiel, and I began writing Ezekiel Jonathan Emanuel on my papers at school. And when high school teachers tried to pronounce Ezekiel, I quickly corrected them and said they could call me Jon or Jonathan.

I finally completed the change when I entered college and no one, except one senior, knew me from high school. Eventually, Ezekiel was shortened to Zeke.

The preparation for my bar mitzvah gave me the time and opportunity to consider my identity. Roughly translated, *bar mitzvah* means "son of commandment" and marks the moment when a Jewish boy becomes responsible for his own adherence to the Torah. Bar mitzvah rites are often mocked and people love to tell stories about the excessive celebrations and the nervous children with squeaky voices reciting portions of the Torah in mangled Hebrew with little or no understanding of what they're saying. But something in me longed for a deeper experience. In part I think this was because my Torah portion comes at the very end of the Bible—it is one of the three "endings"—and is one of the few in the Bible that is written in two columns of poetry and contains a warning and promise to the nation of Israel about how to live.

Our temple offered basic bar mitzvah preparation from a tutor who was knowledgeable and sincere, but focused only on teaching each student how to recite the prayers and his portion of scripture. These study sessions did not provide—nor were they intended to provide—any intellectual insights into the texts or explorations of any existential questions about Judaism. I was vocal and angry about my dissatisfaction with this rote learning of my Torah and Haftorah portions. Deep down I was probably expressing frustration at the fact that I had a horrible voice and—thanks to my mom—could not carry a tune. But I was also frustrated by learning meaningless words in a foreign language without the opportunity to use my brain to figure out what they really meant. I demanded that I stop these vacuous lessons and that we find a bar mitzvah tutor who would do Bible study with me. We were too close to the bar mitzvah, and I had too much to learn to change courses. But my parents agreed to help me find some Bible instruction—after the bar mitzvah was done. In the meantime I buckled down to memorize my portion, and made do with some special encouragement from the Big Bangah.

Grandfather Herman supported me with a symbolic tribute that irritated him but thrilled me. My wish was for him to stop shaving. I liked the way he looked in a beard. It softened his face and made him seem sage-like and more approachable. He didn't like the way it felt on his face or looked in the mirror. Grudgingly, however, he grew the bushy white beard for me.

Around this time, the Big Bangah and our grandmother Sophie moved into my father's study, but not quite by choice. Herman had yearned to live in Israel for some time. He talked about it often, though we were still surprised when he abruptly sold his business, canceled the lease on the apartment he shared with our grandmother, and disposed of most of their belongings.

"It's time," he announced. "We're going to Israel."

There was only one small problem: As a young boy Herman had come to America with no official papers. Once he arrived he never tried to go abroad. So, while he worked, paid his taxes, had a driver's license, and a Social Security number, he never obtained a passport. But without documentary proof of his citizenship he was, technically, an illegal immigrant and could not get a passport. Without a passport, he and Sophie could not emigrate. When he found out about these obstacles, Herman, having made himself homeless by giving up his apartment and selling its contents, decided his only option was to move in with us on Locust Road.

The resolution of Herman's immigration status would require two years of waiting and, ultimately, the intervention of Congressman Sid Yates, who was both Jewish and a Democrat. But even with Yates on the case, the bureaucracy moved slowly. In the meantime, my grandfather's fuzzy face brought tears to my eyes when I spoke at my bar mitzvah. And the moment the service and party were over, Herman's beard disappeared down the drain, never to return.

.....

A year or so after my bar mitzvah, a young Bible student came to Wilmette at the invitation of Rabbi Frankel to serve as a kind of scholar in residence at an old farmhouse with peeling paint that was owned by our congregation, Am Yisrael. For nearly a year Danny

Siegel had a twice-weekly 6 A.M. appointment with me. We would study Pirkei Avot, a famous commentary on Jewish ethics. After these lessons I would cross the road to New Trier West for pre-class swim team practice.

My mother, who thoroughly enjoyed her sleep, qualified for some kind of medal of honor by driving me to these early morning appointments. My study session required that she rise at 5:30 A.M. When she got home after dropping me off there was no chance that she could recover lost sleep—my father and brothers would be dressing, eating breakfast, and getting ready for the day in their "quiet" way. To her credit, my mother did this for a whole academic year with very little complaint.

Danny and I immersed ourselves in Jewish theology and philosophy. Up to that point I didn't know what it meant to really work with a text, striving to unearth all its meanings and context. But with Danny I explored the historical meaning of the words, the literary choices made by the writers, the precedents for the arguments made in a passage, and the implications the words had for the way people of any age, from antiquity to modern times, struggled to live good and moral lives.

I recall one particular morning when we pored over Pirkei Avot and *A Book of Jewish Concepts,* by Philip Birnbaum. "Start reading where we left off last week," Danny said as he walked around the kitchen bundled up in his red plaid dressing gown and sipping his tea. We were somewhere in chapter 3. I took a sip of tea, cleared my throat, and found the right spot in the text.

"Rabbi Akiva used to say: 'Everything is foreseen, yet the freedom of choice is given. The world is judged with goodness, and everything depends on the abundance of mitzvoth.'"

"So what does that mean? How can it be that everything is foreseen and yet you have freedom?" Danny was just asking the obvious question, but the answer was hardly obvious to me, barely fourteen years of age.

"I guess if God is God then He must be able to see everything. Nothing is out of his control, power, or knowledge. But because we are not God, all we see are possibilities and we have to choose among them." I stumbled around like this for a few more back-and-forths with Danny. He then moved on.

"What are mitzvoth? And why does everything depend upon them?"

"Good deeds."

"Look it up."

Here Danny was teaching me to closely and critically examine how words were used, and always have multiple books open when I studied philosophy. I opened the *Book of Jewish Concepts* to the section on mitzvoth and started reading: "In the plural, the term *mitzvoth* signifies specific commands contained in the Torah. In Talmudic terminology, *mitzvoth* is the general term for the divine commandments, computed to be 613." I read on: "*Mitzvoth* is another word for charity. It refers to any particular opportunity to fulfill the comprehensive duty of men toward their fellow men."

Danny kept pressing me about the importance of charity, following commandments, duties to other people, and freedom. "See, in the Jewish tradition, there is no tension between freedom and duty or following commandments. For Jews, freedom is not just doing what you want. Akiva wants you to think differently about freedom."

It was approaching 7 A.M. and Danny told me to gather up my books. He knew I had early morning swim practice at school, which was across the street.

"While you are swimming, think about why Akiva says that everything depends upon mitzvoth. Why doesn't it depend upon faith in God? We are now getting to the heart of what you wanted to know about Jewish tradition. See you Thursday morning."

I put on my puffy orange down coat and walked across the street to my high school, thinking about Danny's questions. The answers wouldn't come immediately, but over time I came to understand that for Jews faith was secondary to practice. It turned out that not believing was no excuse for not doing; even Orthodox Jews could be expected to have a loss of faith, but that did not relieve them of the duty to follow the mitzvoth. This is the part of the Jewish tradition that seemed to have animated my grandfather as well as my mother and father. None of them were believers as far as I could tell; none had a spiritual bone in their bodies; but all seemed impelled to do mitzvoth, which they demonstrated in their public and personal activism. Protest against injustice is a mitzva and so is sounding an alarm about lead paint. These acts aren't about faith in God, or satisfying the ego, they are about caring for others—in a Jewish kind of way. Later in life Rahm, Ari, and I would all fight for public policies and ideas that we believed would benefit all. When we fought to be leaders in academics, politics, and business some would see ego and little else. But anyone who knew how we were raised, in our family and our religious faith, would know there was more to it. We didn't fight so hard—and take so many criticisms—just for ego satisfaction. Somehow, we all feel obligated to do good. Indeed, when interviewed for a story about my work, a reporter asked why I do what I do, especially when I have been subjected to so much criticism as Dr. Death and head of the death panels. I looked at her in a puzzled way, thinking that trying to make the world better doesn't arise from an explicit decision, it is just what I—we—have to do. It is, in the old language, a calling. I wouldn't be me, Rahm wouldn't be Rahm, and Ari wouldn't be Ari if we weren't trying to make things better for our children's and grandchildren's generations.

As Danny taught me, agreement was a rare commodity in the Jewish tradition—and not particularly valued. For every sage's opinion there was another interpretation offered by an equally respected rabbi. The constant argument over scripture within the same tradition seemed, to me, to explain—at least in part—the frequent debate that took place in my family. Danny also sparked in me a great appreciation for what scriptures teach and he helped me imagine an academically oriented life.

Like me, Rahm and Ari were given big bar mitzvah parties with dancing, food, and drink. It was the seventies so the music at these events ran from British Invasion to Motown, and the snapshots of us wearing matching paisley bell-bottoms are proof that no one with any fashion sense made any effort to dissuade us from our efforts to be as cool as we could be. The arrangements for these celebrations varied depending on economic condition. Mine included a lunch for family and adult friends at a restaurant and a party with pizza and records at the school gym for my classmates. By the time of Rahm's big day, my father was making more money and so Rahm got a Saturday night hotel dinner banquet that combined family and friends, and a band that played well into the night.

Rahm's bar mitzvah was also the occasion for one of the more unsettling incidents of our time in Wilmette. During the synagogue service, which was held in the auditorium of a local grade school (our synagogue still lacked its own building), a young man opened the door and screamed some anti-Semitic curses at the crowd. As the guy fled, some of the men in attendance chased him. They caught him outside and held him until an older man who walked with a cane ordered them to leave.

"He said he wanted to talk to him," recalled Rahm, years later. "But everyone knew that the old man abused his own kids and would abuse anyone else who crossed him."

Today, my reaction to the incident Rahm recalled is complex. The response of the men there, who wanted to catch the offender, may have been reassuring to those who felt violated and vulnerable. But what can be learned from their decision to turn a blind eye and leave him with a man who was known for brutalizing his own kids? The men at the temple may have felt justified, but in the long run their behavior cannot be construed as anything but dark.

.....

As we brothers reached our bar mitzvahs we remained, for the most part, the same kids we had always been. Soon enough, however, the self-consciousness that comes with adolescence would make us each rebel at least a little. We began withholding parts of ourselves, retreating from the free-flowing conversation that once held every day together in our home and seeking, instead, privacy and the counsel of friends and adults outside the family. This kind of withdrawal is normal and marks a young adult's effort to become a distinct individual.

However, it was something our mother resisted. She did not want us to stop telling her about our feelings, our relationships, our daily successes and failures.

"Why can't we talk about what's going on with you?" she would say. "I feel like I don't know you anymore."

Her feeling of loss and bewilderment was made worse by the fact that our friends and cousins, especially the boys who had been like fourth brothers, continued to trust her with their deepest and most tender truths. If they could open up to her, she fretted, why couldn't her own sons? With both sadness and anger in her voice she would ask, "What has happened?"

Nothing specific had happened, but everything was changing because we had started to become young men and we needed to begin separating from her and the family and establish our own identities. We did not confide in her as teens for the same reason that we trusted her as little boys: *She was our mother.* As I learned with my own daughters, this is the painful paradox all devoted parents, and especially mothers, must confront one day. The job of being a good parent is inevitably terminal. If you do it well and make your kids confident and ambitious, they eventually grow—must grow—away from you. In those teenage years, when they are trying to become their own people, it's especially difficult. Your kids simultaneously push you away—needing space to explore on their own—and yet still need you in so many ways. It's even harder if you're like my mother and your entire being is wrapped up in being a parent. In the empty silence you are challenged to find a new purpose.

Thirteen

ADOLESCENT REBELLION

"Zeke, you really left the family when you were about fourteen," says Ari. "That's when you started to leave, at least."

"And if there was any sibling rivalry it wasn't after college. It was when we were all living at home," says Rahm.

It's Fourth of July at a waterfront house in Rhode Island and we brothers—all middle-aged men—are gathered around a table on the back porch reminiscing, disagreeing about the details of events, and arguing about our childhood and adolescence. Amid the teasing "Fuck yous" and the ripples of laughter we compare our competing versions of the Emanuel family story.

Rahm, ever the politician, insists that "all the events" we recall are "true" but insists that if we are open-minded we "could give another take on it" when it comes time for making judgments.

Many people might be surprised to hear that of all the brothers it is Ari, who was so manic as a kid, who is most thoughtful and deeply psychological in his approach to life. Indeed, it is because of his struggles as a kid that he has deeply felt empathy for every player in the family drama, including our father, whom he drove crazy, and our mother, whom, he says, "I always love but sometimes don't like." In his eyes, she had been tortured by the way our grandfather Herman withheld his affirmation. "He never really respected her," he explains. "She was always trying to achieve in his eyes and he never gave her his approval."

Exactly.

The Big Bangah, who had been rejected by the machashaifeh when he came to America, had been hard on his own children. Like just about every immigrant father who intends to give his offspring something better than his own childhood, Herman Smulevitz was only able to make so much progress. Having been abandoned by his own father, he had no reference point for what it takes to be a good one. But he did know that life could be a cruel affair and one had better be prepared. To this end, he tried to make his children tough. He did this by withholding his approval, pointing out the deficiencies they needed to address, and demanding that they develop skins so thick that even the most cutting remarks would not draw blood. Under some circumstances, Sophie, my grandmother, might offer her children comfort, but she would not take a firm stand against the callousness and sarcasm Herman directed at his children. She feared him, too.

Our mother would never forget the gruff way she was treated by her father, but she was even more disturbed by the way Herman treated his sons. They may have been favored over her when it came to education, but decades later she still cringed when she recalled how he disciplined them for merely being high-spirited boys. This harsh treatment trimmed my uncles' sails, and they never were able to feel supported for being themselves. This outcome seems even sadder when you realize that the man who undermined those boys was a vigorous, can-do kind of person who should have inspired them to be commanding personalities. This was the Big Bangah as my brothers and I were lucky enough to experience him—energetic, engaging, and encouraging. As his grandchildren, we felt his warmth, and very much wanted him to know about—and affirm—our successes. And we usually received that affirmation—along with a loving smack.

When the time came for her to raise a family, our mother was determined to do better. Still wounded by her father's neglect, she would set aside any ambitions she had for herself in order to focus her time, intellect, energy, and spirit on her children. She considered it her duty to master the modern art of motherhood and give her boys the best possible start in life. And, because the move out of the city of Chicago to Wilmette deprived her of her ability to fulfill her political ambitions, more of her sense of personal worth was wrapped up in our lives than is probably healthy.

But because she was a human being and not a saint, our mother expected—perhaps even needed—affection and appreciation from her family as compensation for her effort. The part of her that so hungered for rewards was, of course, the girl who never got them growing up.

Her need for affirmation was enormous. And because it was based on losses that were long in the past—which we did not and could not grasp—it was impossible for us to fill. As a result of these misplaced expectations, she was always disappointed by the holidays, vacations, and birthday and anniversary celebrations that were supposed to make her happy. No matter what her husband or sons tried she felt disappointed, cheated, and ultimately angry.

Although she generally kept them at bay, the inner grief and anger our mother acquired as a child lurked beneath the sarcasm she often flashed in conversation and in the depressed mood that could grip her for days on end. In searching for an antidote for her unhappiness she often fixed on what she was "owed" as payment for the time she had invested and the personal dreams and ambitions she had sacrificed for us. The price she had paid was obvious and included forgoing her own education and political ambitions and leaving her beloved Chicago for the suburbs. But these choices were not the ultimate source of her obvious belief that she had been treated unfairly by life. That sense of injustice was born much earlier, in her own childhood, which was as insecure as ours was safe and as constrained as ours was privileged.

Indeed, it was the stark contrast between her own experience and ours that explained the depth of our mother's resentments. Every moment she spent watching us grow up and explore the world in freedom and security, the child inside my mother was reminded of her own experience of deprivation. It was not fair that she had been so deprived as a girl and on some level she must have felt sorely cheated by life. The drive for fairness is so deeply ingrained in human beings, and essential to our social nature, that it has been reinforced by natural selection. It certainly helps explain both why my mother readily joined protesters and why she was continually looking for validation from us.

These were not unreasonable expectations, unless you consider that she was relying on some very imperfect fellows to deliver them. Everyday love and affection were no problem, especially when we were young. But lurking in the background remained this sense that we weren't accomplishing enough to affirm her efforts. I got very good grades in school. Rahm was a gifted and dedicated dancer. Ari would show his grit as he adapted to his dyslexia and, later, as a successful athlete. But none of us were "the best" in our grade or high school class at anything—even at getting in trouble. In any case, a child's performance inside or outside the family should not be used as a measure of a mother's success in life. What constitutes an adequate acknowledgment for her efforts?

As we grew older we became frustrated with our own failure to make her happy. Her disappointment, tearfully expressed, made us dread the march of the calendar and feel both guilty and, since guilt works this way, angry about feeling guilty, and about the excessive importance she attached to events like Mother's Day and anniversaries.

Our mother's high standards also sparked resentment as we got older. Try as she did to be different than Herman, she could not do it in every way. For instance, while she loved us unconditionally, we were never able to rest on the laurels of our achievements for more than a millisecond.

Straight A's on your report card, Jonny?

Great. Now what are you doing about the big project due in two weeks?

A victory on the wrestling mat, Ari?

Good going. Now, how are you doing in math?

A standing ovation for a dance recital, Rahm?

Wonderful. Why can't you turn some of those B's into A's?

Besides her demands for performance, our mother also clung to us even as we reached an age when we needed to separate from her. "I was extremely proud of them," she once said about her sons. "I was in love with them."

From an adult perspective it's easy to see how hard it must have been for her to let go of her role—her vocation, really—as a mother. I don't think it's possible to invest more in the mother-child bond than my mother invested. We were her life's focus. As we inevitably pulled away, the pain must have been terrible. I suspect she also feared what we would do if we had full control of our own lives. Adults understand the depth of trouble that waits in the real world. Fortunately or unfortunately, wild teenage boys do not.

I did not try to break my mother's hold until I was into my first year in high school. The transformative moment came when, in the fall of my freshman year, she accompanied me to a folk-rock concert held at my school's auditorium. Seated beside her, in a sea of my fellow students, I got the queasy sensation every teenager feels when he realizes, a moment too late, that he has revealed himself to be a dork.

In that moment, I understood that I would have to push back in order to separate from my mother and father. I gradually but inexorably stopped being open about my feelings and my experiences, and started to spend more and more time out of the house with my school friends.

When their turns came, Ari and Rahm would make the same push for independence, letting go of their own close relationship with our mother and connecting to friends at New Trier West. Rahm, who played soccer for a year, would count a few athletes in his group but stuck mainly with creative types in the theater department and some of the free spirits who attended a so-called alternative program within the regular school. Ari became the boy who knew just about everyone in his high school class but was closest to old friends from our neighborhood and his lacrosse and wrestling teammates. I gravitated toward a crowd of kids who, it turned out, were not much different from me. They were nerds who clustered on the debate team and filled advance science and math classes.

.....

When I arrived at New Trier West High School I set myself on a course to be the top nerd in the class. I also was a little bit of a hippie, growing my hair to my shoulders, and wearing jeans and an army jacket decorated by my artistic cousin Gary with beautiful peace symbols on the back and slogans like "Hell no we won't go" all around. On my feet were a pair of brown Earth Shoes.

Despite having the look of a counterculture kid, I never drifted to the drug scene that was such a part of the 1970s. In the mind of an Emanuel, anything wildly popular is almost by definition worthy of suspicion and probably rejection. This was certainly the case with drugs. When it came to alcohol, I was always afraid of acting the way kids did when they got drunk. I was a control freak and feared what would happen if I was not fully aware and controlling things.

Trite as it might sound, our days were so filled with academics, sports, and extracurricular activities, those distractions just weren't on our radar. New Trier West never allowed me the idle time. The anti-Semites who gerrymandered the district in order to send the growing number of Jewish kids to a new school on the west side of the district didn't want the New Trier name sullied by a second-rate spin-off. So, as Rahm would later say, New Trier was probably the only district in the country where people taxed themselves heavily to send "those people" they did not want their own kids to mix with to a gorgeous school that ranked at the top of all high schools in the country. Indeed, Robert Kennedy spoke at the opening ceremony of New Trier West.

The workings of the place depended in part on something they called the advisory system, which assigned a classroom of students—all males or all females—to a single teacher who would serve as academic coach, personal mentor, and sounding board for their entire four years of high school. These "advisories" were more than traditional homeroom assignments. The teachers were required to visit their students' homes, and meet with their parents or guardians, on a regular basis. They were also the key players on faculty teams set up to detect and address problems that arose for individual students and set the rolls for different courses.

My advisor was the head football coach, Robert Naughton. He also taught mathematics. Initially I regarded him as a stereotype, the kind of muscle-bound guy who wouldn't care about politics and would see me only as a scrawny, long-haired loudmouth. I was partly wrong. Bob Naughton did care about politics. He was a pro-Nixon, pro–Vietnam War conservative who believed American business was the cornerstone of society. We would spend four years arguing over everything from war and peace to taxes and the environment.

Placed in the top academic track at New Trier, I met a group of supercompetitive students who would have a lifelong influence on me. We had a strong academic bent, and paid a little less attention to the usual obsessions of adolescence like fashion, sports, and pop culture. The one exception to this rule, for me, was a car I purchased in my junior year shortly after getting my license.

It wasn't just any car. It was an olive green Volvo 122 stick shift with 130,000 miles on it "but no serious problems," according to the advertisement in the Chicago *Reader*. The asking price was three hundred dollars. Ari and I took cash from my bank account—my bar mitzvah money—and took the Chicago L to check it out. To some eyes it was ugly. To mine it was peculiar, but in a good way. I had seen Volvos during my family's trips to Europe and I thought they were pretty cool. And I learned how to drive a stick shift right from the start, and thought they were much cooler than automatics. Ari and I were sure the price was a bargain and happily agreed to pay it. After the deal was made Ari jumped into the passenger seat and we drove it home to Wilmette. I even let Ari, who was thirteen at the time, do some of the shifting. We pulled into the driveway and honked the horn for the family.

"What are you, a schmuck?" was my father's immediate reaction when he walked out the kitchen door. "What do you want with that old thing?"

"Dad, it's almost an antique," I answered, as if the Volvo were a mint-condition Model T.

"What do you know about cars?" he inquired. "How do you know this one is any good?"

We had long understood my father's mechanical incompetence and our friend Ralph had taught us enough about cars to make us falsely confident. This explains how I wound up with a Volvo that performed nicely moving forward but whose transmission refused to go backward under its own power. No matter what we did, the car could not be put in reverse. We could get it out of the driveway by a gentle push to get it going down to the street, but this was not a long-term solution to the problem. Neither was a repair, which would cost more than the car was worth. My mother came up with the answer. She had Ralph Feldstein sell it to someone for two hundred dollars. Thus ended my fascination with cars. I wouldn't buy another one for almost ten years, and haven't owned one in more than five years.

Fortunately, the kids I hung with didn't care much about flashy cars. Instead we bonded as members of the debate team. As people say, scholastic debate is football for geeks. It's where kids who are smart, aggressive, and competitive but not necessarily strong or athletic can experience something like the aggression and camaraderie of a contact sport. The difference is that instead of bruising an opponent's body you bruise his ego, which is within the rules as long as it's done with proper style and technique. Unlike the dinner table at home, where even profanity-laced tirades were tolerated, being loud and profane actually hurt your chances in competitive debate. What works is the right combination of research and reasoning delivered confidently and persuasively, but not cruelly.

The original New Trier High School had won four state championships in thirty years. New Trier West had won twice in the six years since it had been opened. Pictures of the winners hung on the wall of the team's tiny office, and the competition for a spot on the squad, and the chance to be immortalized on the wall, was fierce.

Our debate coach, Bill Sanders, took an unconventional approach to organizing his team. Others accepted every freshman who applied and used the novice-level competitions to identify the "keepers." Sanders wouldn't let any freshmen onto the novice teams. Instead, students who were interested in debate had to enroll in academic classes in public speaking and communication. The best students from those courses tried out for the debate team and were selected to be debate team novices as sophomores. This approach meant that New Trier West's novices were one year older than their opponents, and had formal public speaking training before their first debate. Consequently, their novice year was always filled with lots of winning. The benefits of this approach continued as they joined the junior varsity and varsity squads. Add Sanders's excellent but subtle coaching and you get a program that was highly competitive year in and year out.

You might think that our devotion to academics was somehow a Jewish thing but it wasn't. Among my friends and classmates were Doug Berger, a Mormon, and Brian Ziv and Suzanne Nora, who were both Catholic. The three of them all came from families who prized achievement and they were motivated to excel at everything they tried.

In my sophomore year I won a spot on the debate team, where I began to learn the differences between arguing at the Emanuel kitchen table and a real debate. Ray Agran, my partner, and I threw ourselves into research, spending hours at the Northwestern University library. For reasons I cannot explain, I loved spending endless hours in the government documents room and reading the testimony and exchanges from congressional hearings, looking for those unexpected quotes that we could use to make our case. We filled thousands of four-by-six cards with facts and quotes. The cards went into little metal boxes. Ray—now a Philadelphia litigator—and I carried six of them into debates like they were crates of ammunition. The intention—and the effect—was to intimidate our opponents.

I further intimidated with my style, which tended toward rapid-fire attacks, plenty of quotes and statistics, and development of unexpected arguments. This approach lacked the appeal of the quiet confidence—Bill Sanders called it "QC"—that our coach tried to instill in us. When I was grown and could absorb what he had to say, Bill Sanders said, "You had an aggressiveness that wasn't mean-spirited, but it was so intense that you didn't notice how it affected other people."

To reach us, Sanders's technique was just the opposite of aggressiveness and volume. A case in point arose during my first major tournament, which was held three hundred and fifty miles from Wilmette, at Southern Illinois University. Ray Agran and I did well in our first debate. We packed up our file cards and left our room. While waiting in the hall we ran into novice debate teams from neighboring schools. We began socializing, which at debate tournaments means arguing at a high volume about which arguments are better and which sources more authoritative.

As the hallway was filled with our voices, Bill Sanders silently approached my side and firmly squeezed my arm. I was so hyped up that I continued the debate without pause. To get my attention, Sanders squeezed harder until it hurt. He said nothing but just gestured me down the hall to the New Trier West room.

"But I want to talk."

"Go to the room," he said almost in a whisper.

Annoyed, I obeyed his instructions. Sanders stayed at my side, never uttering another word. When we arrived at the room I demanded to know why we couldn't talk to the other teams. Sanders would not be drawn into arguing or negotiating. In a quiet tone he simply said, "Quiet confidence," and escorted me to a seat.

Bill Sanders never raised his voice, never argued. Debate tournaments lasted two days, and doing your best and winning was not a sprint, but a marathon. You had to conserve mental and physical energy. Most important, quiet confidence was about showing your talents in the quality of your debate, not trash talking, proclaiming yourself the best, or thumping your chest when you won. What Bill Sanders taught us was Ted Williams, not Muhammad Ali.

Sanders was the first person who ever made a determined effort to smooth some of the rougher edges of my Emanuel personality. Before matches he would talk to me about controlling my tendency toward sarcasm and condescension. It was slow going. I would listen, and grasp it in the abstract, but when the battle was joined I often could not help myself.

When Coach Sanders wasn't allowed to communicate with me,

my partner would try to signal me by tapping his pencil on his desk whenever I seemed to be veering into the aggressive almost-bully role. Even this technique was not very helpful. My senior year, my partner Arnie Grant and I made it to the state quarterfinals, where our opponents were two young women. An excellent debater named Christine Madden had contradicted herself in her arguments, and I used my cross-examination time to rattle off fierce questions. I didn't give her adequate time to respond, instead cutting her answers off. As Arnie tapped his pencil, Christine's face reddened, and several times she seemed on the verge of tears. Turned off by me, and taking pity on Christine, the judges voted two to one for her side even though we had made the better arguments on the merits. My last chance at a state championship was lost.

I was outraged, naturally, but as time passed I came to understand what I had gained from the experience. Where else could I learn, without more serious consequences, about the nuances of public conflict and the limits of sheer aggressiveness? Within the controlled environment of the competition, my excesses were indulged in ways that were instructive to me, and everyone else. In between matches Coach Sanders taught us how to let go of what happened the previous week and focus on the next challenge. We had a tendency to rehash our experiences, dwelling on mistakes made by the judges or the peaks and valleys of our own performances. Bill Sanders helped us learn from the past and then quickly turn to the future.

Another formative academic experience was the Great Books seminar taught by a young English teacher named Raissa Landor. Her class on the great books of Western civilization was conducted as a seminar in a room where the desks were arranged in a circle. She refused to give us letter grades. Instead she wrote detailed evaluations for each of her students and offered suggestions for ways they could improve their reading, reasoning, and writing.

Raissa encouraged us to read deeply and speak our minds about what we read. My classmates and I took her direction to heart. We were excited to compare Alexis de Tocqueville's vision of America with the country we knew and determined to apply Thorstein Veblen's

Theory of the Leisure Class to understand the local wealthy enclave of
Indian Hill.

I was also blessed to have great science teachers at New Trier. The
best was Robert Koonz, who taught chemistry. He was a nervous type
with a coughing tic. He assigned weekly, graded problem sheets and
had a test every Friday. We always groaned about the constant work
and testing, but you couldn't help but learn the material. Koonz was
always nervous about the unpredictability of lab experiments. He
scrupulously insisted we take every precaution, such as goggles and
rubber gloves. He had his hands full with my class. In our very first
laboratory session he had us apply a little electricity to water in order
to separate oxygen and hydrogen and collect the hydrogen to determine how much was created given the energy input. My partner Ray
Agran and I promptly used a Bunsen burner to ignite the hydrogen,
which caused a nice little *Hindenburg*-type explosion and sent glass
from the flasks flying. After scurrying around the room in high anxiety, confirming that we were all safe and unhurt, Koonz flailed his
arms into the air: "No more labs. Laboratory is canceled for the rest
of the year." Maybe this is why I didn't become an experimental research scientist?

.....

Then, and now, Arnie would say that I was not as intellectually gifted
as Brian or Ray Agran but I compensated by outworking them. He
was right. On most school nights I spent at least three and a half
hours—7 to 10:30 P.M.—on homework and never needed to be reminded about it. Ari and Rahm considered this monkish devotion to
books quite strange, but it felt natural to me. While today this amount
of nightly homework seems little for students from the best high
schools, and is much less than what my own daughters spent, then it
was what the best students at the best high schools devoted to their
studies. It was also part of my response to the pressure my parents put
on me to get top grades so I could be accepted at an elite college and
then go to medical school. These expectations had been such a con-

stant in my life that I had accepted them with little complaint. Indeed, I liked excelling at schoolwork, so the hours of studying were not onerous, the way practice is not burdensome for great high school sport stars.

Bill Sanders listened sympathetically when I told him I was not sure I wanted to be a doctor. He also encouraged me to push for admission to my first-choice college, Amherst, even though my father preferred that I attend a college he had heard of like Harvard or Yale. My mother preferred that I stay in the city and go to the University of Chicago, which was close by and where the competitive intensity of the undergraduate program fit well with my personality. But I drew a thousand-mile circle around Chicago and determined I would go somewhere beyond that circle. With Sanders's encouragement I zeroed in on Amherst, in part because one of the smartest New Trier students ever went there, and if it was good enough for him I figured it would be good enough for me. Plus, after having a high school class of nearly seven hundred kids, I thought—wrongly, as it turned out—that I would prefer a smaller institution. I applied early-decision to Amherst, the only college I applied to. By December of my senior year I knew which college I was going to, which relieved a lot of the senior year tension.

Sanders was also instrumental in getting me out of the only serious trouble I ever encountered at New Trier. After our college applications were complete and our first semester finals were over—and so the last grades the college would see were determined—three of us nerds, Brian, Arnie, and I, decided to celebrate by going to Jackson Hole, Wyoming, for a week of skiing. It was early February and we would miss a week at the start of the last semester of senior year. While missing classes might affect our final high school grades, it would have no impact on our college acceptance. Our parents considered us responsible and, more important, deserving of a special treat after long and successful school careers. We had a blast.

Raissa Landor, Bill Sanders, and Robert Koonz were willing to indulge our truancy. However, our gym and calculus teachers did not find our absence amusing, or tolerable. They decided to flunk us and dismiss us from their classes. We could survive F's in calculus, although we wanted the college credits that came with completing the course and scoring well on the AP tests. But, because we needed to complete four years of physical education for graduation, failing gym would actually prevent us from graduating from high school and thus would endanger college admissions. Sensing an opportunity to take some revenge on the haughty nerds, our gym teacher would not let us off easy. We were required to devote many hours to extra PE, which we did by playing endless doubles badminton in order to earn the credit. The calculus teacher, Walter Dodge, presented a more difficult challenge, and was of a mind to simply kick us out of the class.

Thankfully, it wasn't for nothing that Bill Sanders was the debate coach. He convened a nighttime conference at the school involving Mr. Dodge and our parents. Mr. Dodge admonished us that we were throwing away our chance to earn college credit, plus he was disappointed in us because we failed to live up to our role as the classroom's leaders. After much heated discussion, we settled the matter by making a bet that we would earn 5's—the top grade—on the AP test. If we did, we would be forgiven and receive credit. If we did not, he could fail us. Mr. Dodge accepted the wager. We won the bet, and thanks to Bill Sanders's intercessions we were able to graduate and our records remained spotless.

Besides the members of the debate team, Sanders paid special attention to the students in his advisory group, who were in his charge for their full four years at the high school. Before my brother Ari started his freshman year, our mother went to the school and negotiated for him to be placed in Bill Sanders's advisory. The administration agreed to do it and Ari could not have been in better hands.

.....

Although he was every bit as intelligent as most of the kids in the top tracks, by the ninth grade Ari was probably two years behind grade level in reading comprehension and writing, and his grades showed it.

Add a measure of hyperactivity and serious ADHD and you get a smart kid who is full of energy, difficult to engage, and thoroughly frustrated. Knowing what it felt like to be unfairly judged, he looked for opportunities to stand up for people who were being bullied.

It did not take much to provoke Ari, because, to be blunt, he liked to fight. He relished the way that once the battle started all the distractions and diversions that normally bothered him melted away and he could focus on a single simple and obvious task: winning the fight. He also craved the feeling of certainty that comes when you are the good guy fighting a bad guy, doing something as primal as trading blows, until one side has had enough. He actually felt calmer inside when doing battle.

Ari was so good in physically stressful situations because, like most people with ADHD, the chemicals that tend to make other people *more* hyper actually made him feel focused and relaxed. The speed, danger, and risk that make other people nervous make guys like Ari serene.

The paradoxical effect of stimulation on people with ADHD explains, in part, why Ari put so much effort into provoking people. He was bored and if he could get someone to chase him around the house, he loved it. Decades later Rahm's friend Darcy Goldfarb, who was his ballet partner, would recall quite vividly how she would arrive in her orange Oldsmobile Cutlass convertible to take Rahm to the dance studio only to discover mayhem had broken out.

"One day Rahm came out with this grin on his face and said, 'We can't go yet.' I kept saying, 'Why? Why?' Finally Rahm said, 'We can't go because I have Ari tied up in the closet.' We went inside and Ari was locked in a closet and pounding on the door and screaming. Ari would just bait Rahm until he couldn't stand it and then all hell would break loose. But every time it happened Ari looked happy."

With parents who were determined to help him, Ari was one of the first kids in America to take the drug Ritalin for hyperactivity. The drug's usefulness in treating this disorder was discovered in the 1960s and it was introduced gradually in the 1970s. (I would one day study

under one of the Ritalin pioneers, Leon Eisenberg, who would become a professor at Harvard Medical School.) Although the drug
would be a subject of much controversy, it worked for Ari, making him
more focused, and less combative in school. Ari also got lots of help
from school staff, especially Bill Sanders, who was invited to attend a
few meetings at school where the agenda was: What do we do with Ari
Emanuel?

As Bill would recall, the school psychologist and administrators
were concerned about Ari's behavior and performance but unsure
about how to address it. Bill pushed for him to be enrolled in a special
education program inside the high school where he would be treated
as a regular kid who needed a particular kind of teaching. He came to
our house, where my parents agreed on this tack. Days later Ari met
for the first time with New Trier West's first specialist in learning disabilities, a young teacher named Merle Giblichman.

"Gibby," as she was called, had just three years of teaching experience when Ari arrived in her special education classroom. Her long
brown hair made her look even younger than her age. Indeed, she
could have passed for a New Trier student. Since she had grown up in
Wilmette and had gone through the local school system, she knew that
New Trier could be a challenging place for anyone who could not keep
up academically. In this environment, anyone in special ed would feel
tortured by the stigma of needing extra help. For Ari, who came from
a home where reading and scholarship were held in high regard, this
was doubly true.

In Gibby's room, Ari got one-on-one tutoring and a quiet place
free of distractions where he could work on assignments and take tests
under rules that gave him more time and credit for showing he grasped
the content of a lesson even if he had trouble writing out his answers
to questions. The work was not easy. Letters and whole words would
get jumbled between the page and his brain and Ari found it difficult
to admit when he stumbled over material that was easy for others. He
would pound the desk with his fist and kick the walls in frustration.

Fortunately, Gibby did not care much if you banged around and
groaned in misery as long as you did not give up. Her students could

call a time-out to stretch and walk around if they needed to shake off some stress and they got extra time to go back and check their answers or essays. These accommodations, which today are standard in schools across America, were almost unique to New Trier West in the 1970s. At that time, disabilities like dyslexia were little understood and only the best-read specialists used the kind of techniques Gibby deployed to help students overcome them.

Gradually, Ari made progress and gained confidence. When he heard that Gibby had taught French while getting a master's degree in special education he pestered her to give him language lessons. She acquiesced, but only as a reward for his hard work. She also became his advocate. Once, when an enraged Ari leaped off the mat at a wrestling tournament and attacked the referee, Gibby defended him to the faculty and administration. He was allowed to stay on the team and eventually became a top wrestler at New Trier West. In his senior year Ari seemed destined for a shot at becoming state champion in his weight class, but a broken arm suffered at the start of the season kept him out of competition for the year.

Missing his chance to become a champion was a big disappointment for Ari, but he channeled his time and energy into college preparatory courses that Gibby helped him access. She also put up with Ari's anger and subversive activities, which included stealing his own file, which held test results and evaluations from learning specialists. Gibby got it back and actually saw something to admire in his determination.

Like Bill Sanders, Gibby made friends with my parents, who supported every demand she made on their son because they knew she was trying to help him get in shape for college and life beyond. When the teachers' union went on strike my mother joined them on the picket line and when Gibby needed to consult her, my mother invited her to the house for dinner.

Considering what she heard at our house, Gibby knew the Emanuels were highly engaged in political and intellectual issues. So she was a little surprised when Ari revealed his career goal to her during a quiet moment in her classroom. "Gibby," he said, "I want to make a lot of money." He did not know exactly how he was going to do it, or what he might use the money to accomplish. But he was certain that he wanted a fortune.

At a school in the 1970s where the faculty preached idealism and social responsibility, no one else would have been so bold about his desire to be rich. You might privately harbor fantasies of wealth, and certainly there was plenty of money in many of the families who lived in our district. But expressing the desire to be rich was so gauche that Gibby suspected Ari was just trying to be outrageous. He wasn't. In fact, no one in the family was surprised by Ari's ambition. There were plenty of early warning signs.

From the moment he sold that first slice of cheesecake for a tidy profit, my brother was entranced by the capitalist system. The fact that you could make money by outhustling the other guy and by delivering a better product or service more efficiently than the other guy resonated with Ari at a young age. Ari recognized that there were many ways to work this system without having to rely on reading or writing. He was charming, energetic, creative, persistent, and indefatigable. These qualities would be more than enough to get him to the top of almost any business.

For practice, Ari would try lots of businesses on for size, even before he was finished with public school. Like a lot of kids in the suburbs he did lawn mowing and cleanups. But unlike the others, he organized his brothers, friends, and neighbors into crews. Paid $5 to cut the grass on a typical quarter-acre plot, he distributed $3 to the boys who did the work and pocketed $2. When he was older he joined his friends Lowell Kraff and Nate Fineburg in a venture selling T-shirts at rock concerts all over the Midwest. Lowell, who lived a block away, had been Ari's friend since fourth grade. As Lowell would recall, it was at about that time that he made owning a gold Rolex one of his life's goals. His father was a highly successful eye surgeon who made a million dollars a year and drove a Ferrari. Nate, who was Lowell's cousin, became Ari's friend in junior high. Nate would notice that Ari was more driven to succeed than anyone Nate knew.

"He would be up at dawn, honking the car horn outside my house for me to get up and go to work," Nate told me. "If I did not come out he'd come inside and slap me and drag me out of bed," all the while goading Nate in a high-pitched voice. On one level, Nate considered Ari's aggression obnoxious and annoying. On another, he felt entertained by it. "You never knew if Ari the jerk or Ari the nice guy would show up. But somehow I learned to love all of him, including the slaps and the pinches."

Working with as many as a dozen other kids, Lowell, Nate, and Ari bought knockoff T-shirts decorated like the ones sold at concerts for bands like Cheap Trick, the Rolling Stones, and the Doobie Brothers. They would show up outside the theaters and arenas when the bands were playing and in the half hour or so that it took for people to leave a concert sell hundreds of shirts. The trick was to get in and get out before being noticed by anyone working for the band, because they would use force to stop the sale of unauthorized merchandise.

Nate, Lowell, and Ari worked many weekends selling shirts. As time passed, they improved their technique. When their inventory got out of whack and they had too many "smalls" and not enough "mediums" they ripped the labels out and sold them "as is." When a heavy rainstorm started at one outdoor concert Lowell ran to a store, bought hundreds of plastic garbage bags, and sold them as "raincoats" for two dollars apiece.

Of course, it was not all profit and creative problem solving. The T-shirt crew was often chased away from concert sites and they were arrested, more than once, on charges like peddling without a license. In every case, they were detained and released when charges were dropped. Never once did they consider giving up the business. But they did try a few variations. One year they sold big framed photographs that they loaded into the Emanuel family station wagon and hauled all over the Midwest to big office buildings. As Nate would recall:

We'd go into a building and tell the people in whatever offices were there that we had been delivering pictures to the guys

down the hall and had some left over. Before you knew it we'd
be in the conference room setting these things up—they were
landscapes mostly, and skylines of big cities—and people would
buy them to put on the walls or take home. We got 'em for
twenty dollars and sold 'em for forty-five dollars. There were
some days when we would get kicked out of places and never
sell a picture. But there were other days when we would clean
up. At night we would stay out until two in the morning but
then Ari would be back at my house at seven, ready to go again.

Finally came the summer when Ari found more predictable, but
equally demanding work at the Chicago Mercantile Exchange. The
heart of the "Merc" is the trading floor, where different commodities
are bought and sold in areas called pits. Traders in red jackets scream
and use hand signals to make deals that are scratched onto slips that
are then handed to runners, distinguished by gold-colored jackets.
The runners make sure the paperwork gets to the right destination
and at the end of the day reconcile the buy and sell orders they facili-
tated.

For most people who view it from the visitors' gallery, the Merc
floor looks like a dozen cockfights crowded into a space the size of a
basketball court that's been invaded by some hooligan fans of the Ar-
senal football club. As hundreds of traders shout offers and bids, the
prices of commodities are flashed on lighted signs that ring the room.
It's enough to make anyone who doesn't suffer from ADHD feel dazed
and confused. For Ari it was a bit of capitalist heaven on earth. Where
others experienced chaos, he was able to see patterns and understand
exactly what was expected of him. He loved the work so much that he
didn't mind getting up before dawn to drive to work and he gave serious thought to diving right into it as a full-time career. His bosses,
recognizing something familiar in him, would have welcomed him to
train for a full-time job. Ari declined.

It was not that Ari felt ambivalent about the world of business.
He was just determined to go to college. He chose small Macalester
College, in St. Paul, Minnesota. There would be time for big business

successes in the future. Like Lowell and Nate, who would become quite rich and successful in business, Ari was destined for success.

.....

Rahm, on the other hand, was a bit of a quandary. He made friends easily and did well at whatever he pursued wholeheartedly, whether it was soccer or dance. But he was also an underachiever.

I know, it doesn't seem possible that a guy who became famous for his focused intensity and political aggression stayed on the sidelines in high school, but it's true. Some of this hesitance may have been related to his size. He was so tiny in junior high that he participated in trials for a growth-promoting drug. It worked, and he grew about six inches in a year, but even with this increase he remained one of the smallest boys in school. I also think Rahm was affected negatively by living in my shadow at New Trier West, and I wasn't much help.

It was not that I didn't care about Rahm. I loved him. My neglect had more to do with being a teenager—self-involved, immature, and, to a degree that now embarrasses me, naturally insensitive to the needs and feelings of others. I often find it difficult to recognize what other people may feel and what they might need from me emotionally. I've never been good at reading people's faces and understanding what they are feeling. I am pretty sure it's a neurological thing, like color blindness or left-handedness, and the source may be genetic. In the past thirty years, a body of psychological research has confirmed that many animals pass on traits like social awareness and, for lack of a better term, emotional sensitivity. Similarly, neuroscientists have seen that some of us are simply "wired" to catch the subtle, nonverbal cues people send with an imperceptible tilt of the head or a raised eyebrow. This ability is a real advantage because it helps those who have it to work well with others and navigate social situations.

Others, like me, are simply bad at catching on to hints and clues about the feelings of the people around us. We need to be hit over the head with direct statements like "Hey, pay attention to me!" or "Stop it, you're being annoying!" This makes me atrocious at office politics or grasping the hidden messages. I think this inability to read social situations may be why I am so explicit in expressing my feelings and views. Few people say, "I wonder what Zeke is thinking," or "I can't figure out what Zeke means." Social situations are much easier for me to navigate when everything—the good and the bad—is out there. I don't have to work as hard, and guess so much.

I was especially clueless about young women. It wasn't ignorance about sex. My parents regarded sex as normal and healthy. Indeed, having come of age in Europe, my father could never understand the American prudery and obsession with keeping sex hidden. He gave us plenty of information. The problem was that I was so bad at sensing any other person's mood or interest. My numbness was so profound that no amount of attention could reach me.

During the late fall of freshman year of high school, I was sitting in the study hall room on the first floor of New Trier West's social studies building arguing with some friends. A sparky, self-confident young woman came over to me and announced that her friend Melinda Dorner had been looking at me and found me attractive. But, she lamented, I had not seemed to take any notice of Melinda. Indeed, I had no idea who she was or what she looked like. Her friend gestured about twenty feet away to a tall woman, with shoulder-length light brown hair, and suggested that I meet her because she was "interested in you but too shy to come over herself."

Startled, and probably a bit flattered, I rose from my chair, walked over, and awkwardly inquired if Melinda was interested in going for a walk. We coursed through the first-floor corridors that connected the six buildings that made up New Trier West. I learned that she too was a swimmer. We held hands and promised to see each other the next day.

The manner of meeting Melinda—having someone come up and alert me to the fact that a woman found me attractive but utterly failed to seem to catch my attention—would be repeated over and over throughout my life. Of the three women I dated in high school, two asked me out. In college the pattern continued. In my sophomore year, my suite-mate Harold Kahn had to tell me that another woman, Eliza, was interested in dating me. Later, when one of the older women who were admitted to Amherst at the start of coeducation asked me to tutor her in chemistry, I utterly failed to perceive the romantic overtones, despite the fact that she regularly sat with me at dinner in the vegetarian room and she cut my hair because I refused to pay for a barber.

Rahm, on the other hand, is completely different. While today he seems unabashed about saying what he thinks, he was always much better at reading people and elucidating their real motives—even when they did not understand those motives themselves. In high school, Rahm took real delight in the variety of personalities and attitudes he encountered at our big school and not infrequently made fun of their foibles. As his friend Darcy Goldfarb recalled, "Rahm did not want to be mainstream. New Trier was a very traditional community where the cheerleaders and the basketball players were the popular ones but Rahm didn't care about that. Other people did not do the things he did, like ballet, but he didn't care."

The ballet classes were a school-approved activity, which meant that Rahm and Darcy were dismissed early and allowed to go to the Evanston studio on their own. To avoid being seen and subsequently harassed, Rahm generally rushed into the building on Davis Street and ran up the stairs to the studio, where he changed into his tights and shoes. But once he was on the dance floor he was comfortable. As one of the few males in the school, Rahm was valued. However, the teacher, a taskmaster named Phyllis Wills, was merciless in her demands that he improve.

"She sat on the stool and would clap her hands and say, 'No! No! No! That's all wrong.' Rahm would beg her to let us try again. He would give her that smile and she would. 'All right, from the top.' She taught us to be very disciplined," recalled Darcy. "I think it gave Rahm a sense that if you really poured yourself into something you could get an amazing result."

Dance probably was the first place Rahm was really rewarded with success for being passionate and intensely engaged. It is no surprise that dance was as far from anything Zeke-like as you could get. In school Rahm couldn't surpass me no matter what he did, so he decided not to compete. This led him to not try very hard and to dismiss intense academic work. Indeed, he probably dismissed doing anything zealously until he discovered dance.

As one of Rahm's closest friends, Darcy quizzed him on his decision to attend Sarah Lawrence College. He would be one of the few males entering a traditionally all-female institution. She worried about how other people might react to the choice. Rahm, in typical fashion, said he didn't care what people thought. He liked the idea of attending a school where they focused intently on the liberal arts and offered him the chance to continue dancing if he chose. He also liked the fact that girls outnumbered boys by a significant ratio.

I helped Rahm choose Sarah Lawrence over his other main collegiate option, Lewis & Clark College, in Oregon. Both schools would get him far away from home and allow him to test himself as an independent young man. However, I pushed him toward Sarah Lawrence because it was out east and had a superior academic reputation. With two years at Amherst, I had become an East Coast collegiate snob and thought Rahm should graduate from one of the elite schools. Also, I thought at Sarah Lawrence he would get an Ivy-level education and personal attention from outstanding faculty. I pressured my parents to support this choice, even though at the time Sarah Lawrence was the second most expensive private college in the country.

"Remember what Dad would say about the cost?" Rahm reminded me. "He found Lawrence University in Wisconsin, which was much less expensive, and kept saying, 'Why do we have to pay so much more to get that extra name, Sarah?'"

.....

The cost of Sarah Lawrence stopped being a joke when Rahm almost lost his chance to go anywhere for his freshman year. The crisis arose out of a freak accident with a meat slicer at an Arby's restaurant not far from our house in Wilmette.

As I mentioned earlier, Emanuel family policy did not include allowances. While mostly our parents gave us money for things, it wasn't much. Routinely buying pizza, going to concerts at Ravinia Park, and other activities cost more than our parents would indulge, so we worked for spending money. In my senior year I delivered pizzas. I am still not sure I really made much money when I consider the gas and wear and tear on the car. Rahm took the job at Arby's, gamely donning a uniform and hat that Darcy considered especially ridiculous. Rahm was assigned to the machine that turned big slabs of roast beef into slices for sandwiches. At the end of the day, while he was cleaning the slicer he somehow got the middle finger of his right hand too close to the edge of the super-sharp blade. The cut was quick and deep.

After jumping back in pain, Rahm did what you are supposed to do when blood is gushing from a wound. He grabbed a cloth and applied intense pressure. Soon enough his blood began to clot and the flood was reduced to a modest flow, then a trickle. Rahm then bandaged the wound tightly to make sure the flow was stanched. Rahm always had a peculiar relationship with his hands. As a kid he refused to wear gloves even during the coldest winter days or during snowball fights. Painful stimuli on his fingers never seemed to bother him the way they do the rest of us. So the bandage was super-tight and Rahm didn't seem to notice. When he came home Rahm was able to report to my mother and father that he had cut his finger at work and he had taken care of it.

My parents would remember that Rahm did not complain at all about his finger. But why my father didn't insist on examining it to verify Rahm's rendition is still a mystery no one can explain. In any case, Rahm wasn't slowed a bit as he went through graduation and attended the parties and dances that celebrated the New Trier West class of 1977. As part of the festivities Rahm even joined some classmates for a chilly June swim in Lake Michigan. At the beach, Darcy asked him about his finger and said, "Your dad's a doctor. Don't you think you should show it to him?" According to Darcy, Rahm said, "I can't. He's going to be really mad at me because I didn't show it to him to begin with."

The next time Darcy saw him, though, he complained about the pain and looked, to her, to be pale and sweating. A day later he called her to say he was going to be admitted to Children's Hospital in Chicago.

Our father made the decision to rush Rahm to the hospital when his son, lethargic and feverish, finally showed him the injury. When the finger was unwrapped my dad knew right away that Rahm had not properly washed the cut and that he had bandaged it too tightly. The distal phalanx, or end segment, of the finger was blackened by gangrene, and streaks of discoloration were working their way down toward his hand.

At Children's Hospital tests and exams showed that the bacterial infection had invaded the bone, causing osteomyelitis. It was also spreading into his bloodstream and the rest of his body. Rahm was admitted to the intensive care unit, where his fever rose and he drifted in and out of consciousness.

My mother hardly left the hospital after Rahm was admitted. More than once she lay next to him on the bed and prayed for his life. The extremely high fevers made Rahm suffer from hallucinations and episodes of babbling and angry outbursts. He would later tell me, "I woke up one night screaming at Mom, unloading on her about how she loved you more and about how she treated me as the second son. Dad was saying, 'Shh, shh,' but whatever sibling jealousy I had ever held inside me came out. I said everything, plus some more."

Ari, who was sixteen at the time, visited the hospital once, just after Rahm was admitted. He took one step inside the room, which smelled of rotting flesh, glanced at Rahm, who was completely out of it and hooked up to intravenous lines, and broke down crying. Ari is extremely sensitive to suffering, especially when the person in pain is someone he loves. He is also a hypochondriac and a germophobe. Back then, Ari was powerless to help Rahm and traumatized by what he saw in the ICU. Although my parents reassured Ari that Rahm was getting the best care and would be fine in the end, he wasn't any less worried or ready to come back to the hospital. They decided it was best for all concerned that he go to Israel, where family and friends could take care of him and he could spend some time at a kibbutz in the countryside. He agreed to go.

At the hospital Rahm's doctors deployed an array of intravenous antibiotics in high doses to fight the infection. Their main concern was sepsis, an inflammatory response to bacteria circulating in the blood, in which a person's blood pressure drops precipitously and fatal organ failure can occur. As the battle for Rahm's life raged, our parents suffered through every hour. They worried and they also argued. My mother could not understand why my father—a doctor—had not investigated Rahm's injury until it became life-threatening. All he could say was that he had trusted that Rahm, the son of a doctor, knew how to clean and dress a cut.

During this time very few people were permitted to visit Rahm. Darcy Goldfarb recalled that she went to the hospital every day and, on occasion, was allowed into Rahm's room. "He had labored breathing and a fever," she said. "Marsha was crying. I remember I shoved him over and sat next to him on the bed. I whispered in his ear. 'Don't you dare check out now. You have to use every ounce of energy we ever put into every grand jeté we ever did. But don't give up.' He made a little noise like a grunt. I took that to mean he wasn't ready to leave."

When he'd recovered enough to be aware of what was happening around him, Rahm noticed that his roommates, who had cancer or complications from cancer treatment, were extremely sick. In fact, three of them died during his time in the room. After the third one passed away, our mother insisted our father finally pay to have Rahm moved into a private room. Typically, initially he resisted, which led to an argument that was amplified, no doubt, by the terrible stress—and sense of guilt—that both my parents were feeling. Eventually my mother won. In relenting, my father gave some ground without explicitly accepting responsibility for Rahm's condition.

Rahm's general condition improved as the medicine began to take effect. His fever came down and he became more lucid. The nurses caught his eye and he began flirting with them to get their attention and extra helpings of ice cream at lunch and dinner. However, even as

Rahm's sepsis abated and his general health improved, his finger did not get much better. At the point of the injury, where the slicer may have actually nicked the bone, Rahm's bone infection resisted every drug the doctors tried. After about four weeks using intravenous antibiotics, the doctors told Rahm and our parents that the best option would be to amputate his finger and send him home.

As my mother noticed, Rahm had become a different person during his illness. He was still quick-witted and still joked and flirted with the nurses and the girls from school who came to visit. But he was also more sensitive and prone to worry. When a friend, whom he would recall as "a schmuck," said that Rahm was likely to miss his first semester at college, Rahm became so upset that he grabbed a glass bottle that contained intravenous solution and threw it against the wall, smashing it to pieces. He was determined to get out of the hospital and get on with his life.

Faced with the facts, my brother eventually agreed to the amputation. Less than a day later the surgeon discovered that half of the finger was okay, and cut just below the second joint on his middle finger. With no more bacteria breeding in his bone, Rahm quickly recovered. Darcy was startled by his good humor. "When they unwrapped the finger after the surgery the first thing he did was flip the bird," she recalled. "He said something about how he'll have to do it twice from now on, for people to get the full effect."

Between his hospital stay, recovering from the infection, and letting his finger heal, Rahm completely lost the carefree summer between ending high school and starting college. After he recovered, no one ever said much about Rahm's semiconscious tirades or the arguments that raged between my mother and father. Rahm told me much later that "nearly dying was the single most important thing in my life." He said it changed him from a quiet, relaxed kid into a young man filled with the need to succeed and make something of himself. "Before the accident I was very relaxed," he says. "Post the accident: no."

For me, Rahm's hospitalization was both frightening and fascinating. I visited every day on my way home from a summer job as a research assistant in a laboratory at Michael Reese Hospital on the Near

South Side. By the time Rahm was out of the extreme danger zone and intensive care unit, I would bring him a special onion soup he loved from a restaurant near the hospital; we would lie in bed together watching TV and just talking about the attractive nurses. I also recall being impressed by the way a small injury—a cut finger—could quickly bloom into a life-threatening illness. Although no one mentioned it at the time, it was just this process, infection from a small superficial wound, that had killed our father's brother Emanuel back in Israel.

Finally, Rahm was able to leave the hospital after a total of more than six weeks. This would give him less than a month to gain back some of the weight he lost, and hang out with me and Ari, who had returned from Israel.

Fourteen

COLLEGE BOYS

By the time Rahm got to Sarah Lawrence, I was already two years into my education at Amherst. No one on my mother's side of the family had ever gone away to a four-year college. Although my father had studied in Europe, his experience wasn't remotely similar to what an undergrad encountered in the United States in the mid-1970s. At Lausanne he had followed a program that called for lots of independent study, with only three final exams in six years of medical school, and absolutely no campus-style social life. I would be the first in the family to attempt the adjustment to an institutional subculture of dormitories, dining halls, and tradition, which, until recently, had offered precious few opportunities to Jews.

I arrived at Amherst with unreasonable expectations. Given its exclusivity, small size, and reputation for academic excellence, I hoped I would find a bigger version of my New Trier West peer group. In my imagination, most Amherst students would share my rabid devotion to competitive studying, intellectual jousting, and debate about big ideas. I also hoped that extracurricular life would revolve, at least partly, around politics and protest. This was what college looked like to me, through the lens of the media and from my experience on the barricades at Northwestern. This expectation only grew when I heard that the president of Amherst had participated in an antiwar sit-in at nearby Westover Air Force Base and campaigned for women to be admitted to the school. This information reinforced my hope that I would find plenty of like-minded folks who would be excited to talk into the night about democracy in America, affirmative action, and a hundred other topics.

Instead I found lots of really smart students who worked very hard but also devoted themselves with equal intensity to parties, alcohol, drugs, and sex. Ridiculously, I had not fully thought through that I would be in the last entering all-male class, thus within the residual atmosphere of an all-male college. Although a few dozen, mainly older, women transfer students could be seen on campus my first year, female freshmen would only be admitted the next year, and true equality for women at Amherst was still years away. As a result, the college remained a haven for those chauvinists who refused to see women as little more than sex objects and it permitted a level of alcohol consumption that approached both the medical and social definition of poisonous. These elements of campus life were a big disappointment for a kid hoping for an academic utopia where we studied big ideas of every sort and then applied them to life in the outside world through writing, activism, and even public protest.

Of course, when I left home I did not realize that the intense and engaging environment I experienced among an elite group of students at New Trier West and hoped to find at Amherst did not exist there, or at any other college in America in the fall of 1975. According to *The New York Times*, a "puzzling calm" had settled on campuses from coast to coast. While students had not returned to raccoon coats and goldfish swallowing, they seemed nervous and inclined to look for comfort in the status quo. They were also affected by the Arab oil embargo and economic recession that made the mid-1970s an anxious time for anyone concerned about jobs and the future of the economy. Fraternities were reasserting their grip on social life and nerdy, big-mouthed, politically obsessed students like me, who may have enjoyed a brief moment in the sixties when they were respected and even admired, were pushed back to the fringe.

Not surprisingly, I began many relationships at Amherst with arguments. I considered this perfectly normal. Indeed, for me it was a sign of respect. As it turned out, hardly anyone else felt the same way. As Andy Oram, one of my closest friends from college, recalls, "I heard Zeke before I first met him."

> I was coming back from a class or something and I heard arguing coming from our friend Mark Berger's room down the hall. In this high squeaky voice this guy is saying, "You're wrong. You're wrong and you know it!" I ducked my head into the room to see what's going on and this kid, Zeke Emanuel, is arguing about something like his life depended on it. I loved arguing, too, and it never bothered me. But I was one of the few who got it. With other people it inspired a lot of dislike.

Dislike is a kind way of saying it. In fact, I inspired the kind of feeling that moved others to set fire to my dorm room door and ring my phone at all hours of the night. A fair amount of this hostility was, no doubt, aroused by my sharp-elbow personality. Some came because I was a threat to the get-along attitude that necessarily pervades a small institution. And some came as a reaction to the high scores I posted in pre-med science courses like introductory chemistry, which seriously skewed the grading curve. As Andy Oram recalled it, I was the student who made it harder for others to get A's. In my mind, we were scholars on equal footing. But they were worried about making the grades required to earn a diploma and get admitted to medical school. I found chemistry and all science classes easy. Many of them struggled. They deserved my empathy and understanding. I needed help grasping this fact.

.....

"Zeke, no one else thinks this way. This is why half the people in the college don't like you. They think you're loud, aggressive, and obnoxious. And they're right."

It was about 3 A.M. and Andy and I were speeding along Interstate 90 in his '65 Plymouth Valiant, somewhere in the vast space between Albany and Buffalo, bound for the Oram homestead in the little city of Jamestown, New York. Jamestown is just twenty miles from the eastern shore of Lake Erie, which makes the drive from Amherst about eight hours. This was just enough time for Andy to begin explaining what was wrong with me.

If you do it right, your first experience living in the adult world far from family and childhood friends forces you to see yourself in a new light. This does not happen without pain and suffering. (Once I realized it, I told my daughters as they were leaving for college that the most important part of their college experience would entail "suffering," that they would learn the most because of the moments of existential suffering they experienced. Of course, they didn't believe me, especially because their first few years were largely welcoming and pleasant experiences. But they all got the "suffering" part and were the better for it.)

When I think back on how unhappy I was in my first two years at Amherst, I have to conclude that the transformation is ever more painful the longer and more fiercely you resist it. As an Emanuel, I resisted with instinctive, defensive intensity. Who was Andy Oram to say that my way of doing things was wrong? As far as I was concerned, the problem at Amherst was not me, but the other students—their conventionality and unwillingness to ask the "big questions" of life.

"These are privileged people in an extremely privileged place," I told Andy. I, on the other hand, could not afford to go home to Chicago for Thanksgiving and never even ordered a pizza on a weekend. "Most of them come from rich families that gave them everything and now they have the opportunity to get the greatest, most intense education available in the country. And what do they do? These fuckheads

waste their time drinking until they puke. Then wait until the last minute to write their papers and don't do the reading before class."

Fortunately for me, Andy assumed I spoke with the best of inten-
tions, and he was such a good friend that he would listen and argue all
the way from Amherst to Jamestown and never run out of patience—
often laughing at my own narrow naïveté. When we finally reached
Jamestown I discovered that his family was far more reserved and gen-
teel than mine. Andy and I wore ties for dinner with his mother, who
was a widow. But while they were polite, the Orams were also a feisty
group and their conversation sparkled with ideas even while it was
more mannered than an Emanuel dinner. It was a revelation, to me, to
see how a family might enjoy the thrust and parry of debate without
raised voices and four-letter words.

·····

When Andy came to my house I was able to see, through his reactions,
how life on Locust Road might seem to someone with fresh eyes. In the
loud and warm reception we received upon arrival, Andy was taken by
my mother's generous hugs and startled to hear everyone at the house
call me Jon or Jonny instead of Zeke.

The next morning, at breakfast, Andy got the full Emanuel treatment. As he would later recall:

> I had never heard anyone swear or tell an off-color story at
> the table and in the first five minutes at breakfast Rahm must
> have said "fuck" five times. Ari and Zeke punched the shit out
> of each other's shoulders and their dad told this wild story—a
> long dirty joke, really—about two kids growing up in Israel
> who wanted another brother.
>
> I've never laughed so hard in my life. It wasn't just because
> it was funny. It's because it was a really gross story, sexual,
> and crazy, told in this very matter-of-fact way, at the breakfast
> table with Zeke's mother and me, this guy they don't even know.
> That would never have happened at my house but at the Eman-
> uel house it was just normal.

Like just about everyone, Andy was charmed by my father's warm, open, and easygoing personality. My mother, on the other hand, made Andy feel a little bit anxious and on guard. "She always seemed a tiny bit dangerous," he remembered. "There was a certain edge that made you feel like she would say something hurtful and not let someone's pain get in the way of her own need to make a point."

Exhibit A in Andy's critique came after he had known the family for a long time, and my mother, in a careless moment, said something about how he would always be an outsider. According to him, she said, "We love you, honey, but we don't need you." Since Andy was not quite family the statement was true. His point, of course, was that she still didn't have to say it.

In truth, both my parents pushed until you pushed back. For example, the doctor issue. As a youngster I accepted their plan for me to become a doctor, but by the end of high school I had doubts. While I was really good in science, and throughout my high school and college career had never earned anything other than an A in a science course—except first-semester organic chemistry—I had begun doing medical research in laboratories over the summers. The work was interesting, but once I understood the underlying science, I became somewhat bored. All the effort to discover one little piece of a puzzle did not seem worth it. I never liked the process of doing the experiments, and so the notion of becoming a research physician seemed less and less appealing. As a consequence, I began trying to imagine other possible careers. I tried to express my feelings, but my parents did not take them very seriously. They continued to ignore my view, dismissing it as born of insufficient experience. The way they talked about my being a doctor, it was as if I had no choice.

My doubts about medicine reached one peak at the end of my junior year in college when I went home and the three of us went out for dinner at a popular burger place in nearby Northbrook. I tried to tell them that while I found my science classes compelling, I didn't enjoy lab work at all and I could not imagine taking care of patients day in and day out the way my father did. My father delighted in the interaction with people and solving individual patients' problems; I took after my mom and thought about solving people's problems by changing social policies. I was much more intrigued by political theory and political change. I also told them that I was becoming more intrigued by studying and writing about politics, philosophy, and economics. I lacked a clearly formulated alternative to being a doctor. My thinking was pretty vague. Maybe, I ventured, I should start a political magazine or become a political philosopher. These half-baked possibilities were quickly quashed. My parents saw only that I got good grades in pre-med classes and stressed that as a physician I would be well respected and enjoy a good and reliable income, which certainly wasn't likely as a founder of an obscure magazine, they emphasized to me.

Sensing that I might not be satisfied with a life like his, my father said I could combine clinical practice and serious research. "So what if you don't like doing the lab work?" he said. "In a few years you'll have students and fellows to do the work. You'll be the boss."

For once, I didn't have the words to argue with my father. However, while I enjoyed learning about science, I knew I didn't enjoy lab work, even though I was reasonably good at it. I felt a vague sense that while I could not clearly articulate it, I was missing out on something that really appealed to me. I saw the irony that I was easily sailing forward on the pre-med track yet having the persistent gnawing sense that it wasn't right for me, while many of my classmates who truly wanted to be practicing doctors—and would be really good at it—were getting grades that would force them to contemplate other careers. Back at school I continued doing the pre-med track, while also continuing my studies in philosophy and political science. Always a loyal friend, Andy listened to me describe what happened that night in the restaurant and was not at all equivocal in his assessment. He said my parents "were trying to live through their kids too much" and were ignoring my own drives and aspirations. While he did not have an alternative career to suggest to me—after all, it wasn't his role, and because he wasn't sure what he wanted, he was planning to take a year off between his junior and senior years—but he did encourage me to stick to my own feelings. The tendency to push forward until someone screams out in painful resistance was one of the negative aspects of the Emanuel way, he said.

I could understand Andy's point, but it would take more than a good friendship to force me to confront some of the negative aspects of being an Emanuel. For that to happen, I would need to fall in love, marry, and have my own children.

Love and marriage and children were not something our parents pushed on us. Instead they showed us through their example that finding the right person, making a commitment, and having kids can make life more fulfilling and make us into better individuals. However, they clearly communicated to us boys that there was no need to hurry the process, and in the meantime there was no reason to deny oneself life's pleasures, just as long as you were responsible. That's why, in high school, Ari expressed true shock when Gibby told him a classmate was pregnant. "What's the matter with them?" she recalled my brother saying. "Haven't they ever heard of condoms?"

Ari would never be shy about sex, and as the most handsome and charming of us all, he would have an adventuresome single life. Eventually he would meet and fall in love with Sarah Addington, whom he later married, in 1996, when he was thirty-four years old and was becoming a successful agent. Rahm would follow a similar path, holding off on love and marriage until he met Amy Rule in 1990. They married in 1994, when Rahm was also thirty-four and well ensconced in the White House. In marrying late, both of my brothers followed my father's example. He insisted that it was best to complete your education and establish yourself firmly in a career before considering marriage and children. Love can wait.

Considering the fact that I was the brother who was truly tone-deaf when it came to women, it was a bit of a surprise—even to me—when I turned out to be the one who took a romantic detour from Ben Emanuel's route to an early marriage. Certainly my college friends would have never expected me to be the first one to actually find a like-minded soul and win her heart. It would happen in the summer between my junior and senior years, at a place that might be called the Shangri-la for molecular biologists.

.....

Located on the North Shore of Long Island, about forty miles outside New York City, the Cold Spring Harbor Laboratory occupies a small campus on the former company estate of a nineteenth-century whale-oil millionaire named John D. Jones. At its founding in 1890 the lab was involved in many aspects of research, including eugenics. After World War II an influx of immigrant European intellectuals made the lab a leader in the emerging field of molecular biology. By the time I got there in the summer of 1978, Cold Spring Harbor was the home of several Nobel Prize winners and was moving into neuroscience in a big way. The lab was led by James D. Watson, codiscoverer of the structure of DNA.

Ten college students were admitted to the summer Undergraduate Research Program (URP) and were fondly called URPs. The students selected for this work came from around the country, and were notable for being younger than everyone else on campus. We were assigned to work in the faculty labs, and allowed to sit in on classes offered mainly to graduate students and postdoctoral fellows. I ended up working on yeast genetics because my Amherst genetics course included a semester-long yeast lab project. We lived in pretty spartan rooms with not much more than a single bed, an old wood bureau, and a shared nightstand. Cold Spring Harbor was the kind of place where you could sit in on a Nobel laureate's lecture and bump into future prize winners in the hallways discussing new data. We were constantly reminded that a previous URP, David Baltimore, then of the Massachusetts Institute of Technology, had already won a Nobel Prize.

Many of the URPs took their lab work very seriously. My roommate, Jeremy Nathan, a future MD-PhD student and Johns Hopkins professor, worked out the genes that make the proteins for color vision in the eye and worked out the genetic basis of color blindness for his dissertation. He routinely worked until eleven at night, and referred to the lab as his "temple." Because of my doubts about science as a career, I could never get into the lab work that much. A fellow URP, Adam Schulman, was having his own doubts about becoming a molecular biologist. Adam and I reinforced each other on that score. We read Greek philosophy together, traveled into New York City to attend the Mostly Mozart program at Lincoln Center, and organized special discussions for the URPs with some of the outstanding scientists who visited Cold Spring Harbor that summer. Adam and I also organized an URP field trip to the Tanglewood Music Center in western Massachusetts. On many nights we "borrowed" an official Cold Spring Harbor van for late-night swims in the pool of a mansion located across the harbor and owned by the lab. I liked learning about immunology and neurobiology in the Cold Spring Harbor classrooms, but I never really found my lab work compelling. However, I did become infatuated with a beautiful young woman who walked past my lab several times per day as she made her way to the centrifuges to collect samples that were part of her own research.

A couple of years older than me, Linda Wendon was a PhD candidate at University College London but doing her research in Israel. She already had her name on some important neuroscience papers. Linda had come to Cold Spring Harbor with her mentor, Rami Rahamimoff, a world-renowned Israeli physician and neuroscientist who was based at Hebrew University in Jerusalem. Slightly built with silky blond hair and blue eyes, Linda was by far the most attractive young woman I saw at Cold Spring Harbor.

Linda, who had come to New York from Rami's lab in Jerusalem, had been born in Cambridge, Massachusetts, when her father, who was British, was a graduate student at Harvard. He had actually been born into an assimilated German Jewish family. In the 1930s, when he was nine, his parents sent him to a boarding school in England to escape Nazism. He converted to Christianity and became a British citizen. Linda's mother attended Wellesley College and was descended from the artist branch of *Mayflower* blue bloods, the Brewsters. Like me, Linda had seen quite a bit of the world. Unlike me, she did not seem to give a whit about politics or social issues. I was stunned, but also a little intrigued, to discover she did not know the name of the British prime minister and whether he was Tory or Labour. More impressively, she did not seem to care that she did not know.

We had watched each other, but finally met on August 1 and for the next four weeks spent as much time together as we could. During the workweek we ran together, ate dinners together, and went on late-night swims at the mansion pool or at the pebbly beach near the lab. On weekends we often took the train into New York City to visit museums or just walk around. Not interested in politics or social controversy, Linda seemed to me reserved and somewhat mysterious. She was everything an Emanuel wasn't.

When the summer program was over and I returned to Amherst, I was on such an emotional high that I barely ate or slept. I signed up for five courses and worked as a teaching assistant in two others—chemistry and genetics. Linda would remain at Cold Spring Harbor continuing her research through the end of October. During this time we saw each other almost every weekend. If she did not come north to see me, I traveled south to see her.

A long-distance romance forces you to set priorities, and in mine with Linda, I came to question my father's advice about love and marriage. He may have taught us to delay making a commitment until we were fully educated and established in life, but true love is never guaranteed and too many people pass on the real thing while waiting for the "right time" and a host of other variables to align perfectly.

When Linda finally left for England to resume her doctoral research at University College London, we had yet to figure out anything concrete. In the days before the Internet, Skype, and even cheap telephone service, the prospect of being separated by an ocean was daunting. Then there was our age difference. Linda was a quite serious twenty-four-year-old who knew she wanted to have children within a few years. I was just turning twenty-one and not finished with college. She was understandably worried that I wasn't ready for what she wanted. She told me to think hard about my choices. But love doesn't tell you to think carefully. Love leads you to Laker Airways and ninety-nine-dollar fares from Newark to London.

I flew to London over Thanksgiving and then again during Amherst's January term. While Linda worked in a tiny, closet-like lab doing experiments on the effect of tetanus toxin on nerve cells, I wandered through the museums and libraries of London. We stayed at her flat doing domestic things—cooking, reading to each other, and talking, and more talking. She took me up to Cambridge, where I met her parents and some of her extended family, including her uncle Max Perutz, who won the Nobel Prize in 1962 for his work on hemoglobin and had founded, at Cambridge, the world's greatest center for molecular biology. Linda's father, John, was a historian who had not finished his doctorate and wound up working in business and then as a barrister. His style was rather pontifical; he made pronouncements at the dinner table and expected unanimous assent. Being an Emanuel, I failed to grasp the family dynamic and instead of acting agreeable I said whatever came to mind, which irritated John and either amused or frightened everyone else.

.....

The spring break in my last year of college brought Linda to Wilmette to meet my family. She flew from London to Newark and then on to O'Hare Airport, where she appeared looking weary and a little apprehensive about meeting the people responsible for creating the intense, hyperopinionated young man she just happened to love.

When we arrived at my parents' house, my mother, tall and imposing, opened her arms to give Linda a big hug. Volumes are communicated in moments like these. How strong was my mother's embrace? Did Linda return the affection? Was there tension in their bodies? Were any words exchanged? I don't know the answers to these questions but I do know that these were two women from completely different worlds with completely different styles and completely different aspirations.

My mother did everything in a powerful way and even if she tried to hide her true feelings they came through loud and clear. Surely this included a few signals indicating she was uncomfortable about another woman "taking" her firstborn son.

Linda was reserved and so mannered you had to work at getting her to be candid. But she wasn't at all weak. Beneath the reserve she was highly moral and opinionated, especially when it came to interpersonal exchanges.

Inside the house, Linda did not make it past the kitchen before she was met by my father and brothers. Ari, who was then a senior in high school, said something loud and obnoxious about me that was intended to be funny. Rahm, who was in his second year at Sarah Lawrence, asked how she could possibly care about a schmuck like Zeke. My father said he was astonished by the fact that she had traveled thousands of miles to visit me. In *her* usual way Linda listened carefully, and managed an uncomfortable smile.

In fact, a strained smile was the best Linda could summon during her entire stay as she watched my family jostle and kibitz around the house and listened to dinner table chats that became roaring debates filled with comments like "You are an idiot" and "Don't be such an asshole." The put-downs and attacks were sometimes so sharp that it would be hard for an outsider to know we weren't entirely serious. Sometimes one of us would stake out a position just because we knew it would bother everyone else. Ari, for example, became somewhat conservative about economics once he had studied both Keynesianism and the alternatives being promoted at places like the University of Chicago. At one dinner debate he almost came to blows with Rahm when he said that government spending might be too high and that the economy might be boosted by cuts in taxes and business regulations.

"You're an idiot," said Rahm. "You don't know what you're talking about."

"Don't call names," our mother said before adding, "But Rahmi's right, Ari. You don't know what you're talking about."

Besides indulging in this kind of open argument, we also dispensed with most of the social niceties that other people use to welcome guests and establish trust and comfort. Indeed, guests were rarely formally introduced to the family or the house. Whether we had guests or not, we tended to be somewhat grabby with food, and table manners were optional. The only time this ever drew any objections was when my father started eating before my mother sat down.

In retrospect it's easy to see why my mother got upset whenever my father jumped the gun at the dinner table. She invested considerable time and effort in preparing the food and we owed her the courtesy of letting her sit down before we chowed down. Our father didn't see it this way. To him food was fuel and our family dinner was not a slow social engagement but rather a utilitarian exercise embellished with conversation.

As often as not, my father would pick up his knife and fork as soon as his plate was set before him. We would shout, "Dad, cut it out!" and sometimes reach over with our own forks to trap his against the plate. He would complain that he'd worked hard all day and that he shouldn't be constrained by a rule that made no sense. Sometimes this response would be accompanied by a sarcastic joke that made it clear he thought that anyone bothered by his manners was overly sensitive.

Positioned between our parents, we boys took our mother's side. For one thing, we knew she'd worked hard all day and deserved some consideration. We also knew that peace depended on her mood. We wanted to enjoy our food and the time at the table, and this required her being happy when she sat down.

Still, though, I think our father's blasé attitude encouraged us to be somewhat dismissive when it came to the feelings of others, especially women. As our father rolled his eyes at our mother's complaints, we got the idea that women were less rational than men and weren't quite worthy of our full respect. Believe me, this perspective is a liability for any man hoping to love a woman as an equal in a relationship, and this was a lesson we'd each have to learn as adults.

On her first visit with my family, Linda was overwhelmed by the fight-club style of conversation and no doubt detected the sense of entitlement in my father's attitude. I had no real appreciation for so-cial graces and struggled to understand what Linda was experiencing. In response Linda often retreated to my room. She emerged mainly for meals and the occasional outing, which gave me a chance to show her around the North Shore and Chicago. We also went to a movie with my father, which, in retrospect, might not have been such a great idea. He likes to absorb every frame with complete focus while I'm an enthusiastic viewer who laughs easily, and loudly. My idiosyncratic hee-haw inevitably provokes him to scold me and elbow me in the ribs. I think nothing of it, but to Linda it seemed like she was going to the movies with a couple of loudmouths who were more interested in policing each other than watching what was on the screen.

It was a mistake, no doubt, to have Linda stay at our house for such a long time. Although my family considers an extended stay in someone's home simply the way things should be done, three or four days' exposure with nights spent at a hotel would have been a gentler way for everyone to get to know one another. I didn't know any better and my parents would have been insulted if Linda had insisted on staying at a hotel.

And though she tried to be accepting, my mother was never going to be enthusiastic about any woman who replaced her as the number-one female in my life. Inevitably she let her disapproval show. By the end of the visit she and Linda were locked into a pattern of mutual wariness that would last for years to come.

As the man in the middle, I was brought face-to-face with two challenging realities. The first was that my family was uniquely loud, intense, and passionate. And while it was warm, often effusively warm and familiar, it took a rare kind of person to feel comfortable staying in the house. Friends like Andy Oram had said as much, but I'd failed to fully appreciate their insight. But when Linda expressed her discomfort and anxiety every time we were alone together, I was forced to come to grips with the fact that our aggressive, free-form style of relating might strike an outsider as obnoxious, if not assaultive. Worse still was the way we assumed that everyone who came into our orbit should simply adapt and play along. The underlying message was that if you were not skilled at the thrust and parry of kitchen table debate there was something wrong with you. Emanuels did not have to accommodate to the world; the world had to accommodate to them.

After Linda left, I put a great deal of thought into how I might make things work with her despite the difference in our ages, and the physical distance that might separate us as we pursued our careers after I graduated from college. Linda was planning to take a postdoctoral position in London come autumn. I had reluctantly applied to several medical schools. I was rejected at most of them, such as Johns Hopkins and Cornell, without even an interview, but was accepted at just two: Northwestern—where my father was on the faculty—and Harvard. My parents wanted me to be close to home and go to Northwestern. That was not my choice. I was still reluctant to commit myself to becoming a physician and needed more space to make some decisions. Consequently, rather than rush into medical school, I decided to postpone matriculation. Fortunately, the admissions office at Harvard agreed to let me defer, as long as I was doing something that could justify the time off. With a fellowship from Amherst, I decided I would give biomedical research one more sustained period of time to see if I liked it. With the help of one of Linda's relatives I found a research position in the Department of Biochemistry at the University of Oxford. I would be able to see Linda on weekends, try my hand again at research, and have some time—and distance—to assess my career options.

.....

Rahm and Ari felt a little abandoned by me when I went to college, but during the two years when they were both still at home they became closer friends. Then, when Rahm left for Sarah Lawrence, Ari enjoyed special status as the last son at home. Although Ari would deny it as an adult, Rahm and I distinctly recall that he got away with murder. Credit his charming manner or my parents running out of whatever energy made them more watchful with me and Rahm, but for whatever reason, they relaxed the rules and just generally stopped worrying so much. If I had to be home on weekends by 11 P.M. or midnight during my senior year in high school, Ari had no curfew. Sometimes he stayed out until daybreak, and he roamed all over the Midwest working and playing with his friends. On the few occasions when he went a little too far and got into trouble, Ari always managed to do something to change the course of the conversation. In one memorable conflict with my mother, for example, he forced her to stop complaining as he literally picked her up and deposited her in the garbage can on the side of the house. He drove away before she got herself out, but he returned with a bouquet of flowers that she accepted as an apology.

Late in August, Ari and Rahm drove the old Ford wagon to see me at Cold Spring Harbor. From there, I was supposed to accompany Ari to Maine, Vermont, and Massachusetts on his college tour. It was travel according to my father's thrifty style, right down to sleeping in the car and stealing apples from an orchard to eat with peanut butter because we didn't have the money to buy food. We bought the gas on our father's credit card.

The trip did not result in Ari finding the right fit at Bowdoin, Middlebury, Tufts, or any of the other schools we visited. But in his senior year of high school Ari would come east by himself to visit Rahm and practice an early form of "speed dating" at Sarah Lawrence, where the ratio of females to males was heavily skewed in his favor. In the end he wound up focusing on Macalester College in St. Paul, Minnesota. Macalester was quite selective, but with hard work Ari had learned ways to compensate for his dyslexia and improved his grades enough to be accepted. With maturity he also developed better control of his temper and behavior. He was still aggressive and revved higher than most people, even when idling. But he was far less prone to get into physical confrontations and, with the distance, his relationship with my father improved.

All in all, life was progressing smoothly enough. I buried myself in academic work and chased a postgrad position at Oxford. Rahm breezed through college, earning a degree in psychology and soon throwing himself into politics in Illinois. Meanwhile, Ari, after he got his degree at Macalester, took an extended "working" vacation in France, where he made some money but mostly ran up the balance on my father's credit card.

Fifteen

PERFECTIONISM AND ITS DISCONTENTS

It was Oxford, the oldest university in the English-speaking world and the ultimate fillip on an aspiring academic's CV. But I was completely miserable. Adjusting to my new environment had been difficult and now on top of everything I was sick. Alone in the room I had rented in a fashionable North Oxford home, I shivered but couldn't turn up the heat, because the large room was warmed by a coin-operated heater that required a steady flow of five-pence coins. It was in the midst of the oil crisis that followed the Iranian revolution, and the dollar was in the tank at $2.40 to every British pound. I was paid in dollars and was worried about running out of money. Then, when the sweats came and I was miserably overheated, I couldn't leave my room for a cool bath, either, because the house rules forbade running water after 10 P.M. Such was life at the dreary dawn of Margaret Thatcher's rule in Great Britain.

Recession, unemployment, and the traditional British ambivalence when it came to basic comforts meant that my landlady charged for heat by the minute and promised eviction to any lodger who dared break one of her rules. But I was sick, and when my fever spiked at 2 A.M. I couldn't take it any longer. The lukewarm bath made me feel much better and I was able to sleep. The next day, when I came home from the lab, I found a neat, handwritten note on my desk. The landlady curtly informed me that I had broken the rules and must move out. She made it clear that there would be no negotiating on this point. I didn't even try.

That day I began the search for what would, in the end, be a much better living situation. The location was a small house—two rooms downstairs and two upstairs—on the poor side of town, which I came to share with a young couple named Margaret and Danny. Margaret, a Cambridge graduate and grade school teacher, came from a prosperous family. (They got front-row seats to view the wedding of Prince Charles and Diana.) Danny had grown up in New York, where he attended the exclusive Dalton School. After earning an undergraduate degree at Cambridge he enrolled as a graduate student at Oxford. His rooms at the university were the ones Lewis Carroll had occupied as a math lecturer in the mid-nineteenth century.

At the time when I moved in with Margaret and Danny, I was beginning to question all the little steps that had taken me so far from home. Linda and I had seen far less of each other than I expected, even though she was just fifty miles away. In the meantime, I was alienating the people at Oxford in much the same way that I had alienated the people at Amherst, by being myself.

It all started with the way I conducted myself in Raymond Dwek's immunology lab. Accustomed to long workdays, I arrived at the lab early and kept working late into the night. In contrast, the doctoral students and full-time technicians arrived at nine, took the usual lunch and tea breaks, and departed at five. My persistence bothered them, but so did the sound of my loud, squeaky voice and my bull-in-a-china-shop approach to getting things done. If I needed chemicals or other laboratory supplies and none were immediately available in the Dwek lab I scoured the other labs in the building until I found what I needed. I followed the same routine when it came to pieces of equipment, from pipettes and beakers to centrifuges. If someone was nearby, I asked them to lend me what I needed. If I came upon a key item that was unguarded, I simply took it.

Yanks, according to British lore, were always too assertive, action-oriented, and ill-mannered. For a while the fuddy-duddies of Oxford circa 1979 tried to excuse my behavior on cultural grounds. But I was even more obnoxious than the stereotype and it wasn't long before my mentor was hearing complaints.

Fortunately, Professor Dwek, who was thirty-nine and reaching the top of his game, was one of the few in the Oxford faculty who could have tolerated and even encouraged me as I violated one British norm after another. An extremely confident scientist who had worked with colleagues around the world, Dwek was himself a Jew who knew that the British academy did not understand the concept or value of chutzpah. In my own experience, I came to see that Jews were even more misunderstood in England than they were in America. This was made clear to me by the senior technician on Dwek's staff, who held an Oxford PhD. During the spring break he asked me in his Welsh accent what I planned to do to celebrate Easter. I explained to him that I was Jewish. He then said, "That's fine, but where will you be going on Easter Sunday?" Despite working for a Jewish faculty member, he simply had no idea that Jews did not celebrate Easter. He really knew nothing at all about being Jewish.

Raymond actually took more than a little pleasure in the ways that I annoyed those colleagues whom he considered to be stuffed shirts. Whenever the outrage over my behavior grew loud, he explained that I was not ill-mannered but simply "American." He told people to think of me as "the equivalent of John McEnroe," the tennis player who was as famous for his tantrums as for his championships. Raymond viewed this as a double win—the faculty who he thought deserved it were aggravated by me, and he was able to play the "nice" guy without really doing anything to curb my provocative behavior. Raymond's work, which involved deciphering the behavior of specific antibodies that protect us from disease, required the kind of intensity I brought to the task. I may not have been the favorite of my peers but I was an effective research associate, and outside of work, Raymond found me and my broad interests—from philosophy to travel to the arts—to be good company.

A teacher who became a friend, Raymond occasionally invited me to dine with him at his college's high table. This meant donning a coat, tie, and an Oxford black gown and sitting at a long table set on a dais above the undergrad tables in the great eating hall at Exeter College. Raymond saw this as a way to fatten me up with an occasional good meal. Raymond was also kind enough to let me use his faculty rooms in the college for weekends with Linda. And he invited me to dinner at his home. Linda sometimes came with me to the Dwek home, where I hit it off well with Raymond's wife and four children.

In mid-January I served as photographer for his son Robert's bar mitzvah party. When the party ended, I hopped on my bike, the standard means of transportation for just about every student—and many faculty members—in Oxford, and headed for my home, which was down the hill, through the center of Oxford to the other, poorer side of the Cherwell River, about three miles away. It was after midnight, and I shivered a bit in the cold air as I sped down the Botley Road and then onto George Street, which brought me into the center of the city. I turned right on Turl Street near Exeter College and then cut left onto the High Street.

I had not gone more than a hundred feet when a police car overtook me, turned on its lights, and then veered into my lane. I swerved to avoid a collision, and was moving out to pass when the police car swerved again, forcing me to pull over to the curb and stop. The driver, a tall and big fellow in uniform, hopped out.

"Why did you not stop back there?"

"I didn't think you were pulling over for me."

"We wanted you to stop."

"What was I doing wrong?" I shot back.

"Are you drunk?" he said, putting his face closer to mine to intimidate me.

"No. I'm not drunk."

At that time I was a teetotaler, and to demonstrate the fact, I blew into the police officer's face. Not surprisingly, this gesture did not go over well. The officer's partner jumped out of the squad car and came around to where we were standing. He announced that I was being taken into custody for not stopping at a corner and for resisting arrest. They put me in the back of their car and left my bike there to be picked up later.

By the time all the paperwork was completed at the Oxford jail it was well past 1 A.M. and I decided to postpone calling Raymond for help. The officers walked me down to a stone cell already occupied by some guy who had been brought in earlier in the evening for drunkenness and disorderly conduct. They unlocked the bars and put me inside. I slid down the cold wall and sat on the freezing floor, staring at my unknown and incoherent cellmate, who was thrashing on the lower bunk. The only other furnishings in the cell were a toilet and a vomit bucket, both of which reeked.

At 8 A.M. the jailers allowed me to call Raymond, who contacted the law lecturer at Exeter College. They came to bail me out. Before I left with my bike, the charges had been changed, for what seemed like the umpteenth time, to riding without a rear light. Ironically, despite my accent and obvious American citizenship, the Oxford police never asked me for my registration card; every foreigner living in Great Britain had to have one, documenting that he or she had registered with the local police every few months. I refused to register, which was a serious legal violation.

I could have simply agreed to the charge against me and avoided a trial, but I am an Emanuel. I wanted my day in court. Two months after my arrest I appeared before the magistrate. When the prosecutor called for testimony from the arresting officers, the two men gave contradictory accounts of what had happened that night on High Street. Acting as my own lawyer, I nervously pointed out the inconsistencies in their stories and argued that no one could draw a reasonable conclusion based on such varied presentations of the facts. However, this was not a hearing dedicated to fact-finding, truth, or justice. The magistrate confined himself to affirming the charges and setting the fines I would be required to pay. He ordered me to pay 175 pounds, nearly five hundred dollars. This was far more money than I could possibly scrape up. Raymond paid the fine and allowed me to work off my debt to him by teaching Sunday school at his synagogue, giving tutorials in biochemistry to his Oxford undergrads, and grading their final exams for him.

.....

My time at Oxford between 1979 and 1981 was consistent with what many American students there experienced. We were often cold, hungry for decent food, and short on money. This was before Great Britain joined the European Union, imported continental foods, and developed phenomenal restaurants. The only food with any taste was Indian fare. And the combination of the cold and damp penetrated the bones in a way I never experienced in the States. Central heating still had not been installed in many houses; heat flowed from a few coils in small electric heaters that never warmed your body thoroughly. I did, however, enjoy one brief exciting moment when I became famous among the Brits, and also widely despised.

The adventure arose in a roundabout way. BBC television was planning a new show called *Now Get Out of That*. BBC producers advertised in Oxford in the hope of identifying two students—a female undergraduate and a male graduate—to join a four-person "Oxford" team, including a local businessman and farmer, that would be dropped in some remote spot in the Welsh countryside. The Oxford team would compete against a Cambridge team to solve a series of puzzling tasks or missions. If this sounds like a forerunner of the TV show *Survivor,* then you've got the idea. First broadcast in August 1981, *Now Get Out of That* was arguably the world's very first reality outdoor challenge program and it was destined to be must-see TV for four years running.

Raymond Dwek had been dining at the high table in Exeter College with the BBC producer, who complained he could not find a suitable male graduate student for the Oxford team. Raymond considered my daily long-distance running and quirky, assertive personality and suggested me. I didn't hesitate. In a matter of weeks I found myself in the middle of the vast estate surrounding Eastnor Castle with a camera crew and my three teammates. We were given two days to complete a variety of challenges using only our wits, our physical abilities, confusing hints, and the meager supplies provided by the producers.

One of the tasks required us to build vehicles out of a collection of four bicycle frames and various parts and then ride across the countryside. Of course, we did not get enough wheels to construct bicycles for each of us. After much wrenching and tinkering, I decided to simply run ahead of my teammates as they pedaled.

A second challenge found us deposited on a tiny island in the middle of a pond, where we were forced to use a cable system to cross the water without getting wet. Forced to spend the night outdoors in a downpour, we were supplied with just two dead rabbits, some carrots, potatoes, and bouillion, and wood for a fire. Falling into classic, gender-defined roles I skinned the rabbits while the two other men made the fire. The one woman on our team—the law student undergraduate—ended up doing the cooking.

For the finale we had to invade the castle, retrieve a mysterious electronic device called "the Beast," and return to a fixed raft in the castle's lake. I pushed for quick solutions whenever we reached an obstacle and often simply took over a task when things got stalled. I knew as it was happening that I was being much louder and more direct than the others. They were British, which, in my view, meant they were too passive and willing to follow the rules we were given. The jobs at hand required energy, improvisation, and action, which I supplied in abundance while most of the others alternately followed my orders, argued meekly, or sullenly looked on.

The exception was Derek, who was a middle-aged, crew-cut businessman who fancied that as the oldest he should be the team's leader. Initially he tried to take charge. Instinctively, the other Brits deferred to him. But his authority fell apart on the very first challenge when it became apparent that he couldn't read a simple map. I took the map from him and just kept pushing forward. Although we barked at each other continuously, the tension never quite reached the point where any punches were thrown.

I give Derek most of the credit for the fact that we never came to blows. He was a well-meaning bloke and he did appreciate the successes we had. I actually tried hard to be good-natured, even after we had climbed a rope ladder to get into the castle only to discover that we could have strolled through an open door just around a corner. Fortunately, we still got to the Beast first, seized it, and raced toward our final task.

The finish called for us to use a metal frame, wood, and some inflatable tubes to construct rafts that we would paddle across the lake and then, after capturing the Beast, to get to the floating raft. We fired the flare gun and a Royal Air Force helicopter appeared overhead. A sling was dropped down and, one by one, we were winched into the hovering aircraft. It was one of the most exciting things I had ever done. Intensely competitive, I was thrilled when we were informed that we had beaten Cambridge.

After the contest was over, the film was edited and the host, Bernard Falk, added his witty narration. The four hours were aired over the course of four nights during the last week of August 1981 and drew a big audience. And though Derek and the others got plenty of "face time," the voice that echoed constantly throughout the four episodes was not the one speaking the Queen's English.

From the very first scene I was presented as a caricature of the kind of rude, pushy American whom the British love to hate. Overnight, the media decided that I was worthy of scorn and had a field day making fun of me. Russell Davies of *The Sunday Times* of London called me "the excitable Zeke Emanuel" and described my "star turn" this way:

> The camera seldom got a good look at Zeke, as he was mostly a gesticulating blur, but the microphone got no rest from his terrible voice: a high warbling desperate mode of utterance such as might have been heard lecturing its parents in bad feature films of the post–James Dean period. Zeke was that worst of pains, a pain in the ear.

As I recall, Davies was the kindest of the commentators. Summing up at the end of the show, Bernard Falk said, "Zeke is pushy, but where

would Oxford be without him?" Andy Oram insists that people exco-
riated me in letters to the editors published in papers all across Great
Britain and that one of the tabloids elected me the most disliked person in the land. (Ironically, before the show was aired, I had left Britain
to start medical school in the United States. I would not see the show
for another three decades, when my daughters gave me a copy for
Hanukkah in 2011.) The British especially hated that I led Oxford to
victory.

But not everyone viewed me with disdain. A few weeks after the
series aired, some of Linda's friends went walking in the Scottish
Highlands and discovered, inside a hut built as a resting place for hik-
ers, a note advising visitors who faced hardships to "be like Zeke."

In time the experience would help me see, with a bit more clarity,
who I was in comparison with others. I *was* loud, fast, pushy, and incredibly competitive. But I was also the only member of the cast who
would be both indispensable and memorable. I was willing to accept
both the good and the bad, including the bit about how I resembled a
movie character "lecturing its parents," because it was pretty close to
the truth. And I wasn't embarrassed by who I was.

.....

As my brothers made their way into adulthood, they also ran into critics and opponents. In France, where Ari was spending a semester
abroad, he encountered lots of people who challenged his views on life
and how it should be lived. He adapted well enough, learning to speak
passable French and accepting local customs. But he was still the same
old Ari, ever willing to take risks and push things to the limit. When
the Glass brothers stopped to see him during their own trip to Europe,
they found him to be more worldly, but no less ornery. He was starting
to resent the put-downs and dirty looks he got from natives who recognized him as an American and he was veering dangerously close to
the kind of attitude that had meant trouble for him over the years.

When Michael Glass came home he told a story about going with
Ari to a little café for some food. Short on money, they declined the
expensive bottled water that servers tend to push on diners and asked

for tap water instead. The waiter sniffed and walked away. Ari waited for the waiter to pass him three or four times before he called out loudly to remind him to bring the water. Under his breath the man muttered in French, "I'm not your dog." Ari heard him and jumped up, puffed out his chest, and growled, "Tu es mon chien." Thus informed that he was indeed Ari's dog, the waiter hustled off and returned with the water on a tray. All the while, Michael Glass studied the sharp corkscrew tucked into the waistband of the waiter's pants, wondering if he was going to attack. The *chien* turned out to be all bark and no bite and Ari chalked up another victory in his never-ending confrontation with the world.

After college, Ari knocked around in New York for a while, trying various businesses. My father, who considered advanced degrees to be insurance against unemployment and the tyranny of bosses, urged him to get an MBA. Ari could have gone into the MBA program at Northwestern. However, just as I had deviated from my father's advice in order to study bioethics, Ari decided to search for something more exciting and fulfilling than the classroom. Through a friend he was hired by a legendary New York talent agent named Robert Lantz. Already in his seventies when Ari met him, "Robbie" Lantz was the son of a German screenwriter who had escaped the Nazis by fleeing to London. There Robbie had worked for years as a story editor and consultant for American film companies. He finally came to the United States in the late 1940s to work as an agent. He wound up representing a roster of writers, actors, and directors that was the envy of the industry. Among them were Milos Forman, Elizabeth Taylor and Richard Burton, Bette Davis, Montgomery Clift, and James Baldwin. He also represented the estate of Damon Runyon.

Robbie was the quintessential New York character. A regular at the Russian Tea Room, he attended all the important theater openings and frequently wrote letters to the editor of the *Times* to complain about the rude service delivered by ushers and ticket-takers at the theater or about crime rates that kept law-abiding citizens out of Central Park at night.

When Ari met him, Lantz represented the producer of the hugely successful play *Amadeus* and he was trying to help Philip Roth develop a film about the Soviet gulags. The press often turned to him for comments about the state of the entertainment industry or the secrets of successful agenting. He invariably stressed loyalty and constant concern for clients. It was important to accept, he said, that for some actors "a bad haircut can be a catastrophe of biblical proportions."

As an Emanuel brother, Ari understood, instinctively, how to deal with people who were demanding, mercurial, emotional, and dramatic. Because reading remained a chore, he knew he would always struggle to evaluate book proposals or scripts for plays and movies. However, no one would work longer hours on behalf of a client than Ari, who still had trouble sleeping past sunrise, or pour more energy and activity into a single day. Also, the skills and techniques of nagging, defiance, and charm that worked so well for him in the family and allowed him to go up to the line but rarely cross it were perfectly suited to a business where relationships matter more than anything else. He liked nothing more than to be a champion for something or someone he believed in. He was a tireless advocate.

Seeing Ari's potential, and noting the big trends in the entertainment business, Robbie Lantz gave him some serious counsel. New York would remain a big theater town and the center of the publishing universe, but the real action for actors, screenwriters, directors, and producers was in Los Angeles. If Ari wanted to make full use of his talents, earn real money, and represent important artists, he should go west. In 1987, my brother packed and moved to Los Angeles, where, with my father's financial backing, he bought a house in Hollywood and began working on the lowest rung of the ladder: in the mailroom/training program at Creative Artists Agency.

Ari loved the work from the very first day and managed to perform even the most menial tasks—like washing a superior's car—without grumbling. He was so determined to do well that despite his dyslexia, which made reading almost physically painful, he committed himself to reading as many scripts as he could get his hands on. During one family vacation in Costa Rica he actually spent part of each day plowing through a stack of bound manuscripts while the rest of us went swimming and explored the countryside.

In the mid to late 1980s, we three brothers were all pursuing very distinct careers, as far apart as was possible. From the moment he moved west, Ari would never live anywhere else but Los Angeles. I was in the midst of my medical and bioethics training—and raising two daughters—in Boston, more than 2,600 miles away. And Rahm lived in Chicago while taking temporary assignments in Washington, D.C. We would keep in touch by phone but in the coming few years we would spend very little actual time together.

But just as I think it was no accident that we chose three radically different career paths—academics, politics, and business—I think that there were good reasons for us to put so many miles between us. Although Rahm and Ari might disagree, I am certain we needed time and space to develop and succeed as independent adults. Each of us needed to find our own careers and not compete with the others. Rahm needed to get out of my shadow, and Ari needed to prove, to himself as much as anybody, that he could succeed despite his disability. Besides, I don't think there's a city big enough to accommodate more than one Emanuel at a time. Our force fields would have collided and God only knows how many casualties such an event might produce. Once we all began getting recognition in our individual spheres, we could then begin to reapproach one another as equals.

.....

Ever the family negotiator, Rahm possessed the skills required to succeed in politics long before he decided to make it his career. He first joined a campaign in 1980, when he volunteered in Democrat David Robinson's campaign to oust Republican congressman Paul Findley. The district, which was in and around Springfield, Illinois, had been held by the GOP since 1959 and Findley was a powerful incumbent. He was the third-ranking Republican congressman at the time and was also a vociferous critic of Israel. Findley was known as the Palestine Liberation Organization's man in Washington. He spoke in ominous and conspiratorial tones about Israel's supporters in America. This posturing gave Rahm and Robinson, who was also Jewish, plenty of motivation to try to beat Findley. They came very close but lost the year Reagan beat Carter for the White House. Two years later, Rahm helped Richard Durbin finally dislodge Findley. Durbin would go on to a very successful career in the United States House of Representatives, and then the U.S. Senate, where he rose to majority whip.

As Rahm knew, Illinois was a great place to learn politics from the ground up. His first full-time job was at the Illinois Public Action Council, which was conducting a ferocious campaign against utility rate hikes. Focused on working families in both rural and urban communities, the council had volunteers knocking on thousands of doors every day and was raising a war chest worth millions on the basis of ten- and twenty-dollar donations. Already credited with helping to elect several members of Congress in 1982, the council's leaders, including field director Michael McGann, intended to fight the rate hikes and energize the party around issues related to the economy and the environment.

McGann was a skilled and experienced grassroots organizer. He taught Rahm volumes about organizing, fund-raising, and coalition-building and helped him meet the key people in Illinois politics. In 1984 Rahm worked on the campaign of Congressman Paul Simon, who challenged the incumbent Republican senator Chuck Percy. This was the same Percy who had won my mother's vote in 1966. When he challenged Percy the pundits considered Simon's chances to be slim, but he wound up winning with a campaign that showed Percy was out of touch with his constituents and an organization that got Democrats to the polls in droves. As a senator, Simon—who always wore a bow tie—was the exemplar of integrity. He would become one of the main proponents of election finance reform and a staunch advocate for humanitarian intervention in conflict zones such as Rwanda.

In 1985, Rahm became a regional field director for the Democratic Congressional Campaign Committee (the "D triple C" to insiders), the national organization charged with helping the party's candidates get elected to the House of Representatives. In the one newspaper article that mentioned him during this time, Rahm was described as an "intense, high-strung" guy embarked on a "hectic" mission.

Given a territory that included much of the Midwest, Rahm was supposed to help candidates develop into winners. Simultaneously, he advised the DCCC on which ones had a true chance of success and deserved to receive money and electoral support. Then, as now, money played a huge role in elections, and the committee had to be careful about where it sent checks. Candidates were given target fund-raising figures, say, one hundred thousand dollars, and told that if they could raise that amount by a certain date they would be likely to get a share of the committee's funds. Most people are shy about asking for money. To help them, the DCCC provided lists of potential donors with the means and the desire to help Democrats. Rahm would often sit with a candidate, dial a potential donor's number, and hand the candidate the receiver when the line began ringing.

Clayton Lewis, who was the DCCC's man in the Northeast when Rahm worked the Midwest, considered my brother to be a seasoned veteran because he had signed on four months earlier. Throughout the 1986 election season, the two were best friends, often talking strategy late into the night while they ate takeout food inside budget motels like Super 8 and Motel 6. Ever the cheapskate, Rahm could not have cared less about the thread count of the sheets or the number of channels on the TV, as long as he could watch the news. He loved the strategic challenge and he worked with the spirit of a military commander.

When we were growing up, no one would have guessed that Rahm, shy outside the house and reluctant to study for any length of time, would ever be drawn into this kind of fast-paced, detail-oriented life. Maybe we underestimated the effect of growing up in a home where the dinner hour was like the Prime Minister's Question Time in Parliament. Maybe we underestimated Rahm's competitive spirit. Rahm was a natural talent. An eager student of the game, who learned from more experienced players, he also developed his own style. Every bit an Emanuel, he showed emotions openly, spoke bluntly, and frequently raised his voice. Like my father, he was very pragmatic and focused on the essentials, emphasizing problem-solving and winning over intellectual purity. And he vigorously deployed my father's Napoleonic dictum: Offense is the best defense.

For Rahm, it was necessary to balance the passion he felt for candidates who were brilliant and deserved to be in Congress with the practicalities of winning elections. Sometimes the candidates you love face too many obstacles to win. At other times candidates you do not like very much have what it takes to seize a seat for the party. Since the party's goal is to win control of the House, you have to back anyone who can win and cut loose the ones who can't, all without sentimentality.

In 1986, the Democrats added five seats to their House majority and took over the Senate from the Republicans. After the dust settled, analysts noted that it was the most expensive congressional election season in history and that money played a big role in many individual contests. In the five districts where the Democrats picked up new seats, the DCCC had concentrated its efforts and outspent the opposition. The result seemed to affirm the wisdom of selectively funding candidates who had both a fighting chance and the stomach for fund-raising.

Promoted to political director of the DCCC for the 1988 election cycle, Rahm tried to focus workers and spending on efforts that produced measurable results. He tested policy messages to see which ones might move voters to vote for a Democrat and devoted dollars to those activities, such as turning out voters, with obvious rewards at the polls. These methods helped the party gain two House seats during the 1988 election, which saw Republican George H. W. Bush take the White House.

Rahm loved politics and campaigns so much that he stayed in the business during the off years, when most professionals take a break. In 1989 he helped Richard M. Daley Jr., son of the Mayor Daley my mother loathed, win his first mayoral campaign. The younger Daley was a liberal when it came to issues like gun control, the environment, and civil rights but he was no enemy of free enterprise or big business. Indeed, he planned to help those that wanted to expand and bring jobs to the city and he wasn't against borrowing an idea from the Republicans if he thought it made sense. In this way, Daley was the kind of pragmatic liberal Rahm favored.

It was hardly a surprise, therefore, when a young southern governor who called himself a centrist "New Democrat" came to ask Rahm to help him become president. It was late November 1991. The Iowa caucuses and New Hampshire primary were just weeks away and Bill Clinton was in trouble. He was down in the polls and, more crucially, had almost no money. He needed someone like Rahm who had the energy, contacts, and know-how to be his finance director and raise the cash he needed to keep going.

Our father was dead set against Rahm signing up with Clinton. "How can this guy from Arkansas who nobody knows get elected president?" he asked. Of course, my father had not been the most reliable person for career advice. Like most parents he was conservative when it came to his children's careers—he wanted them to pursue tried-and-true paths to success. Fortunately, he raised his children to question authority and received wisdom, and they rarely listened to his cautious advice.

Rahm wasn't so sure that signing on with Clinton was a bad idea. Despite the poll numbers, he knew that Clinton was by far the most charismatic of the candidates. He was a southerner who could appeal to northern liberals and a policy expert who played hardball politics. And anyway, getting high-level leadership experience in a presidential race was worth the gamble.

When Rahm called me we talked about Clinton's overall appeal, which was substantial, and his money woes, which were also substantial. With roughly $200,000 in the bank he was far behind the leading money-raiser, Massachusetts senator Paul Tsongas, who had almost $800,000 in the bank.

By chance Rahm's schedule and Clinton's brought them together at the home of a wealthy Democratic donor in Brookline, a suburb of Boston that was two miles from where Linda and I then lived. We had both had jobs at Harvard Medical School–affiliated hospitals after finishing our training. For some inexplicable reason Rahm asked me to attend the meeting with him.

Throwing in with Clinton would mean Rahm would have to close off the chance to work with other, more plausible candidates, including Jerry Brown and Paul Tsongas. Both would have welcomed him, and other Democratic operatives were picking them to win. Making the right choice at this moment was especially important given the likelihood of a Democrat actually winning the general election. In President Bush the opposition would field one of the weakest incumbents in history, a man who had alienated his base by reneging on his "Read my lips, no new taxes" pledge and energized the opposition with his inability to connect with the American people. The right Democrat could well defeat him, and anyone who was involved in the effort from the start, and at a high level, would be guaranteed a role in the new administration.

.....

Before I met Rahm and Clinton in that Brookline living room I reflected on how far we had all come. At his most recent birthday Ari had turned thirty, which meant that none of us could claim, anymore, to be "young." He had risen quickly in the entertainment business and was already a full-fledged agent, representing movie stars, writers, and directors. Although I didn't understand it at the time, he was already a pioneer in the practice of "packaging," which shifted the balance of power in TV and film away from studios and networks and toward the big agencies. He accomplished this with a combination of aggression, humor, profanity, and impulsivity that would have been ruinous in most other realms but was completely acceptable, and effective, in the realm of egos and make-believe that is Hollywood.

Both Rahm and Ari had decided to wait for career success before committing to marriage and family. By 1991, I was father to three daughters, who were mainly my responsibility during their early years. I was able to function as Mr. Mom because Harvard had let me suspend my medical education to get a doctorate from the Harvard Department of Government, where, thanks to professors Michael Sandel and Dennis Thompson, I was able to focus on the one area where my interest in science and the humanities intersected: bioethics. Although I studied, wrote, and taught, my schedule was flexible in ways that Linda's was not. She was doing her internship and residency training at Massachusetts General Hospital, and writing in the area of medical ethics. In time we would publish many papers and become well-known as the authors "Emanuel and Emanuel." But at the time, my interest in pursuing bioethics struck many at Harvard Medical School as foolish, if not an act of career suicide.

In those days, bioethics was considered a dead-end field and from the start I ran into trouble. One problem arose when a *Boston Globe* reporter did a Sunday magazine feature article on the living will template that Linda and I had created—the Medical Directive. Our view was that patients seemed to want more information and control over end-of-life care decisions. And our Medical Directive was a way to facilitate discussions between patients and their family and patients and their physicians. The reporter interviewed me while I was still a resident at the Beth Israel Hospital, but the article came out while I was training to be a cancer doctor at the Dana-Farber Cancer Institute. Unfortunately, in the early 1990s, cancer institutes were not ready to acknowledge that people with cancer often died and needed help dying well, without pain and with family. They considered themselves cancer fighters, not attendants to the dying. On the Monday after the article appeared I was summoned to the office of the president of Dana-Farber. He was mainly a researcher and he informed me in no uncertain terms to keep my big mouth shut. To be more precise, he said that I could speak to the press and be quoted as a Harvard fellow but not as a physician at the Dana-Farber Cancer Institute.

The president was the type of Harvard character I came to call "bow-tie Jews." These are guys who come from lower-class stock similar to mine but do everything they can to appear more Brahmin than the Cabots and the Lodges. We were oil and water, and after that first encounter I was almost certain that we would clash again, and often, because I was not about to be silenced. Fortunately, I was saved by a couple of other Dana-Farber cancer specialists, Bob Mayer and Craig Henderson, who volunteered to review my work and public statements to be sure they were well supported. Henderson would welcome me to work in the breast cancer clinic, which he directed. In the late 1990s Mayer would become president of the American Society of Clinical Oncology, where he made end-of-life care his major focus and helped change for the better how cancer centers and doctors across the country treated terminally ill patients. At last the medical system would allow people to talk in depth about one of the most important decisions of their life: how to die.

With the support of colleagues like Henderson and Mayer, and with Linda as a collaborator, I got to work in an important new field, while also enjoying the experience of being a very hands-on father. It turned out that like my father, I loved being with babies and little children. I always found playing and talking with them much easier than making cocktail chitchat with adults. After thousands of mornings, afternoons, and evenings soloing with my daughters I got pretty good at reading, games, crafts, and cooking, especially baking. Along the way I finally learned to be more patient and empathetic. Kids will do that to you.

I received a little more smoothing out courtesy of colleagues, students, and friends in the Harvard community. Greg Keating, an Amherst classmate who wound up studying at Harvard Law School, would talk to me for hours about how I needed to make peace with the fact that I was an insider at the type of elite institutions that once barred Jews. He also begged me to put a governor on my sense of outrage, which could emerge at the slightest provocation. During one of these tirades Greg laughed at me and said, for the umpteenth time, "Damn it, Zeke, you don't have to confront everyone, all the time."

In the classroom, I expected a great deal of participation from the students. I badgered them until they showed they knew the material and could both defend their arguments and attack mine. There was no ill will in my technique and everyone was on an equal footing. In fact, if someone said, "You're full of shit, Professor Emanuel, and here's why," I gave them an A. For the most part the students did well and gave positive feedback. But invariably I'd receive a critical evaluation from one of them.

Eventually, a sophomore confronted me about my teaching style. Adam Berger may have been the sharpest student I ever saw at Harvard. A brilliant reader who would one day represent the interests of the northern spotted owl and environmentalism in the courts, he responded beautifully to my rapid-fire style. But he wanted me to know that some of the others felt intimidated to the point where they were becoming unreceptive. One day he followed me out of class and walked me home.

"What's your goal?" he asked me.

"The goal is to make them their absolute best."

"Well, if someone feels humiliated then they aren't going to be able to learn from you. It means you have fucked up."

Adam was right. In order to succeed with all my students, I had to be more careful about showing them that it was all right to be wrong, as long as you stayed in the game, and that they could join the fray without putting their dignity at risk. Again, I'd fallen back on old habits, but I was grateful to Adam.

Still, there were some criticisms I could not contain. I felt the culture of medicine was too often dominated by imperious physicians who intimidated underlings to the detriment of their education and the care of patients. The big chiefs at teaching hospitals could be dangerously authoritarian. I saw this as an institutional problem and began to consider ways that I could work on the system of medicine instead of treating individual patients. I had to accept that despite my parents' expectations and urging, I was never going to be a doctor like my father, with thousands of grateful patients and a long record of clinical victories. But I could dive into the developing field of bioethics and begin to address the problems of structure and the thinking that got in the way of quality care. The course I set for myself was risky. It might even lead me to academic Siberia. But I was no longer Jonny Emanuel moving in a direction determined by my status as the eldest brother. I was Dr. Ezekiel Emanuel and it was time for me to be fully committed to my own path.

Rahm had blazed his own trail, too. He was no longer the fellow my father described as "getting the maximum out of the minimum amount of work." Instead he was a rising star in the world of politics, known for his willingness to do the maximum in order to achieve as much as humanly possible. I had seen the change coming in the mid-1980s, when Rahm was learning the fund-raising trade. He would not shrink from calling anyone, even the parents of our friends in Wilmette, and would press them hard for donations. If they agreed to give a thousand dollars he would say, "I won't let you embarrass yourself that way." Then he would either say that he was going to hang up and let them think about it or say, "I'll put you down for two thousand." Rahm got what he wanted 99 percent of the time. In those few cases when the "ask" failed, nothing anyone said to him ever seemed to hurt him. He just went on to the next objective.

.....

Rahm's resolve was precisely the trait Governor Clinton wanted in a key member of his team. However, on the day that I bicycled to Brookline to sit in on his meeting with Rahm, I knew little about Clinton the candidate, and what I did know gave me pause. The latest poll gave him just 9 percent of the vote, compared with 18 percent for Jerry Brown, the former governor of California, and 30 percent for New York governor Mario Cuomo, who hadn't even declared his candidacy. How, I wondered, would Clinton make up the distance between himself and the front-runners and what risk would Rahm take by joining him instead of one of the leaders in the race?

I was a fifth wheel at the meeting of just four people, but part of Clinton's charm is that he never treats anyone like an outsider. He listened when I explained my work and said something about how I might contribute to his deliberations on health-care reform. I promised to send him my ideas and then kept quiet. As the two of them got down to business, I sensed immediately that Clinton was clearly a master of his craft. Clinton was very good at complimenting Rahm in precisely the way Rahm wanted to be recognized. Rahm impressed me with his focus and seriousness—and his ability not to be sucked in by the compliments.

As they talked, I could feel Clinton's charisma and recognize the way that he was positioning himself to appeal to a segment of the electorate—white, male, rural, conservative—that the party had trouble attracting. Rahm recognized the strength of this strategy, which combined the liberal-leaning politics he favored with a somewhat more conservative approach to issues like welfare reform. Shifting into problem-solving mode, Rahm asked Clinton several questions about his campaign's finances and then began talking about "the two diasporas" that could be tapped for immediate donation. One of these diasporas was the American Jewish community, which Rahm knew well. The other was made up of wealthy Arkansan Democrats, including many who had left the state to find fortune and fame elsewhere in the United States.

Rahm was aware of the Arkansas political elite because he had worked for both Dale Bumpers, one of the state's senators, and for Congressman Beryl Anthony, who had chaired the DCCC from 1989 to 1990. Although he spoke to Clinton with confidence about getting the job done, and agreed to take it on, after the candidate left Rahm was pessimistic about their chances of success in everything he said to me. This is the way Rahm always responds to challenges. He builds a huge and convincing case for a disastrous outcome, and uses the fear this generates to motivate himself and those around him. Rahm keeps up the negativity even as good things happen and polls swing in his direction. I guess it works for him, but anyone who wants to collaborate with him over the long haul must learn to discount most of the gloomy things he says.

In the first weeks of his stint with the Clinton campaign, Rahm contacted every donor and potential ally he could. When he asked me for help I chipped in five hundred dollars, which was a substantial sum for me at the time, and gave him a list of friends and colleagues who might be inclined to donate. Gradually the money began to flow and the campaign was armed well enough to press on through New Hampshire, where Clinton would finish a respectable second, with 25 percent of the vote, compared to 33 percent for Tsongas.

My brother worked for Clinton because he thought he had the

right policies, the best political instincts, and the star power to make a winning candidate. Rahm would serve proudly in the Clinton White House and go on to a career that would require another book to describe in any detail. Time would also prove that Ari found in Hollywood a perfect outlet for his energy, imagination, and ambition. And I, the careful planner who tried to prepare for every contingency, faced a future with more twists and turns than I ever expected. The one thing that would remain constant, and grow stronger with time, would be our connection to one another.

In 1992, in the wake of Clinton's election, Rahm proposed a pact that required us to be together every Thanksgiving. We have kept the agreement ever since, adding spouses and children as they came along. Over the years, we have rotated the venue each year, moving from Los Angeles to Chicago to Washington on a triennial cycle. This tradition meant that even as we distinguished ourselves as individuals our brotherhood was never broken. That, it seems, was perhaps one of the most important values imparted to us by our parents and our experience growing up Emanuel.

WHAT DID MOM PUT IN THE CEREAL?

"Smulevitz, that is S-M-U-L-I-V-I-T-Z."

"No, no," I said. "It is E like Emanuel, V like Victor, I like Idiot, T like Tom, and Z like Zeke. Smulevitz."

I was spelling my grandfather's last name for *New York Times* columnist Maureen Dowd, who was in Chicago to write about my brother Rahm winning election and becoming the city's first Jewish mayor. When we cleared up the spelling issue Maureen said, "Zeke, I have to meet your mother tonight at the party."

"Why?"

"To find out what she put in the cereal!"

"Maureen, how sexist of you! How do you know it wasn't my father who was the critical factor in our success? Maybe it was our genes, not how my parents raised us at all. Or maybe it was the influence of the firstborn. Or the influence of all three of us on each other. Why are you so sure it was my mother?"

I have to give Maureen credit for consistency and perseverance. She has been asking me that question incessantly for the last five years. Not that she was alone. I've heard a version of the "cereal question" hundreds of times, from friends, colleagues, interviewers, and people

I just happen to meet. I understand why someone might be interested in the secrets of our apparent success, but I am more struck by the widely held assumption that the single component most responsible for our success must be our mother.

I suspect this reflex is based on two factors. The first is an enduring, idealized image of the American family before the social revolutions of the 1960s and '70s. The traditional picture suggests that mothers did all the important parenting while fathers existed on the periphery of family life, playing a supporting role at best. Like all clichés, this idea has some basis in overall truth but falls apart when you get down to specifics. My father may have worked tremendously hard and long hours at the hospital and office, but he exerted an enormous influence on us through this example. We were also influenced, in big ways, by our grandfather the "Big Bangah," friends like the Glasses, and the neighborhoods and schools we knew as kids.

The second is the bias that favors nurture over nature. Many people want to believe that parents' consciously imparted influence, in the form of values, education, and even nutrition, determines how their children will turn out. It's a natural point of view. To think otherwise would require us to acknowledge that our ability to shape our children is limited, and that we have little control over many of the traits they will develop over time.

As a scientist I know genes exert real influence not just on our physical and social characteristics, but also in how nurture ultimately impacts us, often by changing how our genes are expressed. Ultimately, it is not either nature or nurture. It is them working together. For example, male assertiveness and its more animalistic cousin, aggression, have a hereditary basis. (Think survival of the pushiest.) The same is true for traits like physical stamina and strength, which still matter in our world despite the fact that life no longer requires us to run miles across the savannah in the hunt for game. In modern life, physical resilience lets you work longer hours and maintain peak performance at your desk or in a classroom. By the same token, an extra-aggressive personality, when channeled properly, will get you closer to the top in most competitions.

In our case, the exuberant energy remarked on by almost everyone who knows us probably comes directly from our father's DNA. Ben Emanuel's workdays often ran to fourteen hours or more and then he would be on call often every other weekend, and yet he never seemed to tire. He also remained slim and physically fit long into middle age, without any formal—or informal—exercise routine. Rahm, Ari, and I all have developed our own workout regimens: I'm a runner and squash player, Rahm's a swimmer and bicyclist, and Ari's a big golfer and weight lifter. Nevertheless, our dad's genes have predisposed us to be high-energy and make it easier for us to stay fit.

Other genetically borne traits common to Emanuels include the dyslexia and attention deficit disorder that afflict the three of us brothers to varying degrees. Here the general DNA connection is well established but we have never formally worked out the precise hereditary pathway. Our mother, while a voracious reader, is a notoriously awful speller. Were she a kid today, I am sure she would be diagnosed with a learning disability. Stories from our father's youth suggest he was the type of kid who was eager for stimulation and had trouble sitting still. My guess is that something in the combination of their DNA brought out more extreme versions of dyslexia and hyperactivity in us. Rahm and I got the bad-spelling part of dyslexia. (It was only in middle age that I learned bad spelling is a manifestation of dyslexia.) Ari, of course, has the classic dyslexia, with his extreme difficulty with reading. All of us had "ants-in-the-pants" syndrome, which made us wilder than most boys and, consequently, more likely to run afoul of authorities. Ari was a perpetual-motion machine, but both Rahm and I were plenty fidgety. I used to bounce my legs throughout the classroom day.

On balance, the traits passed to us through our genes have included gifts as well as deficiencies and have required us to adapt and compensate. However, as much as we recognize our parents in ourselves, we can also see that the transfer of traits has not been entirely consistent. For example, my mother and father are both quite graceful on the dance floor. You could see this trait in Rahm's ballet, but I have to work hard to avoid klutzing up wedding receptions and bar mitzvah parties. Similarly, my father has tremendous auditory acuity. This shows up in his amazing ability to pick up languages and his deep appreciation for music. He can actually identify particular musicians, conductors, and orchestras from a few notes of a recording. Not one of us got his ear. While we might enjoy a night of music, we would struggle to distinguish one classical composer from another. As for languages, it is enough to say that we speak English better than the Bushes, although our vocabulary may occasionally appear limited to four-letter words.

All that aside, it's true that much of our personalities is the result of active parenting. For better or worse, our attitudes, morals, expectations, and behavioral style are *definitely* the product of the way Ben and Marsha organized their household, treated us as children, and showed us, through example, how to live a good life. The key here is their sense of purpose. I'm not saying we were programmed 24/7. On the contrary, we were given plenty of time for open-ended play. However, the scheduled time was devoted to more unusual and frankly adult activities: political demonstrations, ballet, classical concerts, and theater productions.

The money to pay for these experiences came from all the scrimping my mother and father did when it came to everyday expenses. Indeed, if you had visited us when we lived in Chicago you might have looked at our clothes and the furnishings in our homes and judged us to be lower-middle-class at best. We often wore patched jeans bought at Sears; Levi's were out of our price range. At times it felt as if we were actually poor, especially in comparison to the families of some of the kids we met at Anshe Emet. But we were aware that by saving on common comforts we were able to have extraordinary cultural experiences. Living on the cheap made all those summers in Israel and trips to Europe possible—something none of our friends got despite their substantial wealth.

It would be hard to overstate the importance of travel in our upbringing. While our richer friends spent school vacations at expensive overnight camps or on Florida beaches, we went first on very deliberate tours of the American West and then on long foreign excursions, at a time when few families in our social circle did. When it comes to understanding history and culture and putting your own existence in context, my parents firmly believed that travel is absolutely the best teacher. Although many more Americans travel abroad today, in the 1960s jets were still new and between the expense and the discomforts only a small percentage of our countrymen felt motivated to cross the oceans. Most who did went to Great Britain, France, or Italy, where they stuck with a tour group or trundled from one tourist attraction to another.

At home, being part of a minority group also reinforced the way we identified with people who were oppressed and pushed to the margins of society. In word and deed, our parents taught us that we did not have to accept being put down or denied our rights. With that came the notion that no one should be permitted to exercise authority that hadn't been earned and the idea that we should always be willing to defy convention and follow our own inner beings.

Time and again, our parents supported us with supplies and encouragement as we explored interests as varied as ballet, building castles, and hawking T-shirts at rock concerts, which made us fearless when it came to hatching schemes and chasing dreams. Altogether, the escapades, travel, lessons, encouragement, and social encounters made our family life "child-centered" before the phrase came into popular use. Whether we were marching in protests with my mother or trailing after our father at the hospital, our parents made us the focus of their lives and made an effort to instill in us certain values, attitudes, and traits. Some of these efforts worked, and some inspired rebellion. In the category of rebellion, I'd list my decision to give up the practice of medicine, Ari's unabashed pursuit of wealth, and Rahm's practical (rather than radical) approach to politics. In all three cases, we have set our own routes, deviating from our parents' road map.

But even after taking into account the variations and our individual quirks, it's still possible to see a distinct Emanuel blend of strengths, weaknesses, and other characteristics. All human beings are full of contradictions, tension, and flaws. Our critics and defenders would agree that Ari, Rahm, and I can be both benevolent and belligerent, sometimes in the same moment, as when my brothers say, "I love you, asshole." We can also be ambivalent about an issue, especially when we are at our most dogmatic. But passion, energy, and persistence are the hallmarks of the Emanuel style, and it was these three traits that we all exhibited as we advocated for others and ourselves in medicine, politics, and show business.

Laughter was a constant in our childhood home, and it is the sound you will hear wherever any of us go; you would be able to identify me even in a very dark movie theater. However, we are, all three of us, demanding and rigorous when it comes to our work and our ethics. And like our parents, we generally want to mitigate any suffering we encounter, and if we're in the position to help—with family, friends, colleagues, even strangers—we will do it.

In word and deed, our mother and father both offered the clear message that they could not abide bullies and that they expected us to stand up to them whenever possible. Ironically, a deep analysis of our life experience—the kind you might conduct while writing a memoir— would inevitably point to moments when we experienced bullying among ourselves. As much as my mother hated the way her own father pushed her around, she could play the bully with her emotional outbursts and extended silences. Also, it has to be said that our father bullied our mother into moving to Wilmette. And I'm sure that you could find plenty of people willing to recite instances of bullying practiced by Ari, Rahm, and me. Indeed, the impatient, pushy Emanuel style is so well known that during a recent interview for college presidency I was asked, point blank, whether I had the levelheaded temperament the position required.

I know this admission is no big surprise to anyone who's heard about us. Everyone knows that Rahm can be a rough-and-tumble politician and has done his share of shouting and cursing. And there's a foul-mouthed, hyperaggressive character on the HBO show *Entourage* who is modeled after Ari and does little else but bully people. But as obvious as our flaws are to others, it's difficult to recognize them in oneself.

What other shortcomings do we Emanuels share? Sarcasm is one.

Eye-rolling snobbery is another. But, thankfully, as we age these bad habits are fading and our appreciation for the advantages and gifts we received while growing up Emanuel has grown. It is my mother's moral certainty that I hear when Ari condemns the bigoted rants of Mel Gibson. It is my father's sense of humor I see in Rahm's more outrageous acts, like calling out the names of political enemies and declaring them "dead" while stabbing a table with a steak knife.

Finally, I would have to credit the Emanuel brotherhood itself as a major influence on the men we grew up to be. We spent the first ten years of our lives sleeping in the same room, eating at the same table, and strategizing over how to appease our mother's tempestuous moods. Then we spent four summers together in Israel—entertaining ourselves together. The bond we formed growing up together is unbreakable. As adults we are constantly checking in with one another by email and phone. It's not unusual for us to talk four or five times in a week. Indeed, going a whole week without connecting makes us worried that something bad has happened. (It was not until I was middle-aged that I discovered how unusual this is for adult siblings.) And we are able to support one another in a way that is uniquely consistent, specific, and well-informed. We can confide in one another knowing we will receive much more than the generic advice a friend or acquaintance might offer. No one is more critical of me than my brothers, but no one is more supportive and loyal.

.....

As I wrote earlier, Ben and Marsha perfected the art of jazz parenting. But just as in music, their noisy riffs and improvisations were all played within certain rules. Our home may have seemed chaotic, but amid the arguing and the tussling no one was permitted to practice prejudice, cruelty, or stupidity. Every comment received due consideration, no matter who said it. Standards may have been loose when it came to swearing and wrestling, but they were quite strict when it came to values like loyalty and integrity. All that we received depended on us upholding these values, and if we ever failed, we felt the loss acutely. Nothing that other parents did to punish their children, from spanking to grounding to the withdrawal of privileges, could have felt worse than what we felt when the mood suddenly shifted and our mother retreated in anger. The desire for her approval was a powerful motivator. At the deepest level, this anxiety lies behind much of what we have achieved.

The impatient and never-ending expectations voiced by our mother and, to a lesser extent, our father got into our hearts and minds and made each one of us burn with ambition. But while we each set a course toward our own version of achievement, not one of us was able to establish an endpoint. Rahm did not say, "I'll be satisfied if I get to the White House." Ari did not declare, "I want to run a Fortune 500 company." Because we had internalized the idea that life is a matter of constant striving, we could not imagine reaching a point where we would be satisfied. In fact, each achievement, whether it was a published book or an election victory, brought a new, higher goal, which required even more effort.

This insight into the shared source of our success came to me gradually when we began our Thanksgiving get-togethers. Beginning in the early 1990s, they gave us opportunities to check for signs of change, reflect on our lives, and consider the influences that made us—family, Chicago, New Trier, Jewish heritage, the sixties, Americanism, liberal politics. They also let us celebrate some of life's landmarks. In 2009 we used Thanksgiving weekend to have Rahm's fiftieth birthday party and plan for a family journey to Israel, where we would celebrate two bar mitzvahs—for Rahm's and Ari's sons—marking the first time we were there all together since 1970. In 2010, the big news at Thanksgiving revolved around Rahm's departure from Washington and his campaign to be elected mayor of Chicago. I brought to the table, in a manner of speaking, this memoir.

Although no one in the family had read the manuscript, everyone had an opinion. Suspicion, sensitivity, and curiosity swirled in the air as my brothers, their wives, and various children interrogated me for a couple of hours. They wouldn't stop until I agreed to distribute some of the chapters I had finished.

Foraging through the memories of our lives, my brothers and I have decided that there isn't one single thing that our mother, our father, or anyone else added to our cereal to make us this way. Instead it was an approach to life itself, reinforced in myriad different moments, that made us Emanuel boys into Emanuel men.

Hopefully, one day the three of us will reach a point where we are truly satisfied with all that we have as individuals, members of our family, and citizens of our great country. It's not up to our parents, who got us this far, to teach us this one last lesson. No, it is our responsibility. Perhaps when we fulfill it we will be truly grown-up. In the meantime, I have a message for my Emanuel brothers. I love you, you schmucks. And I admire what you have made of yourselves.

Acknowledgments

Family histories are made of stories. For years I had been jotting down random stories and memories I wanted to share with my children. The process of transforming these notes into a family chronicle ultimately became an unexpected—at least to me—journey of self-discovery.

The idea of organizing these disjointed stories into a coherent narrative first came to Richard Abate, then an agent working for my brother at William Morris Endeavor. Such a book is the creation of many helping and critical hands. To each of them I owe deep thanks.

When Richard left, Suzanne Gluck and Jennifer Rudolph Walsh at William Morris Endeavor seamlessly took over as my agents. They offered warm support, ideas, and insightful criticism. Their belief in the value of this book never wavered.

The book benefited from three terrific editors at Random House. nSusan Mercandetti originally acquired the book before joining ABC. She offered insightful ideas about how to structure the stories. Jonathan Jao took over, providing many ideas about how to improve the first draft. Susan Kamil was the hands-on editor extraordinaire. This book is much better because of her exceptional editing—especially the suggested cuts—and discerning emendations.

The real work of writing this book began with Michael D'Antonio, who helped me revisit people and places and feelings that had been far in the past. He also had the great idea of videotaping a discussion among the three brothers during the summer of 2011. This book could not have been realized without his diligent work and collaboration. Our numerous discussions of my family's history greatly enriched and deepened my understanding of my own life and the life of my family.

My parents spent many hours recounting crucial stories that I could not know or whose details I did not fully remember.

There are many people who contributed stories—and they are often named in the book. Special thanks for insights go to my boyhood friend Michael Alter, who has been engaged with our family since he was seven and I was ten, and to Andrew Oram, a close college classmate and the paradigm of Aristotelian friendship for all these many years.

As she drove us along winding roads around the Norwegian fjords, Anne Sovcik endured my reading aloud of the first draft, accompanied by much crying, laughing, and cringing. Fortunately, she was not frightened away by my craziness—or that of my family. My three daughters, always perceptive and critical about their father, were helpful as I worked through draft after draft.

And finally, thanks to my brothers, Rahm and Ari, who were invaluable. While I am an extremely independent person, I could not be who I am without their love and support, which always makes an appearance when you least expect it and need it the most.

Family Tree

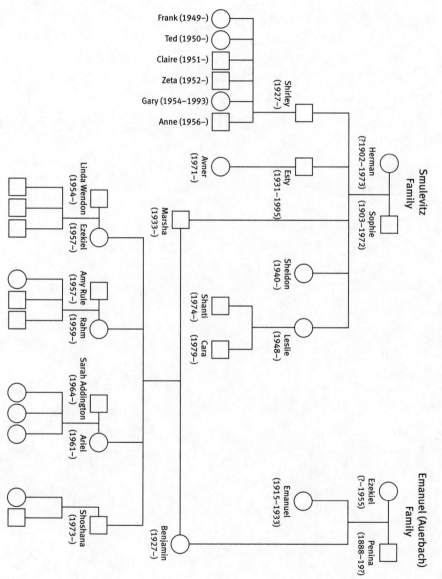

Frank (1949–)
Ted (1950–)
Claire (1951–)
Zeta (1952–)
Gary (1954–1993)
Anne (1956–)

Shirley (1927–)

Herman (?1902–1973)

Smulevitz Family

Sophie (1903–1972)

Avner (1971–)

Esty (1931–1995)

Marsha (1933–)

Linda Wendon (1954–)
Ezekiel (1957–)

Amy Rule (1957–)
Rahm (1959–)

Sarah Addington (1964–)
Ariel (1961–)

Shoshana (1973–)

Sheldon (1940–)

Shanti (1974–)
Cara (1979–)

Leslie (1948–)

Benjamin (1927–)

Emanuel (1915–1993)

Ezekiel (?–1955)

Emanuel (Auerbach) Family

Penina (1888–197?)